345.73
F91c

99118

DATE DUE			

CRIME AND
PUBLICITY

The Impact of News on the Administration of Justice

CRIME AND PUBLICITY

The Impact of News on the

Administration of Justice

by **Alfred Friendly** and **Ronald L. Goldfarb**

THE TWENTIETH CENTURY FUND

NEW YORK · 1967

KRAUS REPRINT CO.
Millwood, New York
1975

Library of Congress Cataloging in Publication Data

Friendly, Alfred.
  Crime and publicity.

  Reprint of the ed. published by Twentieth Century Fund,
New York.
  Includes bibliographical references and index.
  1. Crime and the press. I. Goldfarb, Ronald L.,
joint author. II. Title.
  [KF9223.5.F7   1975]   345'.73'056   74-34427
  ISBN 0-527-02804-5

345.73
F91c
99118
nov. 1976

THE TWENTIETH CENTURY FUND

founded in 1919 and endowed by Edward A. Filene, is a nonprofit
foundation which, through research and publication, seeks to throw
light upon emerging issues of our times. Major fields of interest of the
Fund are economics, social problems and international affairs. The
study of which this volume is a report has been defined and supported
by the Fund's Board of Trustees. The Fund attempts to ensure the
scholarly quality of works appearing under its imprint; the Trustees
and the staff, however, accord the author or authors complete freedom
in the statement of opinions and the interpretation of facts.

KRAUS REPRINT CO.

A U.S. Division of Kraus-Thomson Organization Limited

Printed in U.S.A.

FOREWORD

The Twentieth Century Fund has had many distinguished newspapermen among its Trustees, and a concern for the press and its relation to society has been a recurrent concern of the Board. The opportunity to deal with one puzzling and controversial aspect of the broad field was presented by Alfred Friendly and Ronald L. Goldfarb, one an editor of a nationally known newspaper, the other a trial lawyer who has specialized in writing on legal questions for a lay public. The study was carried out with assistance by the Fund and is presented as the first of what will, we hope, be a series of books upon the press.

The present study represents a true collaboration, so that those who look for heated debates between a newspaperman and a lawyer will be disappointed. Both men are aware of the complexity of the problems posed by the handling of crime news by the press, especially where a sensational case is involved. It is not only that two opposing constitutionally guaranteed civil rights are at stake—the public's right to essential information and the individual's right to a fair trial—but also that newspaper publicity has as often been a factor in achieving justice as in subverting it. Both men eschew easy solutions, whether in the form of rhetorical denunciations or the imposition of "codes."

Not everyone will agree with all parts of the argument here set forth. It would be difficult, indeed, to find total agreement in an area where there have already been so many reports and where defenders of press and bar have so often stood in embattled hostility. But the approach of the authors, in words which they use in a different connection, is "commonsensical and generous." Their efforts to define the problem, to assess its dimension, to weigh the remedies open to the administrators of justice, to evaluate the inadequacies and the dangers of some suggested restraints upon news coverage—all these must gain general assent. The book should also, incidentally, gain the interest of readers not previously informed on the subject. For the reconstruction of notorious cases is inevitably absorbing; and legal arguments, when presented with the combined skills of lawyer and reporter, can be fascinating.

This study is far from being the first word upon its subject. It would not claim to be the last word. But it is of importance in carrying forward the dialogue and presenting an analysis, in one crucial area, of how different interests conflict in our complex society.

AUGUST HECKSCHER, *Director*

The Twentieth Century Fund

41 East 70th Street, New York
January, 1967

ACKNOWLEDGMENTS

Many people helped us in many ways in the preparation of this book. It is not possible for us to mention here each individual kindness. Some friends, however, we burdened so heavily with appeals for information and research that our gratitude to them must be noted: Charles Fenby, of the Westminster Provincial Newspapers Limited, for reports on British press practice; Richard W. Cardwell, of the Hoosier State Press Association, for pioneer work on legal appeals based on prejudicial publication; Dan Morgan, of the *Washington Post,* for an analysis of press coverage of crime in Washington; Leonard Downie, of the same newspaper, for his reports about the Sheppard case; Elizabeth Fudold, of the Justice Department Library, and Mark Hannon and Ann Maples, of the *Washington Post* Library, for generously and expertly responding to an endless series of demands.

Particularly helpful in supplying mountains of information about individual criminal cases were Creed Black of the *Chicago Daily News,* Thomas Winship of the *Boston Globe,* George Rosenberg and Steve Emerine of the *Tucson Daily Citizen,* Robert C. Notson and Peter N. Tugman of the Portland *Oregonian,* Sandor S. Klein of the Boise *Statesman,* Sam Ragan and Colline Roberts of the Raleigh *News and Observer,* Clifton Daniel, Edith Asbury and Sidney Zion of the *New York Times,* Don Davis of the *Denver Post,* Victor Hackler and Odell A. Hanson of the Associated Press, Mark Ethredge, Jr., of the *Detroit Free Press,* George Beebe of the *Miami Herald,* and John P. MacKenzie and Morton Mintz of the *Washington Post.*

We had continuing encouragement and wise counsel throughout from August Heckscher and his associates at the Twentieth Century Fund, particularly Thomas R. Carskadon and Elizabeth Blackert. As sponsors and colleagues they were our major asset.

For their thoughtful counseling, encouragement, and criticism on various sections of the book, we wish to thank William C. Rogers, Peter and Maria Giesey, William Monroe, Paul Oberst, J. R. Wiggins, James E. Clayton, and Lawrence B. Laurent.

We gratefully acknowledge the typing labors of Susan Sprouse, Ellen Sachs, Elizabeth Reimer, Karen Ho, and Eleanor Gomberg. The overwhelming share of that work fell, however, to Mary Green, who accomplished it with unfailing grace and the sharpest critical eye.

The Twentieth Century Fund made it possible for Ronald L. Goldfarb, the lawyer member of this team, to work full time on the book from May, 1965, until August, 1966; the indulgence of the *Washington Post* permitted the newspaperman, Alfred Friendly, to take the time to do his share. This book could not have been written without that support; our gratitude is profound.

A.F.
R.L.G.

CONTENTS

CRIME AND PUBLICITY

The Impact of News on the Administration of Justice

INTRODUCTION

Man's fascination with news of crime is insatiable. The sensational crimes and their trials—those that cause today's free press, fair trial dilemma—engage public interest to a degree matched by little else. To bid the public pay less attention to news of crime and punishment is to play King Canute with the waves.

Throughout history, the trials of grandiose crimes—grandiose because of the persons involved, the enormity of the acts, or the depth and breadth of the implications—have served society in many functions besides the immediate one of determining one man's guilt or innocence. For the individual, they are windows permitting a form of voyeurism, innocent or morbid, into the deeds of one's fellow men; more important, they act as mirrors, terrifyingly hypnotic, in which each man may see the dark parts of his soul. For the society as a whole, trials are often the crystallization and the high point of its conflicts. They are the essence of the drama and dynamics of the culture, and may well provide the clearest view of them. As Sir John MacDonnell has put it, "Faithfully reported, a trial is a living picture; it brings us nearer to life than the best literature; you hear the voices; it is life itself."

The criminal process, beginning with the crime and continuing through the arrest, the indictment, the trial, and the verdict, is frequently the particularization in a form the layman can understand of matters so grand as otherwise to be almost beyond comprehension. The issue is confined and sharpened, made concrete and played out with a set of characters whom the citizen can identify and relate to his own experience and thoughts. It has shape. And however much it may be deplored—however much it is really deplorable—the crime and the trial contain the essentials of theater, often great theater.

3

As abstractions, concepts like anarchism, treason, or prejudice are hard to get one's hands around, but put them in terms of Sacco and Vanzetti, the Rosenbergs and Leo Frank, and the dimensions become fathomable. Better than any textbook, the trial of Bill Haywood makes clear the struggle over the organization of labor; the trial of Aaron Burr is a distillation of post-Revolutionary American politics; and even the trial of Christine Keeler evokes the kind of ferocious interest that a hundred disquisitions on lust cannot produce.

In periods of great tension over issues under furious debate, a criminal charge, the ensuing developments, and finally the trial seem fated to come to pass as the climax. The raid, the capture, and the trial of John Brown were not phenomena emerging from a vacuum; they came as the culmination of three decades of abolitionist strife; the resultant judgment poised the nation for its imminent plunge into tragedy. The case of Captain Dreyfus was both the apogee of an anachronistic and corrupt social system and the beginning of its reform. The Scopes trial not only marked the end of the American fundamentalist cosmography but was a notably significant cause of its death.

The great trial is often the device by which the conscience and the philosophy of the society are enunciated. Whatever one's views about the merits of the war crimes trials in Nuremberg or Eichmann's in Jerusalem, they were vehicles for the declaration of profound legal and moral judgments. The great trial can illuminate theological principles, as did St. Joan's, or voice the heart of a nation about to be born, as did Gandhi's.

Finally, the trial is often the cornerstone of the institutions of the future. The case of John Peter Zenger formed part of the foundations on which freedom of political expression was erected. The bomb in the Haymarket and the trial that followed were to change the course of the American labor movement.

Almost from the beginning, writers have recognized the criminal act as a posing of an issue, great or small, and the courtroom as the place for its dramatic decision. They are the climax and the denouement, the moment of crisis and resolution toward which the novelist builds. Satirists from Rabelais to Anatole France to Mark Twain, social critics and novelists of all nations from Dickens to Dostoevski, from Kafka to Capote, the articulators of the conscience of the people, have used for their purposes the commission of a crime—or its allegation—and its resolution in the courtroom.

Interest in news of crime and punishment is much too powerful an impulse to be beaten down; heavy-handed suppression or even enforced postponements of accounts that measure the flow of life itself are simply not feasible this side of a dictatorship. The problem, of course, is that public interest in crime inescapably brings public influence upon the administration of justice. As the scientist dealing with small nuclear particles knows, a thing observed is a thing disturbed; as society watches the processes of crime and punishment it cannot avoid carrying extraneous material into what, in theory, must be a quarantined courtroom where processes are carried out by perfect and objective rules.

To be sure, society has come a great distance since the days when public interference with the law came close to being the law itself. Socrates was tried by the mob, masquerading as a jury for the city of Athens. The public of Jerusalem—or at least its Establishment—blackmailed a judge into delivering over for execution a man in whom the judge had thrice found no fault: "If thou let this man go," the accusers cried, "thou art not Caesar's friend." But to ask for the ideal of a judicial system dealing with crime in which the public climate of the time and place has utterly no impact in the courtroom is to ask for the impossible.[1]

The suggestion that secret administration of the law can produce a better form of justice than can an open society is, of course, absurd. But it would be equally absurd to pretend that the public's impact on the administration of justice does not cause some deeply troublesome problems. Its tendency is to distort in greater or less degree the rigorous and impartial procedures that a civilized society has decreed for judging persons accused of crime.

Those procedures are designed to provide justice by due process of law, protected from the whims of men—the passions of the mob or the influence of the master. They are to guarantee that the accused shall be

---

[1] And perhaps for the undesirable. It was public opinion rather than the law that forced Zenger's acquittal. It may well be that the force of emerging moderate opinion in the American South serves the cause of justice to Negro and civil rights defendants better than it could be served by a Southern judge and jury isolated from the pressure that the news engenders.

judged on the basis of fact and not of rumor, on a specific act and not on reputation, for a given deed and not for episodes in his past; that he not be coerced into incriminating himself; that he have the opportunity to confront the accusers and try to refute the accusations. Of equal importance among these and many more guarantees in American criminal jurisprudence is the command of the Constitution that a defendant enjoy a trial before impartial jurors.

But those jurors, by prescription, must be members of the public before they become jurors. In a case where public interest has been lively, they may have been exposed to public emotions and judgments and information that have no place in the courtroom, that are nonjudicial. And even after the jury is empaneled, its members may not be able to escape hearing the public's views. Thus, public interest in a crime, public discussion of it and of the suspect, public debate over the suspect's guilt or innocence, and public craving for complete information about the episode before the case comes to trial and during the trial itself, all combine into a force that may diminish or even corrupt the prescribed objectivity of the jury.

This is the essence of the free press, fair trial problem. On the one hand is the contention that the public interest in news is justifiable and irresistible, at least in a democracy, and to the extent information about crime is denied the public, or minimized or even delayed, to that extent injury is done to the public; on the other hand is the assertion that the public interest can itself contaminate certain of those procedures of the court, specifically the objectivity of the jurors, that assure a defendant a fair trial.

As with other problems, the clearest illustrations are at the extremes: At one end of the spectrum are the secret trials of the dictatorships, where public scrutiny is utterly denied, and only the verdict, if that, is made known. At the other extreme is publicity so flamboyant that, as the phrase has it, "trial by newspaper" occurs, wherein no one can be sure whether the verdict was reached on the basis of evidence properly introduced in court or as a consequence of the hue and cry in the press and the nonjudicial material it published that may have influenced the jurors' judgment.

The horror cases that come to mind are the publicity-ridden trials of Hauptmann, Hall-Mills, Finch and Tregoff, Samuel Sheppard, and Jack Ruby; or where the press performed equally scandalous public mischief in the (supposedly prejudice-proof) British cases of Christine Keeler, Stephen Ward, and the Moors murders.

How far, on the one hand, may society go to limit public observation, and, on the other hand, how much impact on the processes of justice resulting from publicity about individual criminal cases can society tolerate? How can the conflict be resolved or diminished? What accommodations can be made?

These are the questions that this book will examine.

CHAPTER 1

THE COMPLAINT

WEREWOLF
 FIEND
  SEX-MAD KILLER

FATHER OF FOUR ADMITS STRANGLING LOVE

"HE'S SICK—AND I'M SO ASHAMED"

KNIFE-KICK YOUTHS SLASH 3

TWO GIRLS ADMIT #2 HOLD-UP KILLING
 MET IN REFORM SCHOOL
  LAID PLANS THERE FOR CRIMINAL CAREER, POLICE SAY

BEAST HUNTED IN ROBBERY AND
 RAPE OF WIDOW, 71

ACTRESS, 16, IS SLAIN:
 HUNT "MEAN" STEPDAD

EX-CON ADMITS
 HE'S MAD DOG KILLER OF THREE

PRESIDENT'S ASSASSIN SHOT TO DEATH

The headlines above—inflammatory, tendentious, laden with prejudgment, salivating—are real, and unfortunately all too typical of a considerable portion of the American press in its handling of sensational crimes. Together with the textual material introduced by them, they constitute the publicity that, it is charged, corrupts the fairness of criminal trials.

The classic indictment was made by the Warren Commission, the President's Commission on the Assassination of President Kennedy: "The

Commission believes that a part of the responsibility for the unfortunate circumstances following the President's death must be borne by the news media." The Commission declared that the "experience in Dallas is a dramatic affirmation of the need for steps to bring about a proper balance between the right of the public to be kept informed and the right of the individual to a fair and impartial trial." It recommended that representatives of the bar, the law enforcement associations and the news media "work together to establish ethical standards" on the dissemination of crime news "so that there will be no interference with pending criminal investigations, court proceedings, or the right of individuals to a fair trial."

Whether the performance of the nation's press—and by "press" here and throughout this book we include radio and television—during the tragic week in November, 1963, was typical of its treatment of criminal affairs, whether it was dreadful interference or brilliant performance, or whether it was only an exception brought about by an unbelievable cataclysmic happening is for the moment immaterial.[1] What is beyond dispute is that this performance was widely denounced as an illustration of the evil the press is charged with committing regularly against the due process of law in criminal procedures and as a glaring demonstration of the need for remedial action.

The criticism of the press for its behavior at Dallas (and later at the trial of Jack Ruby) and for the hypothetical injury it inflicted on Lee Harvey Oswald's chance for due process of law was only the culmination of a growing American concern about what has come to be labeled the "free press, fair trial" dilemma. The enormous growth of the press, the extent and vividness of its impact (compounded through the pervasive medium of television), its ability to blanket not merely a community but the whole nation with its views, its opinions, and the force of its reports have made its potential for injury more overpowering than ever before. The big eye peers into every closet; the big voice and the big headline proclaim the findings to the expectant, attentive millions.

The thrust of the press, moved by its imperatives for newsworthiness, salability, speed, and excitement, is posed against the solemn, dispassionate, calculated rules of evidence and the punctilious rules of court. The press stands charged with overwhelming the law. The injury that

---

[1] The episode is considered more extensively in Appendix C.

the press is seen to inflict on the administration of criminal justice is, preponderantly, in its asserted denial to a defendant of his Constitutional guarantee of fair trial before unbiased jurors; to a much less extent—at least insofar as the volume of complaint provides a measure—the press (especially television) is accused of corroding the dignity and scrupulous procedure of the judicial process itself and the objective, impersonal environment in which it operates.

Press coverage of crime and trials is seen to make its harmful impact in two principal ways: One comes from bringing to the attention of the actual or prospective jurors, outside the courtroom, information and opinion that is "nonjudicial" (or "extra-record" or "extra-judicial"), namely, material they are not allowed to consider under procedures society has designed to govern the fair adjudication of a defendant's guilt or innocence. The second comes from creating an over-all atmosphere in the community, by the sheer volume or sensationalism of publication about a case, that tends to contaminate the objectivity of the jurors and the court and to subvert the dispassionate attitude prescribed for the trial procedure.

Today's concern with the effect of news coverage on trial procedure had its beginnings in the events of the 1930's in Flemington, New Jersey. There, Bruno Hauptmann stood accused of kidnapping the Lindbergh baby. He was tried and convicted in an atmosphere of circus sensationalism that outrageously degraded the judicial process.

The interest of the public and the press in the trial was obsessive. The prosecutor did not disguise his intent to bring the inflamed public opinion to bear upon the jury. He said in his summation:

> I am not concerned about what the mob is clamoring for, as counsel refers to it, but you can bet your life that if there is a clamor from the people of this country for this man's conviction I have sufficient faith in the American people to know that it is their honest belief and conviction that he is a murderer. Otherwise, there would be no clamor, if there is one.

During the trial, pamphlets were circulated showing Hauptmann's earlier criminal record in Germany. Newspapers reported the opinions of eminent lawyers about his guilt. The prosecuting attorney gave constant newspaper interviews. Present in this otherwise quiet little town to cover the case were 141 news reporters and photographers from all over the world, 125 telegraph operators, and 20 messengers. The presiding judge forbade photographs while the court was in session but allowed newsreel cameras with sound equipment to be installed in the court-room. The inevitable happened. One photographer muffled his camera in a soundproof hood, installed in it a recording device with a remote control, and recorded some of the testimony. When the court was not in session sightseers were admitted. Placards were placed around the courtroom showing where principal participants in the trial sat. How-ever, as a sign of decorum, "members of the Rotary Club kept sight-seers from cutting their initials in the judge's bench." At the trial, the public applauded state witnesses. The whole proceeding was wild, rau-cous, and unrestrained. The court itself scarcely attempted to correct it.

When the issue of prejudicial publicity was raised on appeal, the ap-pellate court said, "It was inevitable," and upheld the conviction.

After the trial, the organized press and bar agreed that something had to be done about lurid publicity of trials. Speeches were made and committees were formed, but very little was accomplished. While the bar's unilateral prohibition of broadcasting and photographing trials was a direct result of that case, the basic problem went unresolved.

In the years that followed, the media grew larger, their impact be-came more pervasive, and their taste for sensation, it would appear, in no way abated. The temptation to gain circulation through the elaborate and voluminous reporting of scandalous and shocking criminal cases remained.

The Hall-Mills case stands out as a classic early example of sensa-tionalism gone wild. Actually, more than three decades after the event, it is clear that there was nothing wild at all about the manufacture of the sensationalism: It was contrived coldly and deliberately as a weapon in William Randolph Hearst's circulation war with Joseph Patterson.[2] Since then, the formula for the sensational case has remained standard, cut on the tried and tested Hauptmann and Hall-Mills pattern: Major circulation magazines and newspapers and broadcasters dispatch their crews and chroniclers; the whole country is treated to the details of the principals' love life, Broadway and Hollywood columnists' curbstone

[2] The story is deftly told in William Kunstler's *The Minister and the Choir Singer* (New York: Dell, 1965).

opinions about the law and the lawyers, artists' sketches of distraught defendants, vindictive victims, pompous prosecutors, and jejune judges.

In the now classic Dr. Samuel Sheppard case, the Supreme Court of Ohio described the proceedings in Sheppard's first trial in these words:

> Mystery and murder, society, sex and suspense were combined in this case in such a manner as to intrigue and captivate the public fancy to a degree perhaps unparalleled in recent annals. Throughout the pre-indictment investigation, the subsequent legal skirmishes, and the nine-week trial, circulation-conscious editors catered to the insatiable interest of the American public in the bizarre. Special seating facilities for reporters and columnists representing local papers and all major news services were installed in the courtroom. Special rooms in the Criminal Courts building were equipped for broadcasters and telecasters. In this atmosphere of a "Roman Holiday" for the news media, Sam Sheppard stood trial for his life.

The Sheppard case is, if extreme, illustrative of the mid-twentieth-century free press, fair trial problem, and is the subject of one of its major judicial declarations. It thus warrants consideration in detail.

In the early morning hours of July 4, 1954, Marilyn Reese Sheppard, twenty-nine years of age, pregnant wife of an osteopath, Dr. Samuel H. Sheppard, was murdered in her bed in her home in Bay Village, a lakeside suburb of Cleveland. She had been beaten to death by an undetermined blunt instrument. She was stripped, but had not been sexually assaulted.

Dr. Sheppard, a well-known local socialite, said that after friends spent the evening with him and Marilyn at their home, he fell asleep on the couch downstairs. He was awakened before dawn by his wife's screams. He raced upstairs, grappled with one or two shadowy forms in the bedroom, was struck on the back of his neck, briefly examined his wife and found her dead, went downstairs, saw an intruder ransacking his desk, chased him outside, ran down to the lake front behind his home, wrestled with a man on his private beach near the edge of the lake, and fell unconscious there. When he came to, he went back into the house, re-examined his wife, wandered about in a daze for a while, and finally called a neighbor and friend, the Bay Village mayor. The rest was public.

The police theorized that after the guests left, Sheppard had an argument with his wife over the fact that he was having affairs with other women; that in a rage he fatally struck her with one of his surgical instruments; and that after realizing what had happened, he made it appear as if someone else had done it.

The wealthy Sheppard family was well known in the area. They traveled in the best circles. There were rumors of daring social activities in which the Sheppards took part.

The case caused tremendous competition between local law enforcement agencies from Bay Village and from Cuyahoga County. One local coroner, a well-known sleuth who took great pride in his murder investigations, became intensely involved. Eventually, nearby Cleveland officials came into the case. Not irrelevant to an understanding of the great public play in the case is the fact that at the time, the trial judge was seeking re-election and the assistant county prosecutor who spearheaded the prosecution was running for a vacated judgeship. Both were supported by the newspapers and eventually won their elections.

The *Cleveland Press* was the largest paper in Ohio and at that time had a circulation of 310,000. Throughout the pretrial and trial period, circulation went above that level; the increase was climaxed by a complete newsstand sellout of 30,000 extra copies the day the verdict of the case was announced. The other major paper was the *Cleveland Plain Dealer*.[3] It was the first to publish (on the morning of July 5) after the crime. It gave the story an eight-column banner headline on page one. Between then and Sheppard's arrest, the *Plain Dealer,* the morning paper, accorded the Sheppard murder story a page-one banner headline on twelve out of twenty-six days. On nine more days the murder was still the lead page-one story, but without a banner. On four other days it was on the front page but not as the lead story. On one day of the twenty-six, no Sheppard story appeared in the *Plain Dealer*.

The *Cleveland Press,* the afternoon paper, used the Sheppard case as its lead page-one story on each one of the twenty-three days it published during the prearrest period (the *Press* did not publish on Sunday). Nearly every story commanded an eight-column banner headline. On at least three occasions, the Sheppard case (a lead story and several sidebars) consumed nearly all of page one and several inside pages. On three days, the *Press* ran front-page editorials on the case (it printed no other front-page editorials during this period).

[3] Coverage by a third Cleveland paper, the *News,* was mostly unexceptionable.

It was not only the quantity and prominence of the coverage but also the intrusion of the newspapers into the merits of the case and the effect of the *Press*'s editorial position on the administration of justice that have made the episode the subject of such continuing concern and comment.

The prime mover in the *Press*'s coverage, editor Louis B. Seltzer, describes in his autobiography, *The Years Were Good,* his rationale in the Sheppard case:

> For mystery, for suspense, for painstaking putting together of fragmentary clues by the most scientific methods, the Sheppard murder, which was to become one of the country's most famous of modern times, had within it all the elements of the classic criminal case.
>
> It had one other element, which set it apart from most murder cases of this type. That was the deliberate effort to prevent the law enforcement authorities from finding the killer. The case became both a murder and, in a very real sense, a roadblock against the law. . . .
>
> Dr. Sam was fenced in by his family, his friends and the public authorities of Bay Village. The protective wall had been put up quickly. It was almost impossible to penetrate it, and then only at the will of those who controlled the encirclement—and on their terms. The pose seemed obvious—to hold the wall secure around Dr. Sam until public interest subsided, and the investigating authorities turned their attention elsewhere.
>
> The newspapers began to lose interest—except one. The *Press* kept the Sheppard murder case in top position on page one. It kept steadily prying into the case, asking questions, trying to break through the wall around Dr. Sam.[4]

During the first few days after the murder, both papers supplied voluminous coverage containing large chunks of partisan information that could have been revealed only by the police authorities doing the investigating. At the outset, Prosecutor John J. Mahon took over the investigation and suggested to the press, "There is too much delay here." Detectives complained that Dr. Sheppard was being shielded from them. Competition between different police authorities developed. And the Sheppard family, in the middle of an intercity jurisdictional squabble, found themselves criticized for shielding Dr. Sam.

From the beginning, favorable information seems to have been played down or buried. Newspapers placed police comment on the front page; they relegated to page four, and confined in a small story, the favorable

[4] World Publishing Company, Cleveland and New York, 1956; p. 267.

news that the Sheppard family was offering a reward for information leading to the arrest of the killer, and a statement by Dr. Sheppard that he was ready to cooperate in the investigation in every way. Coroner Samuel Gerber began to supply the *Press* with every shred of evidence and every opinion from his investigation, referring derogatorily and with subjective conclusions to the "inconsistencies in Dr. Sheppard's 'version of what happened.'" Preposterous stories cropped up from all manner of sources around the country, which the police consistently leaked. Only later were they discredited.

On July 20, the *Press* appeared with a front-page editorial entitled "Somebody's Getting Away with Murder." It asked, "What's the matter with the law enforcement authorities?" It called the investigation "studded with fumbling, halting, stupid, uncooperative bungling." It asked, "Why all this sham, hypocrisy, politeness, criss-crossing of pomp and protocol in this case?" It argued that the case was being botched. It complained that in the background of the case were "friendships, relationships, hired lawyers, a husband who ought to have been subjected instantly to the same third degree to which any other person under similar circumstances is subjected, and a whole string of special and bewildering extra-privileged courtesies." It went on to guess that the killer "must be laughing secretly at the whole spectacle." And then, pointing clearly to Dr. Sam, it said, "Why shouldn't he chuckle? Why shouldn't he cover up, shut up, conceal himself behind the circle of protecting people?"

The pressure was on. After the editorial the Bay Village city council voted to hand the investigation over to the Cleveland Police Department's homicide squad. The police asked aloud why there was no inquest and why Dr. Sam would not take a lie detector test.

The doctor's marital infidelity was heavily publicized both before and during the trial—detectives had told reporters about his affair with another woman and the information was promptly published. The *Press* added cartooning to its editorializing about Dr. Sheppard, and at one point printed a front-page article on his deferment from military service.

On July 30, 1954, Dr. Sheppard was arrested. Arrest and pretrial coverage continued from July 31 to September 23. In its fifty-three days of publication during that period, the *Press* gave the story a banner headline twenty-three times, lead position twenty-six times, and a place on the front page thirty-one times. On two other days, the Sheppard story appeared elsewhere in the paper. The newspaper was silent about the case on twenty days. In the *Plain Dealer*, the treatment and display were slightly less generous.

In all the papers on July 30, the arrest of Sheppard was praised and favorable official comment on the action was reported. The police chief was quoted as saying, "It's about time." The mayor lauded the arrest. There were pictures of Dr. Sheppard on his way to jail.

On August 2, there was a long story about a twelve-hour grilling of Dr. Sheppard which could only have been written from detailed accounts by the police. The *Press* said, "They have smashed through cover-up techniques of the killer," and added that Dr. Sam could no longer be given a lie detector test even if he requested it, because "this man has schooled himself completely and any reaction now would be unreliable and not indicative of his true feelings."

On August 7, the prosecutor was quoted as saying, "There is a strong circumstantial case against Dr. Sheppard." On August 10, the *Press* said, "The police have virtually completed their investigation of the July 4 murder of Mrs. Marilyn Reese Sheppard. Their conclusion is that they have convincing evidence to prove that Dr. Sam Sheppard . . . was the killer."

Leaks continued. The authorities were as eager to offer pretrial disclosures as reporters were to extract them. The police chief was quoted as saying he was convinced that Sheppard was the right man. New evidence was appraised as being damning to Sheppard. The point was reached where the *Press* was printing previews of the following day's grand jury testimony. An outline of what the prosecution's case would be was published. The court's refusal to grant bail to Dr. Sheppard was interpreted in the press as the growing "presumption of Sheppard's guilt." Finally, on September 23, in the *Press*'s last story until the trial in October, the names and addresses of all those picked for the jury panel were printed on page one.

Under Ohio law the jury panel is chosen a month in advance of the trial date. Thus the sixty-four possible jurors, their names and addresses made known to anyone who read the newspapers, were exposed to a month of pretrial discussion from a wide variety of sources. In fact, as

one observer put it, they became "minor celebrities." Jury selection took
two weeks, with the *Press* reporting each choice. Even during the selection proceedings the jurors were exposed to unusual publicity:

> When Judge Blythin came to court Tuesday morning he found his
> courtroom overrun by cameras and cameramen representing newsreels,
> television, magazines and newspapers. Flash bulbs were popping and
> huge lighting devices backed by powerful reflectors were sprouting
> from chairs, tables, and floor to near-ceiling height, their cables twist-
> ing and coiling over the carpeting.
>   [Defense counsel] Corrigan rose to protest that no trial could be car-
> ried on amid such hubbub. "They're standing on tables, sitting on rail-
> ings, and hanging from chandeliers," he asserted. "They're even taking
> motion pictures of the jurors—that is, when they can get their lenses
> past the assistant prosecuting attorneys trying to get into the picture."
>   Judge Blythin was angry, too. He sternly ordered all photographic
> equipment removed forthwith from the courtroom and ruled that no
> pictures of any kind could be made in the courtroom for the duration
> of the trial, even when the court was not in session. Glum and sullen,
> the photographers picked up their gear and transferred their activities
> to corridors and nearby courtrooms. Later in the trial this rule was fre-
> quently and openly disregarded.[5]

After four prosecution peremptory challenges and five by the defense,
as well as thirty-nine challenges for cause, Judge Blythin declared,
"Gentlemen, we have a jury." The judge ruled that the best proof that
there was no need for either continuance or change of venue was that
a fair jury had in fact been obtained. Thirteen prospective jurors were
not seated because their opinions based upon pretrial press coverage
were by the time of the trial unalterable. One woman, an alternate
juror, swore she knew nothing about the case. Five of the empaneled
jurors had admitted upon examination in the process known as voir dire
that they had read a great deal about the case, but swore they would
not allow what they had read to influence their decisions. The rest had
heard or read something about the case, but similarly swore they could
put it aside and make their decision on the evidence. The jurors were
allowed to go home at the end of each session but were admonished not

⁵ Paul Holmes, *The Sheppard Murder Case* (New York: Bantam, 1961); also
see Stephen Sheppard with Paul Holmes, *My Brother's Keeper* (New York: McKay,
1964).

to discuss the case and, after a few days, were finally instructed not to read the newspaper reports of the trial.

On October 8, ten days before the trial began, the *Press* published on page one results of a public opinion poll showing an overwhelming consensus favoring a verdict of guilty, and a lengthy story giving the details of the state's case. Defense motions for change of venue were characterized as frivolous and dilatory. The trial judge was praised for his determination that opinionated jurors would not automatically be banned so long as they could listen to and be guided by the evidence and the court's instructions in reaching a verdict.

On October 18, amid front-page-banner hoopla in all three papers, the trial began. The prosecutor outlined his case for the newspapers and said, "We think we have a strong case." A few days later the *Press* ran a feature story on the prosecutor's campaign for judgeship. It also printed brief biographies of each juror.

On October 23, the *Press* printed a feature story on page one, under an eight-column headline reading: "WHO WILL SPEAK FOR MARILYN?" Lineups of the witnesses, thumbnail biographies, pictures, and predictions of testimony found their way into the papers during the trial. Picture-taking was allowed in the courtroom at times when the trial was not in process.

Derogatory descriptions of defense witnesses and the defendant were paralleled in the *Press* with glowing descriptions of the prosecution. The *Press*'s tone is exemplified by such reports as, "Six laboratory detectives prepared today to throw a scientific harpoon into Dr. Sam's version of how his wife was murdered." "The state plans to use Dr. Hoverston and Miss Hayes as 'Sunday punch' witnesses to support the prosecution's contention of the motive for murder." "The jury will hear . . . Police Chief John Eaton tell how the authorities checked out numerous suspects and found the evidence always pointing to the victim's husband."

Prosecution witnesses were described as soft-spoken. The defense lawyer was described as belligerent. It was predicted that someone's testimony would show Sheppard as "a regular Dr. Jekyll and Mr. Hyde." Many of the damning developments reported as imminent never, in fact, emerged in trial. Much of the information about events supposed to take place could only have come from the prosecutors or the police. The constant leakage from prosecuting officials to the press was obvious.

The jury found Sheppard guilty (it was disclosed later that two jurors voted for acquittal on the first ballot).

In the words of District Judge Carl Weinman in 1964, "If ever there was a trial by newspaper, this is the perfect example." He said that the *Press* "took upon itself the role of accuser, judge and jury."

After almost a decade in jails and in appellate courts, suffering from and appealing the verdict of his highly public trial, Dr. Sheppard secured from the United States Supreme Court a reversal on the ground that publicity had deprived him of due process of law.[6] A retrial was ordered, and Dr. Sheppard was acquitted.

An example of the frightening capacity of crime coverage to defame and never adequately to make amends is provided by an episode in California in 1952, when John Alvin Rexinger was arrested in connection with the rape and torture of a nineteen-year-old nurse. The facts, as summarized in a magazine article:

> At about 10:30 P.M. of a Saturday night, a pretty young nurse and her escort, James Lonergan, were approached by a stranger as they stopped their car in Golden Gate Park. At knife's point, the stranger bound Lonergan with cord and gagged him with adhesive tape, manacled the girl with leg irons, cut off her hair with a pair of scissors, burned her with a cigarette, raped her twice and, before leaving, pricked her and Mr. Lonergan with his knife. To top all, he stole Mr. Lonergan's wrist watch.[7]

Needless to say, the ugly circumstances of the crime lent themselves to press exploitation. When Rexinger was arrested all four San Francisco newspapers featured his picture with the headline: "THAT'S HIM!" The newspapers smacked their lips over the details. The *San Francisco Chronicle* called the attacker a "torture kit rapist." The *Examiner* called him "the mad rapist" and the *News* called him the "Fanged Fiend" because he was described by the victim as having canine teeth that protruded over his lower lip. Coverage of the Rexinger case, according to the same article, "might be compared with the rising strains of a huge orchestra, swelling from crescendo to crescendo."

Rexinger, a parolee from San Quentin, had come under police suspi-

---

[6] This decision is discussed in Chapters 7 and 13.

[7] Decca M. Treuhaft, "Trial by Headline," *Nation*, October 26, 1957. See also John Lofton, "Trial by Fury," *Nation*, November 25, 1961.

cion because he had a record of sex crimes and resembled a police sketch of the assailant. The victim identified him as her attacker. Both she and her escort had given varied descriptions of the assailant, and admitted that they were somewhat incoherent and under shock at the time of the attack. As a matter of fact, Rexinger had been found guilty of forgery in the past. But his sex conviction was for statutory rape, and he had never been imprisoned, because no violence had been used.

Newspaper stories told of tape recordings of Rexinger's literary compositions, which police found in his apartment. Though police criminologists had turned up no incriminating evidence, the *Examiner* quoted a police inspector who, acknowledging that he was no literary critic, said that the tape of the defendant's poetic ramblings "clearly indicates he, Rexinger, is a sexual psychopath and sadist." Buried by the same newspaper was the fact that another qualified official stated that after intensive psychiatric examination there was no evidence of any sadistic drive in Rexinger.

The newspapers compared Rexinger with another criminal who had been executed earlier the same year for murder and rape of a fourteen-year-old girl. They pointed out the physical resemblance between the two men and said that the means Rexinger used were reminiscent of the manner of the other man.

Rexinger meanwhile steadfastly denied any role in the case. The press crusade against him continued for eight days after his arrest. Every police move was headlined. Interviews with the suspect in which he protested his innocence were eclipsed by police comments that sought to undo them. He was described as "testy," "suspicious," "con-wise," "withdrawn," and "evasive." Information favorable to Rexinger received scant notice.

The *Examiner* printed evidence discovered by its reporters that was later discredited, but only after its damaging publication. The *Chronicle* saw fit to publish on page 24 the remark of a district attorney that the case was weak.

A week later, another man, picked up for a different offense, confessed to the crime when it was discovered that he possessed James Lonergan's watch. When charged with the crime, he showed police the tools he had used in the attack. Microscopic examination of them confirmed his confession. Interestingly, the real criminal did *not* fit the description that had been given by the victim.

The *Chronicle* thereupon noted that *the police* had created a case "strong enough to send an innocent man to San Quentin for life." The *Examiner* also criticized the police for being more interested in a conviction than the truth. The *News* was even more aggressive, blaming Rexinger for his own predicament: "Above all, Rexinger lied. . . . Had it not been for his falsehoods, police would never have been able to build up a case against him." Thus the *News* absolved the press and police, blamed the victim himself, and even took credit for the press's notably creative role in the affair. With awesomely gymnastic logic, the *News* then pointed out that the "spotlight of public interest" saved Rexinger because "our kind of society demands facts. Spurred on by public interest, police could produce the facts—and clear him." Indeed this was so. But only after the newspapers indulged in the most intensive efforts to convict him. Inordinate amounts of news space were given to all aspects and fantasies of the case. The police even furnished the tape recordings from his room, and the newspapers promptly published them. That Rexinger was cleared was in no way thanks to the press; for more than a week his arrest was never off the front pages. No newspaper came to his aid or presented his side.

That the publicity failed to subject Rexinger to unfair trial and unjust conviction is, of course, no exculpation of the press; he was injured seriously enough, and in a way that permitted precious little possibility of amelioration.

It is perfectly true that some of the most hair-raising examples of prejudicial publication have had, so to speak, "happy" outcomes, as in the Rexinger case; the juries failed to convict, some fortuitous circumstance arose, or some *diabolus ex machina* providentially emerged to take the rap.

The press is inclined to argue from this pattern of experience that there has been no proven case of a guiltless person having been imprisoned or executed because of justice-warping publicity. The claim may be at least arguable with respect to executions, but there are some examples—mercifully only a few—where prejudicial publications seem to have sent innocent men to prison or to have played a part in causing them to linger long and miserably in jail until justice was ultimately done them.[8]

[8] Edwin N. Borchard, *Convicting the Innocent, Errors of Criminal Justice* (Hamden, Conn.: Shoestring Press, Inc., 1932); Jerome Frank and Barbara Frank, *Not Guilty* (Garden City: Doubleday, 1957).

But even if the claim were true, it misses the crucial point. What *is* at stake, and concerns the press and the common citizen as much as the legal philosopher, is the essential requirement, fundamental to the safety of all men's rights, that a trial be conducted according to the legal rules prescribed for it, not according to simplistic notions of rough justice. Punctilious observation of the legal processes is not merely the hallmark of civilization but its safeguard. To treat this notion cavalierly is to put one's foot on the path that leads to drumhead courts and vigilante proceedings.[9]

The free press, fair trial issue has to do with just that: fair trial, not simply a conclusion of guilt or innocence. The distinction is not captious, but basic.

In the trial process, it is not the defendant alone who may fall victim to the sensationalist press. Although as a matter of Constitutional law a fair trial is guaranteed the defendant, certainly as a matter of social policy the state deserves a fair trial as well. And the reporting of criminal cases may work to prejudice the government, too. An example is the trial in September, 1960, of "Tony" Accardo, well-known Chicago underworld figure and alleged heir to the Al Capone rackets kingdom.

After a long, expensive, and exhaustive investigation, the United States government indicted Accardo for criminal tax evasion. The government, wanting to protect its case, scrupulously avoided leaks, did not make public pronouncements, and generally discouraged publicity. Yet the Chicago newspapers, not because the case itself was interesting —it was not—but because of Accardo's reputation, had a field day. They never left it alone. During the empaneling of the Accardo jury, the newspapers reported that the notorious defendant had been arrested fourteen times without conviction; that he had been convicted of disorderly conduct, indicted for carrying concealed weapons, charged with conspiring to defraud the government by using an alias when visiting "syndicated hoodlums" in Leavenworth. As a measure of their fairness,

---

[9] Press spokesmen reveal themselves at their unlettered worst when they complain of the courts' "coddling criminals" or freeing guilty men on "legal technicalities." The legal system is, by definition, a set of procedural technicalities—technicalities to achieve justice by law, not by caprice. As Oliver Wendell Holmes put it in his uniquely precise prose: "The substance of the law is secreted in the interstices of procedure."

they reported, "He beat both charges." "THERE'S A CAPONE ECHO AT ACCARDO TRIAL," was the headline of an article which went on to compare Accardo's trial with Capone's: "In the villain's part this time was Chicago's jet-age Capone—stony-faced . . . Accardo, the master of muscling legitimate business."

After a long jury trial, Accardo was convicted. But on appeal the conviction was reversed, in part on the ground of prejudicial publicity. On the subsequent retrial, Accardo was acquitted. It can be argued that the reversal was wise in that the conviction might well have been based on the prejudicial publicity. On the other hand, it might be true that the imponderable vicissitudes of the trial system worked to Accardo's advantage the second time around. We will never know. But the government and the public are entitled to stable verdicts—especially in important cases (which are usually the most heavily publicized). To win its case, the government should have to convince only twelve jurors beyond a reasonable doubt—not twenty-four.

The Accardo case is an example of the press prejudicing the trial process, first apparently hurting the defendant and ultimately hurting the government.

The confounding kernel of the problem is the lack of consistent cause and effect. For every case where a newspaper destroyed a man by front-paging a charge and burying his acquittal, another exists where a press exposé showed that the wrong man was convicted. For every lynching tirade there is a valuable revelation of corruption or injustice.

Furthermore, how does one account for the perverse results of publicity in weighing the effects of press coverage of criminal cases? Does pointing the finger make a villain or an underdog? Does criticism cause hostility or sympathy? Is the jury contaminated, or in the face of raucous publicity does it bend over backward to do what is expected of it?

These questions arise in their most perplexing form in the Gosser case in Toledo, Ohio, where there appears to have been an intentional attempt by the press to produce a particular verdict, favorable to the accused.

Toledo has two daily newspapers with common ownership, the *Times* and the *Blade*, the latter having far greater circulation and general influence. Coverage of the Gosser case by the *Times* was unremarkable except for its contrast with the other paper's coverage. An examination of the timing and nature of pretrial publications of the *Blade* discloses a singular pattern of news, editorials, pictures, and feature articles. Interestingly, the later reports of the trial proceedings themselves, if partisan, were not biased, even according to aggrieved government representatives.

Richard Gosser was a long-time labor leader who eventually rose through the ranks to a high position in the AFL-CIO executive council; he was the top United Auto Workers official in Toledo, his home town. Long suspected by Federal officials of having rackets affiliations, he was arrested in 1962 and charged with criminal conspiracy to defraud the United States. Gosser and others had paid a secretary at the local Internal Revenue Service office to smuggle reports of investigations to Gosser and certain associated local rackets figures. The secretary had been caught at her task; she told all to government authorities, and continued her work under the eye of the Department of Justice. As a result of government surveillance, Gosser and others were caught and arrested with the incriminating evidence.

Two days after Gosser's arrest, on November 14, 1962, the *Blade* published a front-page statement by Gosser denying guilt and charging a frame-up and Gestapo methods on the part of the government. On the following day, November 15, the *Blade* published a lead editorial the thrust of which was that the prosecution of Gosser, an important citizen in that community, was undertaken for political reasons; that the then Attorney General, Robert F. Kennedy, was carrying water for UAW president Walter Reuther against his long-time enemy Gosser, even as Kennedy had done against another Reuther foe, Teamster president James R. Hoffa; and that there was some question whether a grand jury would indict and bring about a trial.

On January 8, 1963, the date set for hearings on the defense motions to suppress the evidence in the case, the *Blade* printed two articles about Gosser. The first, apropos of no prior or current event, was a front-page report that he had issued a statement saying plans had been made to build an adjunct to the UAW Health and Retiree Center. The other article, on the front page of the second section, was headlined: "GOSSER URGES HIRING ABLE, WILLING FROM RELIEF ROLLS." It described a proposal Gosser had made at a UAW luncheon to form a booster committee and noted the fact that he was under indictment and, though voluntarily suspended from union duties, remained active in the administration of the Health and Retiree Center. The apparent newsworthiness of all this was that Gosser was continuing his community affairs even though he was in the toils of the law.

On January 23, six days before trial, amid public discussion by Gosser that he was framed and was the victim of Gestapo tactics, the *Blade* editorialized on the prosecution of Major General Edwin A. Walker in Mississippi. The editorial called for the observance "of the most scrupulous standards . . . from Federal legal officials." It said, "If highhanded procedures are followed against a Walker, others are also exposed to such treatment." This editorial, though pertaining to someone else, was peculiarly applicable to the defense that Gosser was raising and the paper's earlier editorial about Attorney General Kennedy.

On January 27, two days before the trial was to begin, the *Blade* published on the first and third pages of its editorial section (of which eighteen thousand extra copies were distributed free in the schools) a large feature article about Gosser. It contained a pictorial history of his rise in the labor movement, and an account of his maturity as a statesman who enriched his community and who was now, in the twilight of his career, facing a tragic trial based on what he characterized as political persecution. Photographs showed Gosser breaking ground for the Retiree Recreation Center, at a UAW summer camp, and at a Democratic political rally. The article was capped by a picture of him in a benign pose.

The next day the *Blade* editorialized that the Gosser case was the product of a lack of integrity on the part of the Federal government and resulted from a personal vendetta and the connivance of UAW president Reuther and Attorney General Robert F. Kennedy, with the aid and comfort even of President John F. Kennedy. Entitled "A Case of Conspiracy," the editorial read in part:

> . . . What have they got against Dick Gosser? . . .
>
> If something was stolen from the IRS office, why was the person most directly involved in it—an IRS employee at the time—never even indicted?
>
> And was it solely by chance that a small army of top federal agents converged on Toledo for the arrests in what might otherwise appear to be a routine case?
>
> The man who commands the Federal Government's civil forces in these matters—and sometimes, as in Mississippi recently, its military

forces as well—is no shrinking violet. With all due respect for his reso-
lute sense of purpose in high office, we can't overlook Attorney General
Kennedy's demonstrated capacity for political strategy and forceful
maneuver. . . .

Has [Robert Kennedy's] failure to nab Jimmy Hoffa moved him to
seek a new target, possibly more vulnerable?

Or, does Walter Reuther's increasing disenchantment with his senior
vice president in Toledo present a more convenient outlet for political
ambition?

For all Mr. Reuther's labor statesmanship, he is not above moving
obliquely against those with whom he has differed in labor circles.

Wouldn't it be quite a feat for the Attorney General to clobber a labor leader at last—and have it conveniently please a labor politician
who worked most assiduously in behalf of the Kennedys during the
1960 presidential campaign? . . .

Dick Gosser belongs to Toledo, is a part of this community. Certainly we have disagreed with him in the past and have said so in no
uncertain terms. But we also have recognized his many contributions to
this city, which he loves.

During the last decade, in particular, he has exercised a maturity of
leadership in Toledo's industrial economy that this city has sorely
needed. If that offended Mr. Reuther, it was Toledo's gain, including
UAW members whose jobs were protected.

And with his Sand Lake summer camp for children, his health clinic
the year round, his retiree center for older folk, his influential voice
endorsing many civic improvements, Dick Gosser has been a mighty
power for good in this community.

As the trial progresses, a large segment of Toledo will be most interested in what kind of conspiracy is involved in the case against Dick
Gosser.

Were these articles a calculated attempt to influence the potential
jurors, who were up to this point part of the public but who were
close to becoming a part of the trial process? The *Blade* had never behaved similarly. Government attorneys categorized the flow of information in this case as a partisan and progressive build-up which reached
its peak just before the trial.

One editorial attacked the trial judge. Editorials after the trial also
attacked the ultimate verdict of guilty. One was entitled "Law Triumphs
Over Justice." In the words of the government trial attorneys, it con-
doned the perjury of the defendants, confessed that the paper had
known all along that the defendants were guilty of wrongdoing and ex-

cused the wrongdoing as human nature, and then attacked the system of justice that could imprison men for such action in this unfair manner. The *Blade* then ran a Sunday feature article on the pitfalls of the law of conspiracy, neglecting to point out the pains taken by the court to avoid them. Although these latter articles appeared after the verdict, they are relevant in assaying the continuous, over-all pattern of the *Blade*.

Almost every juror admitted on voir dire that he had read of the case, specifically the January 27 feature piece. But they all swore that they could discard from mind anything they had read and could judge the case upon the evidence and the law.

Gosser's conviction came after a long, hard trial. While on the one hand it could be argued that the guilty verdict renders void all criticism of these publications, on the other hand it could be asked whether or not the press here created a substantial danger which the government managed to overcome.

Better than most, perhaps, the Gosser case raises a perplexing question that can only be speculated about, not finally resolved.

Does the verdict show the adequacy of voir dire? The integrity of juries? Publicity may work in perverse ways. Could a jury exposed to this volume of partisan and sustained coverage have set it aside? Presumably it did. It could be that while the publicity did have an impact on the jury, the voir dire and the instructions dissolved it.

Is the time to weigh the culpability of publicity before the verdict? If the measure may be taken only after the verdict, the Toledo *Blade* has an irrefutable defense to any claim of wrongdoing.

The quandary lies in the realization that while a verdict itself may be an empirical measure of the impact of the publicity, in some cases the verdict may come at a point in time too late to help the victim. A defendant who is the subject of extreme pressure for conviction could point to a verdict against him as evidence of prejudice; but by that time the damage to him would already have been done. And how could he prove that the verdict was not the product of a dispassionate judgment of the trial record alone? Should the fortuities of the verdict absolve a publication that intentionally (assuming intent could be proved) seeks to pervert the trial process? Should its failure be its salvation? Or is this wrong a wrong itself, demonstrable notwithstanding an inconsistent verdict?

Does the Gosser case indicate that the press's power is overestimated; that publication is only one inconclusive current that works upon the trial process's inexorable move toward truth?

The favorable publicity that preceded Gosser's appearance in court seemed to have benefited him in no way. For a contrast, however, consider the case of William Van Rie, brought to trial in Boston in February, 1960, accused of murder.

Months before, the brutally beaten body of a wealthy, well-educated, and beautiful twenty-three-year-old divorcée was found floating in the waters of Boston Harbor. Her half-nude body had been thrown overboard from the Dutch freighter *Utrecht,* on which she and chaperoning friends had been returning from Singapore. After a long and well-publicized investigation, Van Rie, the ship's radio operator and a Dutch citizen, was arrested and charged with the murder. He admitted having had an affair with the woman during the crossing and having struck her on the night of her murder; but he denied any knowledge of her death.

The Netherlands Consulate General secured defense counsel for Van Rie and brought to the United States his wife, Nella, his childhood sweetheart whom he had married. The heavy coverage, police-and-prosecution-oriented, typical early in the case then took a turn, and began to stress Van Rie's youth and good reputation in Holland, his tearful reunion with his devoted, loyal wife who had come three thousand miles to stand by her husband. In the words of one reporter:

> One friendly story after another recounted their tearful reunion in Charles Street jail in Boston, her semiweekly visits to her husband, her repeated assertions of her belief in his innocence.
>
> "In this case," says a Boston attorney, "the defendant has turned the tables on the prosecution. He has got a better play in the press than the government."
>
> In fact, he adds, the Van Rie side has received so much sympathetic attention that "there would be very little possibility that a prospective jury would be unfairly influenced, unless to the detriment of the Commonwealth."
>
> Attorney W. Langdon Powers, who with his brother Walter will defend Mr. Van Rie, admits the publicity in this case has "helped tremendously."[10]

[10] Emilie Tavel, *Christian Science Monitor,* January 26, 1960.

Headlines changed from captions like "THOSE BLUNT-FORCE INJURIES—HOW DID LYNN GET THEM?" "POLICE FIND DISCREPANCIES IN UTRECHT MAN'S STORY," "OFFICER ADMITS SLUGGING LYNN," "HEIRESS CALLED TO HER FOR HELP, PROFESSOR SPECTER'S WIFE REVEALS," to such defense-oriented titles as "NETHERLANDS GOVERNMENT EYES CASE," "VAN RIE CALLED 'GENEROUS BOY' BY NEIGHBORS," "GIRLS PACK CORRIDORS FOR COURT APPEARANCE," "COME AND STAND BY ME VAN PLEADS WITH WIFE," "SLEEPING ACCUSATION VAGUE, COUNSEL FOR VAN RIE SAYS," "VAN RIE HUGS WIFE, BREAKS INTO TEARS," "VAN RIE'S WIFE CALMLY CONFIDENT," "TWO LEGAL-MEDICS EXPERTS WILL TESTIFY FOR VAN RIE." Developing sympathy with the defendant could be sensed from the news stories as well.

Van Rie was acquitted. The spectators burst into applause as he left the courtroom. That a community which had banned books of Theodore Dreiser on grounds of obscenity could applaud an admitted adulterer just acquitted of murdering his paramour offers an interesting view of human nature. It may be that Van Rie's popularity with the jury and the courtroom audience resulted from his popularity with the press, which treated him better than most charged murderers and admitted adulterers. Or perhaps his success derived not from the fact that he was popular and made better copy as an attractive underdog than as a vilified accused, but rather from a certain peculiar, perverse public reaction to some crimes and criminals that cannot be explained or predicted.

Another sensational case, raising the same puzzling questions, had to do with issues almost mystical in their impact. In the 1966 "Krebiozen trial," promoters of the drug were pitted against the power and prestige of the Establishment, medical and governmental. Not only the inherently interesting merits of the medical dispute itself, but also human predilections about miracles and the defiance of authority gave the case electric overtones.

The anti-cancer drug Krebiozen provoked an intense controversy in the United States. Such professional groups as the American Cancer Society and the American Medical Association, along with many others, found the drug to have no medical value. Yet it had its champions within the medical profession, among high and reputable public officials, as well as among cancer victims, hundreds of whom passionately maintained they had been cured by the drug. After many protracted and vitriolic clashes, the Food and Drug Administration finally forbade interstate shipment of Krebiozen. Its developer, Dr. Stevan Durovic; his lawyer-brother, Marko; Dr. Andrew C. Ivy, a well-known doctor and former vice president of the University of Illinois; and another associate were indicted by the United States government for criminal conspiracy and mail fraud in the development and distribution of the drug. After a controversial nine-month trial (and about four million words of testimony), all four were acquitted.

The lay onlooker could only conclude that the issues of the case were irresolvably confounding; the government argued that the drug's curative powers were dangerously and deceivingly absent and that the defendants bilked the pathetic public and made personal fortunes; the defendants presented specialists who disagreed and patients who testified they were cured by the drug. What could a jury do? And how could the press or the public resist involvement in such an intriguing trial?

The point of the Gosser, Van Rie, and Krebiozen cases is that we simply do not know about the effects of public information upon juries; nor can we predict the results of crime and trial news with any degree of certainty. The general, and we admit very logical, assumptions that are made about partiality and unfairness inevitably following heavy press coverage are not supported by scientific or even consistent evidence.

The bitter complaint of "trial by newspaper" arises principally from these and many other notorious cases whose names have become almost household words in the debate: Finch and Tregoff, Chessman, the Scottsboro Boys, etc., plus those made famous in landmark Supreme Court decisions (discussed in Chapter 7).

If all were the subject matter of sensationalist press treatment, it is also true that the crimes involved were themselves sensational. They were newsworthy (to use the word without any morally prescriptive connotation), which is to say they grasped the public interest; and the cause was not merely press treatment. They were "naturals" to begin with. Almost all embraced one or more of those elements which the Ohio Supreme Court noted were present in the Sheppard case: suspense, mystery, social prominence or important position of the principals, extreme violence and, for the most part, sex.[11]

[11] To dally for a moment with moral value judgments about what should and should not be of public interest, it can be conceded that fascination with lascivious and prurient subject matter is deplorable. But, lamentable or not, it is a powerful fact; to ignore it, pretend otherwise, or resolve that everyone should rise above it is futile.

If the interest of cases like these to the public was rendered kinetic in part by the press, it was only because potential interest was inherent. They were sensational because they were extraordinary, provocative, shocking, and utterly fascinating. Their dynamics were not to be gainsaid.

But when public interest occasions private injury, a decent society cannot simply throw up its hands, shake its collective head mournfully, and, without trying to do anything more about it, accept the situation as inescapable and irremediable. Nor, of course, has society done that. It has sought remedies by means of law and by a multitude of other corrective proposals. Increasingly, since the assassination of President Kennedy, it has complained of the press and has questioned the propriety and purpose of acts by the news media that offer injury to the Constitutional rights of defendants.

Yet, in one way or another, each of the proposals and all of the complaints have collided with the legal imperatives and social values of maintaining a free untrammeled press in a democracy. The consequence has been the most intense debate on the free press, fair trial issue in the history of the Republic, and, it may be hoped, one of the most productive.

Its resolution, we suggest, is not nearly so simple, nor are the merits of the argument so overwhelmingly on one side or the other as the extreme partisans of the debate appear to believe.

CHAPTER 2

IS CRIME NEWS

FIT TO PRINT?

Directly or indirectly, almost all the proposed solutions to the free press, fair trial dilemma require delaying the publication of potentially prejudicial news until it is introduced in open court or until the case is disposed of. In chapters that follow, we shall consider in detail this "solution by postponement" of publication, which has been offered in several forms. All of them make judgments about what the press ought not to publish before or during trial; they go on to provide that the press be prevented by law, or refrain by voluntary means such as codes of ethics, from publishing the proscribed material, and that enforcement measures be used to stop police, prosecutors, and counsel from uttering it. But before we discuss these suggestions, it is necessary to clear a certain amount of underbrush.

Among many critics of the press, especially those concerned with the fair trial problem, there is a conviction that the press has no business publishing the volume of news about crime that it does and with such sensationalism. The conviction is often unvoiced and sometimes not even consciously recognized. At first glance, the contention seems self-evident; on examination, it turns out to be extraordinarily complex and by no means easy to sustain, much less to put into practice.

But until the broad issue of the press coverage of crime is dealt with, consideration of specific solutions to the free press, fair trial problem is impossible. For the man who wishes to limit news coverage or the flow of information finds it almost irresistible when discussion about his measures grows intense (or, more usually, rancorous) to fall back on the argument that the publication he objects to on specific fair trial grounds is really objectionable on other, social grounds.

Moreover, some of the ramifications of the "solution by postpone-ment" bear directly on the larger question of the social purpose of publi-cation of crime news in general; and they deeply affect the operations of the press in matters far removed from coverage of crime. Measures that appear to be narrowly focused only on postponement of crime news actually entail extraordinarily worrisome practices affecting audience confidence in the media; they raise troublesome issues on the proper purpose and function of the press and its effectiveness as an instrumen-tality of society. As will be shown later, many cases of postponement of publication, however limited in theory, mean actual nonpublication in practice.

Lest the statements that follow be misunderstood, it is necessary to antic-ipate at this point some of our conclusions:

1. American press coverage of crime news often is excessive and offensive, pandering to the lowest taste and unnecessary even for the most basic commercial reasons. The press should move to clean house on its own initiative and through persuasive means available within its institutions. Public resentment grows, and may be succeeded by meas-ures more punitive than wise.

2. A great deal of information about crimes and those accused of them that is seemingly prejudicial could be postponed until it emerged during trial or thereafter without serious loss to the media and their audience. This is true particularly with respect to publication of evi-dentiary matters such as the existence of confessions, the pretrial com-ments of police and prosecutors about indications of probable guilt and, in many cases, about the defendant's criminal record.

Our opposition, then, is not to general objectives, but, as will be seen, to proposals that are universal in scope and absolutist in implementa-tion. For the moment, our argument is simply against the underlying notions that crime and police news is per se deplorable, and that if only the press acknowledged the fact and acted upon it, the threat to fair trial through prejudicial publication would virtually disappear.

The standard complaint of critic to news-media owner or publisher about the sensationalism of American crime-coverage is expressed in words something like these: "Why publish all that news about crime anyway? It serves no social purpose; indeed, it is, if anything, injurious to the morals and behavior of the citizenry. Its publication merely breeds more crime and perversion. You publish it because it means more circulation, more money to you . . . and for no other reason."

The standard response of the owner or publisher is a knee-jerk reflex exalting the noble purpose of the news craft.[1] The answer is likely to be triggered as much by commercial as by high moral considerations, and it is the dissembling of the fact, not the fact itself, that is offensive. The commercial purposes of the press are valid, indeed indispensable. Press owners, however, seem to have so impressed themselves with their social responsibilities that they are embarrassed about publicly acknowledging the perfectly praiseworthy economic aspects of their business. What is worse, the answer is rarely convincing or well expounded.[2]

However abusive the charge, however clumsy the reply, the contention deserves attention, and at the beginning of the argument rather than at its usual angry conclusion. There is little point in trying to discover whether or not publication of crime news injures an individual defendant if it is demonstrable that it does injury to the entire community; it is a waste of time to explore various specific remedies for lesser ailments if a larger illness stands in need of universal treatment.

The inquiry will be speeded if both the critic and the respondent shed sanctimoniousness and hypocrisy. There is a great deal of both for each to lay aside. Day in and day out, as readership surveys make brutally clear and as common knowledge confirms, the best-read items in a newspaper are those about crime. This fact is no doubt a sorry reflection on the level of American taste and a cause for melancholy tongue-clucking by everyone dedicated to moral uplift. But it is a fact.

Every editor knows it. With or without readership surveys, he knows that crime news is the hottest article on his counter. Within limits—within rather far extended limits, to be honest about it—the

---

[1] Except that the owner, the publisher, and also the editor and the program director—and possibly even the reporter—will refer to it as a profession. It is not, and a very good thing, too, for the sake of freedom and diversity of expression. Those who wrote the First Amendment understood the danger that would ensue if everyone who was allowed to put word to paper for public exposure had first to undergo some sort of professional training, examination, qualification, and perhaps licensing.

[2] This is curious, for one would expect press executives to be the most adept at marshaling words, the stock in trade of their business, to make their case. The failing is general, and not just in this argument.

publication of crime news bolsters readership and circulation. It is safe to say that no general-circulation newspaper can survive without rather abundant news about crime, even though this cannot be proved, there being no example (the *Wall Street Journal* and the *Christian Science Monitor* are not general-circulation papers but are directed, instead, to special-interest groups). Even the august *New York Times* prints extensive crime and police news, although, of course, in less volume and flamboyance than the *New York Daily News*.[3]

In a competitive situation where there are bound to be occasional or continual battles for readers and revenue, the usual weaponry is the reporting of crime. Even in a one-newspaper community, the editor knows that the most effective leavener to a diet of such wholesome subjects as United Nations debates and suburban zoning decisions is a dash of reportage about a love-nest killing or the heist of the night's receipts from an after-hours drinking club. There are, it will be contended later, essential reasons for the publication of news of crime. But when an editor defends his printing of crime news solely on noble pretensions and as if he entertained no commercial thoughts, he is being transparently disingenuous.

At the same time, he need not be steeped in cynicism to suspect that the critic who denounces his sordid motives in publishing matter of such unelevating content is himself hypocritical and self-righteous: hypocritical because it is doubtful that when he sees a headline over a crime story he reads no further but moves on, uninterested and disdainful, searching for the report of yesterday's contretemps between the Federal Reserve Board and the House Banking Committee; self-righteous in the conviction that somehow he is entitled to judge for the masses below what is fit reading for them, wholesome, edifying, and virtuous, as against what will do them harm.

"The trouble with crime and punishment as it concerns the press," Walter Lippmann has noted, "is that it is too interesting and too absorbing and too convincing because it comes out of real life."[4] It is indeed "too interesting," and the editor who claims to be printing it only to

[3] To draw conclusions about the consequence of that difference from their circulation totals (*New York Times*, daily, 767,239; Sunday, 1,473,981; *News*, daily, 2,122,982; Sunday, 3,135,151; data as of September 30, 1966) is not to indulge entirely in *post hoc, propter hoc* reasoning.

[4] Speech to the International Press Institute, May 27, 1965.

serve the processes of the democratic society, and the bluenose who would suppress it for its entirely too attractive excitement and its lack of uplift, are both deceiving themselves, if nobody else.

But even after the cant has been removed from both sides, the basic argument remains and needs to be pursued much further. News of crime and punishment, thievery and violence, murder and sex—these are what excite interest and rivet attention. But to say that this is so, that it is, indeed, painfully evident, is not to end the argument. It is not the same as saying that the editor and the news director must be slaves to the basest pressures. The ancient excuse that the editor must give the reader everything he wants was never acceptable in the first place and is now too shopworn to warrant refuting. A responsible editor must concede that he is not required to fill his paper or program with such trash and filth that he cannot look at himself in the mirror.

The proper recipe for remedy here is surely *modus in rebus:* moderation in all things. For the extreme of disinfecting a newspaper to complete sterilization is as unreasonable as the extreme of sensationalism. In pointing to the journalistic imperatives of "real life," Lippmann was stating a fact, to be ignored by the press—and by the press critics—at their peril.

Who is to set himself up as the tribunal to decide what the public should read? To an extent, everyone, but also no one. What emerges as the daily diet in the paper or on the television screen is, as it should be, a vector of several forces, some more worthy or more admirable than others. Among them are the pressures of the gentlefolk and the upper class, the well educated and the well born. There are also those of the semiliterates, the vulgarians, and the numbers players at the other end of the culture spectrum. Between these extremes are the pressures of everyone else.

The pressures are positive and negative, commanding that some items be on the bill of fare and that some be prohibited. There are pressures of good taste, of community needs. There are also the heavy pressures—and only a fool would belittle their importance—for a news organ to survive. These are the ones that require a decent regard for the legitimate needs, demands, and interests of those who use the news medium, which is to say the audience and the advertisers. All these pressures are mixed in editors' minds and consciences, by whatever economic and moral computers they use to guide them. Depending

on the pressures, on the economic circumstances, and on the afore-
mentioned consciences, some good and honorable and responsible products emerge, and also some dreadful ones.

A would-be epigram has it that every city gets the kind of newspaper
it deserves. The famed nineteenth-century newspaper editor Charles
Dana is quoted as having said that he was not too proud to print anything that divine providence permitted to happen. The notions are amus-
ing and have some truth to them, but they are surely not the final
answer. Throughout history, society's judgments of excellence have not
gone to him who supplied the most of what the largest number of people
wanted. The calling of editor or program director must have some worthier purposes than passive response to what appear to be audience desires. The news executive denigrates his role when he contends that he
is prisoner to the tastes of his viewers and readers. It is a compliment,
and he should recognize it as such, and be pleased, when the cultivated
or educated critic insists that the press should be a leader, an exemplar,
an advocate in the area of taste; it is even a compliment when the press,
alone of commercial ventures, is denounced for betrayal of its noble
purpose if it seeks to sell as much of its product as it possibly can.

The argument here treads on swampy ground and the view is murky.
It is not likely to be settled in these pages, and it has not been settled
anywhere else.[5] In some way or other, each press proprietor, editor, or
news executive has to make an individual choice, there being no one else
who can make it for him.

But when the editor exercises what is essentially a fearfully autocratic
power to decide the contents of his medium, he is not as alone as he
might seem. The era of the old-fashioned newspaper tyrant is dead; today's editor must reflect to a considerable degree the preferences, needs,
and demands of his community. With whatever degree of success, the

---

[5] Another murky area, also unsettled, is whether crime news is itself criminogenic.
There is little evidence that it is not, which is natural in view of the difficulty of
proving a negative; but the evidence on the other side suggesting that news and
portrayals of criminal acts encourage their imitation is also inconclusive. It consists
largely of individual examples. Although the statistics would be hard to come by,
it may be that for every man whose unlawful acts are determined to be the consequence of stimulus from a television show, there may be two others who were
kept on the straight and narrow by the never varying demonstration, in every
television show and most newspaper accounts, that the criminal comes to a bad
end.

editor seeks to strike some sort of balance between what he knows are the majority wishes of the general public and what he senses are the imperatives of the community's leaders and elite—and what he himself judges is right.

A decent shopkeeper will not sell shoddy goods or cheat his customer; if the editor is decent, neither will he. The decent news executive tries to put himself in tune with the public as best he can, sensing not only what it wants, which may be scientifically determinable, but making some judgments by himself of what it should have for its own and society's good—which cannot be scientifically determined.

Despite the dreadful programs and newspapers and periodicals, is there a better way to determine the content mix? Given what the audience thinks it wants and doesn't want, and given the economic imperatives of the business, can there be designed, even in the hypothetical absence of the First Amendment, a better way of selecting the content mix than by subjecting the individual elements to whatever news sense, conscience, practicality, good taste, decency, and social responsibility the editor may possess? Is any group likely to do a worthier, more useful and responsible job? An editor or committee named by the government? Someone from the business community, or the labor unions, or the university faculty? A committee of judges? A jury?

Should there be an examination to qualify every press owner, or director—or reporter or announcer? The idea is as repugnant as it is ridiculous. Moreover, there is no indication that, man for man, those of the Fourth Estate are notably inferior in morals or performance to those of the licensed professions. To wander even farther into a dream world, one might ask if all editors should be elected. That is to say, should there be a vote on who ought to operate the news media? The very idea is, or should be, as offensive to the citizens of today's democracy as it was to the men who created democracy in America not quite two centuries ago. They decreed that any man who wanted to had a right to disseminate his views as widely as his resources permitted, without asking anyone's leave.

To be sure, in another but vastly different sense, editors are in fact "elected," in that those whose product fails to satisfy the desires of the readers are removed from office by an economic vote: the subscribers, the audience, and the advertisers pass their products by, with varying degrees of effectiveness. Lord Francis-Williams, the distinguished British philosopher of the press, has noted: "A newspaper's readers are its constituents. They cast their votes for it each day they buy it."

In the area of the press, where absolutism is forbidden, where diversity is to be encouraged, and where values are inescapably subjective, each reader can make his own judgments of what he wants and what he abhors; each can campaign for his likes and dislikes at the top of his lungs. But none is entitled or qualified to set himself up as the arbiter or director of the other fellow's product.

We may grant the injury that can be done to due process of law and the fate of a criminal defendant, but an uneasy feeling must attach to any proposal for limiting publication of crime news. To single it out for special treatment, distinct from that given other categories of news, on grounds that it can sometimes do harm is to argue that potential prejudice to criminal defendants is a thing apart. Publication of a huge variety of news items can cause harm: to the chances of a pending piece of legislation, to the campaign of an office-seeker, to the flotation of a new stock issue, to the sales of a store or a product, to the composure of a concert singer and to his box-office returns—even to the security of a nation. Publication of a Senatorial critic's speech may harm the foreign policy of the President or may undercut the effectiveness of the Secretary of State. Yet no one suggests prohibition or even reduction of that sort of news. It is justified not alone on grounds of truth; its issuance is sanctioned even if the news or the opinions are in error. For it is apparent that controlling its publication (legally or extra-legally, and by whatever set of criteria or value standards one could devise) would be the end of the free flow of information, opinion, and advocacy that is the heart of the democratic system and that American democracy has insisted on since its birth. The risks are part of the dynamics.

There are unpleasant events that take place in the life of society, just as there are pleasant ones. No good reasons exist why society should be shielded from knowledge of what is ugly and be informed only of what is beautiful. Crimes take place; laws are broken, violence is committed, often horribly. But the presumption surely rests on those who would suppress news about these aspects of communal life to demonstrate why they, as distinct from all other aspects of life, should not be included in the people's knowledge of the events in their midst. The handling of crime news may require special techniques, but eliminating it is not one of them.

The precept that citizens of a democracy must know what occurs in the society from day to day is so fundamental as to need no demonstration here. It is very difficult to prove that for some reason or other crime should be an exception, a special case to which the principle does not apply. In fact, of course, the opposite argument, to be taken up in a moment, is nearer the truth: the citizen finds crime to be of intense personal and, equally important, civic concern.

The interest is natural and it is also legitimate for persons who live as neighbors in a society in whose governing they have a vote. There is no need to impute individual or collective paranoia to the community to explain it. To be sure, both common sense and the psychiatrists tell us that the dark aspects of all of us are engaged, in ways we find unpleasant to admit, by accounts of greed, trickery, violence, and sex, and the more flamboyant, the more the engagement. To deny this is hypocritical, to ignore it is foolish.

But, whether in dark ways or bright, news of crime and punishment comes closer to being the stuff of "real life" to the average citizen than news of almost any other field of human action. In the long run, the success or failure of a disarmament conference in Geneva, the perfection of a device to desalinate water, an uprising in Poland, or the demonstration that energy equals the product of mass and the square of the speed of light may determine the survival of each person and have more to do with how his life will be lived than the fact that a woman was bludgeoned to death in the next block. But no one need puzzle for long over which event evokes the average man's instant concern. He may be in error in how he bestows his interest, but he is surely not in doubt.

We assert that there exist no a priori standards that determine (for most of the spectrum) what volume and treatment of crime news are proper for the public to see and that there are no groups entitled to establish universal standards to forbid publication of material that does not meet them. We have suggested that editors do about as well as anyone else might be expected to do in selecting the contents of their publications. We have contended that every venture into news suppression is pregnant with danger and difficulty.

The argument to this point has been essentially a negative one: that the case *against* publication of police and crime news is not tenable. But is it possible to make a positive case in favor of such publication? To say that the average man appears to want a hearty diet of crime news, and that he is entitled to it if he wants it, is not to say that its publication therefore serves a positive, useful purpose. The question may be academic in a democracy where the First Amendment is operative, but it is nevertheless worth answering.

As noted above, some of the citizen's interest in crime springs from sordid if not psychopathic roots. But some grows from the perfectly proper need to know what is happening in his community. In theory and also in practice (for one may not underestimate the depth of the average man's concern about how his government is working), the citizen has as much stake as the mayor in the peace and quiet of his street and in the probity of the city's employees, as much stake as the Pinkerton guard in the safety of his money and property, and perhaps more stake than the cop on the beat in his and his family's personal safety.

Crime of almost any sort is a threat to him. He has a need to know about it, its detection, its prevention, its punishment. He is not willing, being sensible as well as democratic, to turn the whole area over to the officials who have been designated to cope with the subject, and never watch what they do and how they do it. Nor should he be willing to. Merely to know that a crime has occurred, that a suspect has been arrested and, many weeks or months later, found innocent or guilty, is not always enough to satisfy him. Nor should it be.

The people of a community that purports to be self-governing—the average man and the leading men—need news of crime in appropriate detail (which often means abundant detail) to satisfy their interest as persons and as citizens. The personal interest is not ignoble per se; the civic interest is essential.

Of all the institutions of a democratic society, the police and the court-house complex is surely the most susceptible to abuse and the most needful of continuing outside scrutiny and public chronicling of its actions, down even to the picayune details. It is not that judges, prosecutors, trial court lawyers, police, and jailers are less worthy human beings than anyone else, but the very nature of their jobs means that their working life is confined to the ugliest, most degraded and brutal aspects of the society. The objects of their attentions are men whose acts are transgressions, whose habits are furtive, whose deeds are violent, and whose dialect is falsehood. The police response to them can scarcely be expected to be one of daintiness; the police environment is not conducive to niceties. The concern for punctilious observance and modern-day conceptions of Constitutional guarantees to defendants that does honor to so many judges of the higher courts and so many distinguished legal scholars and advocates is nowhere given a more hostile and derisive reception than among some police and functionaries of the courts. In view of their work and whom they work on (and over), their attitude is understandable. But the fruits of that attitude are precisely those which most abundantly breach the guarantees of fair trial and due process in the first instance.

Nowhere is the positive role of the press more necessary than at the threshold of the administration of criminal justice. Its function is to focus public attention and condemnation on official lawlessness—or, better, by that scrutiny prevent its occurrence. The greatest injury to a defendant's chance for fair trial may well arise from what is considered almost routine practice by police and prosecution in the few hours or days following arrest.

Professor Yale Kamisar has referred to the evils that take place at this beginning stage of the judicial process:

> In this "gatehouse" of American criminal procedure—through which most defendants journey and beyond which many never get—the enemy of the state is a depersonalized "subject" to be "sized up" and subjected to "interrogation tactics and techniques most appropriate for the occasion"; he is "game" to be stalked and cornered. Here ideals are checked at the door, "realities" faced, and the prestige of law enforcement vindicated. Once he leaves the "gatehouse" and enters the "mansion"—if he ever gets there—the enemy of the state is repersonalized, even dignified, the public is invited, and a stirring ceremony in honor of individual freedom from law enforcement celebrated.[6]

It is here that the "voluntary" confessions are coerced, the prolonged and illegal interrogations are made, the intangible but real threats are

---

[6] "Equal Justice in the Gatehouses and Mansions of American Criminal Procedure," in *Criminal Justice in Our Times* (Charlottesville: University Press of Virginia, 1965).

mounted, and the brutality committed—in too many jurisdictions, brutality in the physical sense; in many more jurisdictions, brutality in the sense of degrading a man and demeaning his dignity.

That public scrutiny of all phases of police and prosecution activity is essential should be obvious. It *is* obvious to every veteran police reporter representing a news bureau in any metropolitan area. The reminiscences of Gene Blake, a reporter for the *Los Angeles Times*, are all too typical. In the course of a debate over police disclosure of information to the press, he said:

> In Los Angeles about 15 years ago an amateur photographer walked into the *Times* office with some pictures showing police in the act of arresting a group of men. A reporter recognized the men in the picture as being henchmen of the notorious mobster, Mickey Cohen. A routine phone call to the police division where the incident occurred drew a blank. The detectives in charge professed not to know anything about it, said no such arrest had been made and there was no report on it.
>
> The *Times* knew better and pressed the matter, finally succeeding in bringing out the truth that the men had been apprehended but that the police had ordered that they be released without any record being made of it.
>
> This case resulted in indictments on conspiracy charges of several men, both policemen and civilians, plus disciplinary action against the police officers involved. The indictments did not result in convictions on the conspiracy charges, which I think again helps to prove another point. All of the pretrial publicity which was given to this case apparently did not prejudice the jurors to the extent that they decided to convict the defendants without regard to the legal evidence in the case. . . . But . . . the police officers were disciplined.
>
> Another case involved the notorious Bloody Christmas beating of several Mexican-American prisoners in the Central Jail a little over 10 years ago. Newsmen were in the vicinity and were aware that something was going on but were given the run-around by the police. The matter was brought to light and evidence that the prisoners had been beaten was presented. Grand jury indictments were returned, partially on the basis of newspapermen's testimony. This resulted in conviction of several of the policemen and disciplining of several others.[7]

Examples of this kind of service that the press renders to the cause of justice are voluminous; they help make the reporter's craft a noble

[7] From an address at the Center for the Study of Democratic Institutions, January 26, 1965.

venture. The moviegoer will remember, for example, one dramatic instance that was the basis for the film *Call Northside 777*, in which a reporter, working through the years on his own initiative, proved the innocence of an unjustly convicted prisoner.

There is a second unfortunate circumstance about the apparatus of criminal justice in America: it is pervaded by politics in its least attractive form. With some exceptions at the higher levels, most state and local judges are elected. Characteristically, so are the prosecuting attorneys and the county sheriffs. At no other place in the political structure of the state or city or county are the temptations for political expedience, chicanery, and corruption so great, simply because at no place are the opportunities so voluminous and the scrutiny so difficult.

In *The American Commonwealth,* Lord Bryce entertained no doubts about the need for public opinion as a pressure on the courts. He referred to its influence "which not only recognizes the interest the community has in an honest administration of the law, but recoils from the turpitude in a highly placed official."

"The judge himself is made to dread public opinion in the criticism of a very unreticent press," Bryce continued. "Democratic theory, which has done a mischief in introducing the elective system [for selecting judges], partly cures it by subjecting the bench to a light of publicity which makes honesty the safest policy."

Corruption and political dirty work at the police and lower-court level come usually in small dollops, and too often the tendency is to ignore them as either inconsequential or inevitable, or both. Too long ignored, they flourish like the green bay tree and ultimately ripen into roaring scandals.

Typically, the dishonesty takes the form of graft and payoffs from the large or petty gamblers, the narcotics dealers, the prostitutes and their madams; too often, the police themselves become involved, taking a piece of the business for their own. At the level of the court, money dishonesty often is replaced by political dishonesty. Where this occurs, the man seeking election makes deals with the shadiest and most powerful of his parishioners—a lighter sentence for the relative of a friend or the friend of a relative, a not quite vigorous prosecution, a compromise on a scapegoat—in return for support at the polls or money for his campaign. The debauching of lower courts during the Prohibition era stands as a reminder. Or the corruption may take the opposite form:

furious and flamboyant prosecutions, dragnet operations, a flood of coerced guilty pleadings, a massive slapping in jail of every drifter who cannot give a good account of himself, and all this to win votes for a posture of vigorous law enforcement, or—as when Bull Connor had political ambitions in Alabama—as the staunch defender of white supremacy.

In his book *The Predicament of Democratic Man,* dedicated to exploring the citizen's moral involvement in the misdeeds of government, the late Professor Edmond Cahn of New York University gave the classic illustration of injustice beginning at Kamisar's "gatehouse" and persisting through the "mansion" itself:

> Not long ago a couple of masked bandits entered a store in a large American city, pointed their guns at the woman who owned the store, and demanded the contents of the cash register. It happened that a policeman was visiting her at the time. When the bandits saw the policeman, they shot and killed him, took the money, and disappeared. Incensed by the murder of one of their comrades, the police rounded up a number of unemployed young men of the neighborhood. The woman identified two of them as the burglars. Although they protested their innocence and offered credible evidence that they were elsewhere at the time of the crime, the district attorney prosecuted them zealously, the jury believed the woman's testimony, and on their being convicted for the robbery and killing, the judge sentenced them to ninety-nine years in the penitentiary.
>
> One of the young men, whom I shall call only by his first name, Joe, had come from Poland to America as a baby in the arms of his mother, Tillie. After Joe's conviction had been affirmed on appeal and all hope of legal redress had been abandoned, it was Tillie, a simple scrubwoman, who caused the truth to come to light. She posted a newspaper advertisement offering a reward of $5,000, which represented eleven years of savings from scrubbing floors. The advertisement intrigued newspaper reporters, who began investigating and soon discovered that the entire prosecution had been baseless.
>
> The prosecution's key witness, the woman who owned the store, had originally refused to identify the two defendants. She had changed her testimony and identified them only because the police, knowing that she had been selling liquor illegally, had threatened to send her to jail if she did not lie as they demanded. But the conspiracy was not confined to the police; at its apex stood the district attorney. Why had he been so eager for a conviction and so ruthless in securing one? Because, at the time of the crime, a great international exposition was about to open in the city, and visitors and customers must be reassured that the prose-

cutor and police were efficient and the streets of the city entirely safe.

After these facts were exposed in the newspaper, public clamor brought it about that the two young men were pardoned and released. By then, of course, the exposition was long since over, and the district attorney had been honored at many community meetings and lawyers' banquets, had received the usual certificates, tributes, resolutions, and diplomas, had eaten and digested his meals, smoked and enjoyed his cigars, and delivered solemn speeches at his church.[8]

It is, finally, the court and its appointees and patronage system, especially in middle-sized and small American communities, that are the heart of the political machine. Too often, the court and police complex serves the purposes of that machine corruptly. Perhaps of all institutions in the American democracy, it warrants the most intense public scrutiny and the most careful chronicling. The connotations that attach to its collective sobriquet, "the courthouse gang," are too seldom undeserved. As of old, Boss Hague's Jersey City or Boss Tweed's New York are illustrations of the tight machine controlling all public agencies, including the police and the courts. In more recent times, the history of the courthouse gang in Conway County, Arkansas, which destroyed a newspaper editor who sought to expose its corruption,[9] gives a warning to anyone of imagination how handily a powerful group can refuse to respond to legitimate inquiry on the transparent excuse that their answers might jeopardize the trial of a defendant. In Conway County, the judge, the jury commissioners who select the jury panels, the sheriff, the politicos with local and state power, the principal administrative officer, the county tax assessor, and the lieutenant governor of the state of Arkansas made an unbeatable team.

It would be nice to believe that in every instance of corruption some handsome cub reporter, spotting the injustice, effected the rescue by shouting the injustice to the world. This is unfortunately remote from reality. But it is true that some lawyers and police reporters, without any particular Galahadlike trappings, do function to suppress abuses. Their impact on removing the temptation of the police to take short cuts and

---

[8] Reprinted by permission of The Macmillan Company from *The Predicament of Democratic Man* by Edmond Cahn. Copyright © 1961 by Edmond Cahn.

[9] The story is told in horrifying detail by Roy Reed, in "How to Lynch a Newspaper," *Atlantic Monthly*, November, 1964.

ride roughshod over prisoners' rights is very great. It is accomplished by speaking aloud to the community—or simply by having the potential to do so.

It is interesting, and ironic, that at the very moment when the press, according to the conventional wisdom, was supposed to have behaved at its very worst, it performed, by its mere presence, this preventive role. With reference to the arrest of Lee Harvey Oswald, Eugene V. Rostow, then dean of the Yale Law School, wrote: "The presence of the news media in the police buildings was not entirely a negative factor in the course of events, however. A Texas lawyer has said in his 40 years of experience at the Texas bar, Oswald is to his knowledge the first man who was held overnight by the police, and did not confess."[10]

Not much imagination is needed to picture what would happen to Bill of Rights guarantees for criminal defendants if police and prosecutors operated without continuing public scrutiny. And, for better or worse, the press provides the overwhelmingly large proportion of what public scrutiny there is of the police and trial process.[11]

The point is not neatly demonstrable by a recitation of all the instances where the press has saved an innocent man from jail or even execution, or has prevented a criminal from escaping the law when at-

[10] *Book Week,* November 22, 1964.

[11] A letter to the *New Republic* (October 16, 1965) from Nicholas Horrock, of the Baltimore *Evening Sun,* states the point with some passion:

"Prosecutors, police and other mechanics of the law enforcement business spend much of their time and effort now in endeavoring to conduct their business with as little public scrutiny as possible. Any metropolitan police reporter can vouch for that. To arm these officials with a legal means of cutting off the news and barring the newsmen is to encourage the squadroom investigation and the third degree, the 'quickie' magistrate's trial where the defendant is afraid to ask for a jury. Give the desk sergeant or chief of detectives the right to hold back data on these cases or rule out interviews with prisoners and you hit one more nail in the boarding up of the individual's civil rights.

"Some years ago a veteran reporter for the Gannett-owned Plainfield Courier News spelled it out for me at 2 a.m. in a New Jersey police station. The police had just arrested a Newark Negro for the rape of a suburban housewife. The reporter put it this way—'look around—do you see any lawyers—anybody from the ACLU? Sure you don't. You and I are it.'

"Newsmen are often the only 'third force' in the investigation of a crime, the arrest and the interrogation. And often they fail this responsibility and become mere apologists for the cops, passing on unquestioningly the State's Attorney's version of the case. But just as often they're the people who point out that the prisoner was arrested a week ago—how come no lawyer? No booking?"

tempts were made to put the fix in for him. There are, to be sure, many such dramatic instances, and every year some newsman wins one or another of the seemingly endless national and local journalism prizes by just such an act. But the real job is performed in a negative, preventive, and much less readily demonstrable way.

One instance, where the demonstration is clear, is worth recounting. Beginning about 1963, reports began to grow about a judge in the District of Columbia who insisted on demanding unnecessarily explicit sexual details in divorce proceedings in his court. The ugly reports grew in volume, but casual newspaper coverage of his court was unable to produce enough solid details to demonstrate a scandal. The *Washington Post,* accordingly, determined to switch from casual to systematic coverage. For two weeks, a reporter attended every session of a divorce court that otherwise deserved scant attention. But the judge immediately recognized the presence of the reporter; his behavior became a model of Victorian delicacy. The reporter was relieved from an assignment that appeared fruitless, and soon the reports of the judge's prurient questioning resumed. Shortly thereafter, a United States Senator publicly denounced the jurist for lascivious prying in the course of a divorce action involving one of the Senator's constituents. Discussion of what further action should be taken was ended soon afterward when the judge died.

It is overstating the matter to say that the press functions to uphold the law as the pre-World War I British Fleet-in-Being functioned to uphold the Pax Britannica, but there is a similarity. Until Skaggerak, British battleships did not have to destroy the navies of other powers; the fact that they were in a position to do so was sufficient to keep marauders from mischief to the empire. The public eye in the police station, outside the grand jury room and inside the criminal court room, does for the process of law precisely what any monitor does in any situation where the temptation to break the rules is great. Judge J. Skelly Wright, of the U.S. Court of Appeals for the District of Columbia, put the matter in a nutshell when he said: "Public officials, including judges, prosecutors and the police, function best in a goldfish bowl."

The hypothetical situation of what would happen in the absence of continuing crime-reporting can be visualized best, perhaps, in the South of the mid-1960's, where police and lower courts appeared to be of all elements in the society the most hostile to the desegregation decreed by the Supreme Court and to the measures enacted to grant Negroes their civil rights. In a multitude of instances, the police, sheriffs' offices, and local magistrates acted as evaders or violators of the law rather than as its enforcers. The negative is hard to prove, but can there be any doubt of what the situation would have been without a steady reporting of these acts, a continued publication of the victims' complaints, a systematic reportage that substantiated them? If there was ever a reason for reporting news of what are declared to be criminal acts, of the arrests, the further police procedures and trials—in all of their details, including police comments or lack of police comments—it has surely been provided by the civil rights events of the past few years.[12]

In some instances, the local press of the South has done heroic service in exposing brutal and illegal police action and denial of justice in the lower courts in connection with civil rights agitation; that exposure tends to deny respectability to the violators, to reduce the community support they enjoyed, and generally to diminish official lawlessness, which otherwise might continue unchecked. But the press outside the South has also played a powerful role to this end, even though one

---

[12] One may suspect that nothing would make a segregationist law officer in Alabama happier than a prohibition similar to that, for example, of Dean Erwin Griswold of the Harvard Law School (pp. 127–128) forbidding law enforcement personnel from making any comment whatsoever once an arrest was made. Whether the person arrested was an integration activist or a segregationist bully who had beaten him up, the ban would vastly facilitate the railroading (or at least the intimidation, brutalizing, and prolonged detention) of the first and the whitewashing of the second. In the January, 1965, issue of the *District of Columbia Bar Journal*, W. Theodore Pierson made the point with respect to the latter situation:

"Must we not admit, on the basis of experience, that the fair administration of justice and the rights of the accused are seriously threatened by police brutality, improper investigatory procedures and isolation of the accused from counsel and friends? Consider, conversely, what a great boon such a procedure [exclusion of the press from police offices and distribution of criminal information only by press releases] would be to the power structure of closed communities which apply a double standard of justice—one for whites and another for blacks.

"Recent developments in the case of the [1964] murder of the three civil rights workers at Philadelphia, Mississippi, afford us some insight into this possible injustice. It has been reported that in Mississippi's history, no white person has ever been convicted for the murder of a colored person. In some instances, this conspiracy against equal protection of the laws seems to include judges, juries, police officers, attorneys and the white public. Here our concern is not for the accused. He has everything going for him. Our concern is that he is not called to account under the laws of the land."

might think at first glance that what a Northern paper had to say about events in a rural Southern county would be a matter of complete indifference to a sheriff bent on suppressing Negro rights. For today, as in John Donne's time, no man, not even the redneck sheriff, is an island. Once the spotlight of attention focuses, even from a distance, the violator's path becomes harder. Publicity can injure a bad cause and serve a good one, as well as the other way around. It forces, at a minimum, unwelcome scrutiny; on occasion it forces corrective action from an embarrassed or outraged community, from a harried governor with ambitions that rise above racist victories in his state, or from a finally aroused Federal agency.

The manifest imperfections of the law enforcement agencies are such as to shout for the need of the press to report every last step of their processes. Yet the sensationalism of the press, in its too frequent conversion of what should be a punctilious search for criminal justice into a vulgar piece of voyeurism or vaudeville, and its potential for destroying a defendant's (or the state's) right to fair trial, urge the conclusion that the press has no business publishing what it does.

The temptation is to find a way out of the contradiction by fixing on some standards of what is good and bad to publish and to require action conforming to those standards. One looks for a middle course between Lord Acton: "Everything secret degenerates, even the administration of justice; nothing is safe that does not show it can bear discussion and publicity," and Aristophanes: "Horrible facts should be buried in silence, not bruited abroad." But attempts to find a compromise and reduce it to writing or regulation tend to end in systems that are intolerable or ridiculous in an American environment.[13]

Sensationalistic crime coverage cannot be defined, but it can be sensed and it can be illustrated; its examples are almost always glaring. Bad press, like good art, is hard to define but easy to see. The editor who

---

[13] An example of an attempt to substitute mathematics for matter is offered by a 1964 Chilean law. It provides jail sentences of up to three years for "sensationalistic" coverage of criminal trials, sensationalism being defined as a story "giving prominence to crime or criminals" and consisting of more than five hundred words, headlined over three columns, or printed in larger type or different color ink from the usual. For radio and television the limit is three minutes of news on a single crime story per hour of transmission.

picks up the story of a police raid on a perversion palace in a distant
state and splashes it in print or on the air deserves more criticism than
he usually gets—not because he is injuring the defendants' chances to obtain a fair trial, which he is obviously not doing at that distance, but
because he has been pandering. His readers know it, and so does he.
But the potential of harm to the public is far greater from an editor's
failure to watch intensively the processes of crime and judgment in his
community or to report on them fully. At present in America the charge
of laziness and lack of sustained vigilance of the acts of police and courts
rests far more heavily on the press than the charge of sensationalism.
To quote Rostow again:

> President Taft said 60 years ago that the administration of criminal
> justice in the United States was a disgrace to a civilized country. . . .
>   In this setting, I suggest, we could hope that President Kennedy's
> tragic end might become a prod to progress we know to be long over-
> due. As part of the general movement to reform criminal law, Congress
> and the courts can hope to deal with many problems which press upon
> our consciences quite as much as the excesses of the press—much as
> those excesses threaten the possibility of a fair trial—or the absence of
> a statute making it a Federal crime to kill the President; the selection of
> juries, for example; the control of wiretapping and like offenses as a
> form of search and seizure; the availability of counsel; arraignment, bail
> and a hundred other practices where our customs still widely justify
> President Taft's harsh verdict.[14]

It is by reporting those evils and the "hundred other practices" that
the press can serve the goal of obtaining fair trials—and does, though not
in the volume and with the stamina that it should. But it cannot help
at all if it labors under some sort of precious philosophy holding that
reporting about crime, criminals, police, and prosecutors is a nasty
thing, to be cut to a minimum.

Jeremy Bentham had a word to add on secrecy. The "proceedings" he
refers to in the following passage are those of the trial itself, but his
point is valid for all criminal proceedings, beginnning with the discovery of the crime and the arrest of the suspect:

> . . . suppose the proceedings to be completely secret, and the court,
> on the occasion, to consist of no more than a single judge . . . that judge

[14] *Book Week*, November 22, 1964.

will be at once indolent and arbitrary; how corrupt soever his inclination may be, it will find no check, at any rate no tolerably efficient check, to oppose it. Without publicity, all checks are insufficient; in comparison of publicity, all other checks are of small account.[15]

The foregoing discussion does not refute the continuing complaint that a great deal of the treatment accorded crime by the American press is atrocious. The critic can concede that sizable amounts of press coverage of crime are essential, salutary, indeed indispensable; he can concede that attempts to impose regulations or laws governing the style, volume, and contents of that coverage may do more harm than good. But he can still maintain, and accurately, that some large percentage of published crime news is pure and simple pandering. He can charge, correctly, that the Los Angeles papers' screaming stories about the Sheppard case in Cleveland, or the Cleveland papers' equivalent treatment of Finch and Tregoff in California, are indefensible. If he cares to, he can assemble a horrifying dossier of hundreds or thousands of examples of crime coverage for which there is no excuse of social value, no exercise by the press of the public watchdog role, no service to the cause of justice, no justification for its relative volume and prominence, no performance consonant with the proclaimed essentiality of a free press in a democratic system. He can go on to demonstrate, with an appallingly large volume of evidence, that local crimes will go unreported—especially those which victimize Negroes and other low-income or low-status groups —while a sex crime involving a bosomy Delilah a thousand miles away will receive lavish display.

It is all true. But it is simply not germane to the issue considered here. El Paso's coverage of Buffalo's murdered blonde does not injure the chances of a fair trial for the defendant charged with murdering her. Argument about this kind of excessive crime coverage is interesting, it concerns a matter of importance, and it is worth pursuing for the sake of making America's press a much better and more useful instrument. But it is an argument about taste. It has nothing to do with the problem of free press, fair trial. Because it is irrelevant, it should not be allowed to intrude on that problem, which is difficult enough as is.

[15] *Rationale of Judicial Evidence* (Bowring's edition, 1843), p. 343.

CHAPTER 3

A MEASURE OF
FREQUENCY

The basic complaint that the free press plays havoc with fair trials is a proposition that receives much homage and almost no examination. In today's confrontation between press and bar, the worry begins on the note that there is a serious problem which arises frequently and is on the increase. Not only, it is usually posited, are things bad but they are getting worse, and now answers are urgently needed. All this is stated peremptorily or, when not, omitted only because of the presumption that the fact is so well known and beyond dispute as to need no declaration. The frequency of the problem has been taken for granted.

The late Justice Felix Frankfurter's concurring opinion in *Irvin v. Dowd* stands as the classic exposition of the thesis:

> Not a term passes without this Court being importuned to review convictions had in states throughout the country in which substantial claims are made that a jury trial has been distorted because of inflammatory newspaper accounts—too often as in this case with the prosecutor's collaboration—exerting pressures upon potential jurors before trial and even during the course of trial thereby making it extremely difficult if not impossible to secure a jury capable of taking in free of prepossessions evidence submitted in open court.

The latter-day particularization of this sentiment was propounded at the time of the assassination of President Kennedy in a letter to the *New York Times* by a group of Harvard Law School professors. With reference to the possibility of Lee Harvey Oswald's receiving a fair trial had he lived, they wrote:

Not only would it have been virtually impossible to impanel a jury which had not formed its own views on those facts which might come before it, but much of the information released, such as statements by Mrs. Oswald, might have been legally inadmissible at trial.

We cannot comfort ourselves with the notion that this could have happened only in Dallas. It is too frequently a feature of our process of criminal justice that it is regarded as a public carnival. And this reflects our general obsession that everybody has a right immediately to know and see everything, that reporters and TV cameras must be omnipresent, that justice must take a second place behind the public's immediate "right to be informed" about every detail of a crime.

This same assumption, as noted earlier, underlay the conclusions and recommendations about the press in the Warren Commission Report on the assassination of President Kennedy.

Do the quantity, certainty, and consistency of these comments bear a realistic relation to the proportions of the problem? Although the seriousness of any complicated legal issue like this one may not lend itself to exact analysis, certain quantitative data—while not mathematically exact—can provide some measure of the frequency with which the problem arises, and thus help to put it in a proper perspective.

Unfortunately, merely to raise the question invites the suspicion that the purpose is to show that the incidence of adverse effects is so small that the problem may be ignored or at least dismissed as insignificant. Nothing of the sort is here intended or attempted. The argument would be intolerable that because ours is an imperfect world we can look the other way at injustice provided it does not occur too often. A system of justice that is resigned at the outset to occasional instances of unfair trial, uncorrected and uncorrectable, is a contradiction in terms as well as an affront to human values. Any denial at all to fair trial is too large to be ignored. In terms of law and logic, of decency—in any terms that anyone of good will would postulate—the argument is unacceptable that infrequency justifies complacency. Rather, the following inquiry about frequency is made as a first step toward considering the burdens of various kinds of remedies and judging their fairness and appropriateness as they weigh upon the several elements of the society—the state, its officials, the court, and the accused—as well as the press and the public.

If the press jeopardizes the fairness of trials so much that no adequate correctives can be found in existing court procedures, or endangers them so often that those procedures demand an intolerably heavy tribute in terms of court costs, of difficulty of prosecution and defense, and of protracting the defendant's agony and uncertainty, then it is clear that some new and severe revisions and prohibitions must be instituted. But the costs of those measures must also be weighed. In seeking a balance the values of suggested remedies must be placed alongside the price they exact in the curtailment of public information. It seems clear that the more often publication in fact undermines the right of fair trial, the more wide-ranging or universal must be the kind of remedy capable of dealing with it, and the heavier the cost society is justified in paying. But if the incidence is rare, then different remedies, less extensive in their impact, may be suitable and effective.

The Supreme Court shares this judgment in its treatment of First Amendment cases. It has declared that it is incumbent on anyone who would limit First Amendment rights "to demonstrate that no alternate form of regulation would combat such abuses without infringing First Amendment rights."[1]

Accordingly, we shall look here at what evidence exists of the frequency of the danger to fair trial from the press. Subsequently, we shall examine the various remedies, the weight of the burdens they entail and upon whom they fall, the feasibility of putting them into operation, their effectiveness, and the degree of protection they afford.

There have been only a few attempts to obtain a statistical measure of the frequency with which the problem of prejudicial publication arises, and there is relatively little literature on the subject.

We may begin to put the matter in perspective by noting that only about 8 per cent of Federal cases go to a jury trial.[2] And the monumental study, *The American Jury*,[3] by Professors Harry Kalven and Hans Zeisel of the University of Chicago Law School, reports that only about 15 per cent of all state felonies, and of course a much smaller ratio of misdemeanors, reach a jury verdict. The authors note: "A fundamental fact about the jury trial is that it is the mode of final disposition for only a small fraction of all criminal prosecutions."

---

[1] *Sherbert v. Verner*, 374 U.S. 398 (1963).

[2] Speech by Attorney General Nicholas deB. Katzenbach, American Society of Newspaper Editors, April 16, 1965.

[3] Boston: Little, Brown, 1966.

In a 1965 speech about the free press, fair trial dispute, Judge J. Skelly Wright of the U.S. Court of Appeals for the District of Columbia said that the problem of prejudicial publication "does not exist at all in the great majority of the hundreds of thousands of criminal cases" brought each year in this country. "Less than 1 per cent of those cases receive a line of notice in the press. Of that 1 per cent, between 75 and 90 per cent of the defendants plead guilty. . . . We are dealing, therefore, with possible prejudicial publicity in only a small fraction of the less than 1 per cent of the criminal cases brought. Moreover, even as to that 1 per cent that do receive press notice, the notices are not all prejudicial."[4]

The most thorough attempt on the part of a representative of the press to assess the frequency of the problem was made by Richard Cardwell, counsel for the Hoosier State Press Association.[5] He compiled a list of cases involving the issue of trial publicity in all of the state and Federal courts during the two-year period from 1963 through 1965 that went to appeal. There were a total of sixty-nine cases in which the issue of *pretrial* publication was dealt with on appeal. In only about 5 per cent of the cases, Cardwell found, did this objection lead to a reversal on that ground. Furthermore, during the period between February, 1963, and February, 1965, the issue of prejudicial publication *during trial* was raised on appeal in only thirty-two cases. Of these, in only three cases did reversals result.

This compilation is based only on reported cases in the state and Federal courts found by Cardwell in the official law reports. The figures obviously do not indicate how many times the prejudicial-publication issue was raised at trial where there was no verdict, where there was an acquittal, where the issue was not raised on appeal, or where appellate courts did not deal in their decisions with the issue, however it may have been raised. To that extent, his statistics are not complete. He does represent, however, that his tabulation includes all reported state and Federal cases where appellate courts dealt specifically with the issue of prejudicial publication. It is thus likely that those cases where the issue was legitimate and serious would have been included in his compila-

---

[4] *Fair Trial—Free Press*, 38 Federal Rules and Decisions 435–7 (1966).

[5] Most of his report and statistical analysis was published as an appendix to the statement of Paul Fisher to the Senate Subcommittee on Improvements in Judicial Machinery and may be found in the published hearings of August 17–20, 1965, on S.290 at pp. 307–311.

tion. At the very least, his collection provides a realistic approximation of frequency.

In full recognition of the difficulty of arriving at any absolute tally showing either the volume or the rate of occurrence of potentially prejudicial publication, much less its actual effect on all trials, we have nevertheless attempted two approaches of our own to provide objective evidence. The first was a detailed analysis of one newspaper's coverage of criminal cases in one city in one year; the second was a nationwide survey of the views of state and local prosecutive officials.

In the first of our studies, we examined the records of the District of Columbia felony court for the calendar year 1963 in conjunction with the coverage given those cases by the city's largest newspaper, the *Washington Post*. The research followed this route: The names in all cases were taken from the Federal District Court's indictment list for the year 1963; these were then checked against the *Washington Post* name index file; the articles in which the names were mentioned were then culled from the library files, read and analyzed for timing, content, and frequency; finally, court records were followed for the next two years to determine the disposition of each case covered.

Although there is no such thing as a typical city or a typical newspaper, the choice of the District of Columbia and the *Washington Post* is unlikely to produce a picture varying widely from that of the rest of the country, save in some few cities plagued with journals notorious for their heavy crime coverage.

Washington's court system is atypical in one respect which needs mention but which does not affect the interpretation of the results unless it is to overstate the incidence of publication. On the one hand, all felony cases are tried in the Federal District Court, with the United States District Attorney as their prosecutor; thus, we are dealing with the sophisticated, and probably more restrained, Federal trial system for what elsewhere would be local crimes. On the other hand, the statistics relate only to felony cases, the most serious crimes and those most likely to be publicized in any community. Because most crimes are relatively simple, minor misdemeanors and petty offenses less likely to command press attention, the percentage of all criminal cases to receive press coverage in an average city would be much lower than even those reported here.

Washington provides a fair example of a major city experiencing the crime, court, and communications problems common to the rest of the nation; if anything, its felony court probably has proportionately rather more than less crimes to consider than courts of other cities, inasmuch as the formal borders of the District of Columbia enclose what would be, for any large urban area elsewhere, the "downtown" or central city only, in which the incidence of crime is relatively heavier than for a typical metropolitan area as a whole. The District of Columbia has no suburbs within its city boundaries; statistics for other cities, where the relatively less crime-ridden suburbs are included, thus tend to be lower.

The newspaper, in turn, cannot fairly be classified as sensationalist or notorious for its exploitation of crime news; nor is it famous for excessive reserve in covering news of crime. It seeks to report community affairs as diligently and thoroughly as possible and is not guilty—if that is the proper word—of above-average prudishness. During 1963, the newspaper did not operate under any special, exceptional, or experimental reporting and writing procedures that could have made its coverage either unusually flamboyant or unusually demure. The *Washington Post* appears to give about the same amount of space to crime news as the *Washington Star,* the more conservative evening paper, and a considerably larger amount than the third paper, the smaller, tabloid *Washington Daily News.*

During the year studied, the *Washington Post's* circulation in the District of Columbia, from whose population all juries in District Court were empaneled, was about 146,000 daily and 154,000 Sunday. With 252,000 occupied housing units in the city in that year, the newspaper accordingly reached about 57 per cent of the family units, a record high figure for morning newspapers in America. Thus, no paper could have been chosen for this study that exposed news of crime and courts to a larger proportion of potential jurors.

It is highly unlikely that the other two newspapers—or for that matter the radio and television stations—mentioned very many criminal defendants who went unlisted in the *Washington Post,* or supplied coverage significantly different, more detailed, or more potentially prejudicial. In short, it is unlikely that other coverage notably affected the administration of criminal justice in more or different ways than that of the largest paper. Ignoring the speculative effect of repetition—similar stories in more than one paper, and presentation of the account again over radio and television—one may conclude that the articles in the *Washington Post* represented the near-totality of pretrial and during-trial publication likely to have come to the attention of prospective jurors.

In 1963, District of Columbia grand juries returned 1,231 felony indictments, naming (since some indictments listed more than one individual) a total of 1,509 defendants. Only 312 of them—about one out of every five—were ever mentioned *at any time and to any extent* in the *Washington Post*. Of these 312 defendants whose cases were covered at all, the *Washington Post* wrote a total of 578 stories. This coverage included all stories or mention of any kind from arrest to ultimate disposition, but excluded reports of verdicts or pleas and stories following the trials, such as appeals, remands, etc., inasmuch as reports about these latter events could not have influenced the outcome of those cases and thus could have had no bearing on the question of prejudicial publication.

The following table indicates the point of time and at what stage in the judicial or prosecutorial sequence of events each defendant was mentioned in the news stories:

At arrest	248	defendants
At arraignment or preliminary hearings	37	"
At coroner proceedings	19	"
At indictment	101	"
At subsequent pretrial stage	23	"
At trial (before verdict)	25	"

NOTE: Since some defendants were mentioned at more than one stage, the listing totals more than the 312 cases covered.

The bulk of all the coverage came, it is clear from these figures, at the time of the initial public contact with criminal cases, that is, at arrest. In determining the potential impact of arrest coverage, two points should be borne in mind. First, to whatever extent it may be prejudicial, the reporting of an arrest would almost invariably be prejudicial to the defendant, not the government. However, this factor may be discounted by a second consideration: the average time lapse between arrest and trial in the District of Columbia is six months for defendants incarcerated before trial and longer for those free on bond before trial. Unless coverage continues after the report of arrest, it is unlikely that a first report would affect a jury empaneled half a year or more later.

This initial coverage was usually simple and minor, and follow-up stories at the pretrial and even the trial stages were rare. Of 312 covered cases, in 225 instances the extent of the coverage was one story; in 45 cases, two stories; in 10 cases, three stories; and in only 32 cases (about 10 per cent of the total 20 per cent of all defendants mentioned by the *Washington Post* in this year, or 2 per cent of all the cases in Washington) was the coverage repeated four or more times. Of the 225 one-shot reports, 36 involved simple reports of the indictment, and the others were merely single stories at the time of the arrest (as noted above, many months before the trials were due to be held). Most of these 225 one-shot stories were brief, mundane, not prominently placed, and likely to be forgotten if noticed. Most reports were two paragraphs or less. In some gambling cases, a defendant's name was merely reported on a list.

During 1964 and 1965, almost all the cases covered by the *Washington Post* were processed through the District Court, so that it is possible to examine their outcome. Of the 312 defendants mentioned by the paper, only 86, or somewhat less than 28 per cent, ever went to trial (3 by the court, 83 by juries). Of these, 11 (13 per cent of those tried or 3.5 per cent of those mentioned) were acquitted. And of the total 312 cases covered, there were findings of guilty (by plea or trial) in 234, or 75 per cent. Cases of 55 of the defendants were dismissed and there were other dispositions for the remaining 12. Of the cases of the 226 persons mentioned by the newspaper but who did not stand trial, most were disposed of by pleas of guilty; the remainder met with government dismissals, removal to other jurisdictions, death of the defendant, findings of insanity or incompetency to stand trial, and, in one instance, a mistrial (not caused by publicity). Prejudicial publication was not a factor in any prosecutor's discretion to dismiss any of these cases.

What does this show? A major newspaper in a major city in a recent year did not even mention with so much as a line of type 80 per cent of those accused of committing major crimes in its own back yard.[6] Of the one-fifth who were mentioned, 72 per cent were written about in only one story, and with few exceptions, these appeared long before trial at the time of arrest or indictment. The notion that this kind of brief, mostly routine story, appearing long in advance of the empaneling of a jury (for that small percentage that even went to trial) constitutes a real threat to the accused's chances of getting an unbiased jury is patently absurd. Any realistic consideration of the effect of this coverage on these cases, then, can refer at most to only 2 per cent of these defendants who received enough press mention to raise even the possibility of prejudicial fallout. And that potential exists only on the artificial assumption that the printing of four or more newspaper stories about a defendant is per se prejudicial.

In all of the thirty-two cases reported by the *Washington Post* four or more times there was a note of the extraordinary, the bizarre, the especially frightening, or the humorous—or, to get down to it, the interesting. Some of the incidents:

—The homicide of a seventy-seven-year-old minister in the course of robbing him of some change amounting to less than two dollars.

—A mail fraud by a former Michigan Democratic State Chairman who bilked G.I.'s.

—A scholarly collector of erotica for inclusion in books on sex and culture (the coverage in this case, while frequent, was sympathetic to the defendant).

—A fratricide, the murder of a twin brother.

—An international whiskey smuggling syndicate and the seizure of contraband liquor in a situation that had other exotic elements.

—An attempted jailbreak murder by prisoners who were repulsed with tear gas.

—A police duel with an escapee of a local mental institution who was a rapist and a robber.

---

[6] The managing editor of the *New York Times* has pointed to a more extreme statistic: Of the 11,724 felonies committed in New York City in one month (January, 1965), only 41 were mentioned in the *New York Daily News*, which is noted for the attention it gives to crime, writing more about it than any other newspaper in the city.

—A threat to the life of the President of the United States (resulting in civil commitment instead of a trial).

—An escapee from a mental institution who was charged with murder and who was caught in the Bronx Zoo after stealing the cars of a United States Congressman and a famous journalist.

—A fifty-one-year-old attorney and former policeman who killed a young divorcée client who would not marry him.

—Igor Cassini, charged with being a lobbyist for Trujillo and the Dominican Republic without registering with the government. (Cassini was a society columnist and well known to the Kennedys, whose administration indicted him.)

—The robbery of a United States Congressman in an alley in a Negro section of town.

—A seventy-three-year-old physical therapist charged with abortion and a notorious local criminal lawyer charged with perjury in the course of a grand jury investigation of the case in which he was counsel to the abortionist.

—A layman charged with fraudulently masquerading as a child psychiatrist.

—The murder of the son of a well-known local attorney.

—The bugging of a luxury hotel room by three private detectives to eavesdrop on the conversations of an attorney using the room while handling a case before the Federal Power Commission.

—The sexual molestation and murder of a nine-year-old girl.

In all thirty-two cases there was one common element: unusualness. None of the newspaper coverage was of the kind that could be labeled sensational. None of it was boldly emblazoned or headlined. Rarely was a picture used. All of the coverage was factual and, with few exceptions, unemotional and nonpartisan. None of the articles demanded a verdict or ventured opinions on the merits or demerits of any of the cases or the evidence or the guilt or innocence of the defendants. None contained the kind of extraordinary coverage that was found in the Sheppard case, which could warrant the accusation that the press was (1) overcovering cases out of morbid or prurient curiosity or (2) attempting to sway the administration of justice. All these cases simply amounted to relatively full coverage about generally interesting and unusual newsworthy events.

There is nothing in the dispositions of the 312 cases covered by the *Washington Post,* or in the thirty-two given the heavier coverage of four

Felony Indictments in the District of Columbia:
Disposition of All Indictments and of Those Covered by the WASHINGTON POST

| | Covered by *Washington Post* in calendar year 1963 | | | | All indictments, by year of disposition | | | |
| | At all | | Four or more times | | Fiscal year 1964 | | Fiscal year 1965 | |
Disposition	Number	Per cent	Number	Per cent	Number	Per cent	Number	Per cent
Guilty	234	75.0	23	71.9	1,184	68.6	1,050	59.0
Not guilty	11	3.5	1	3.1	106	6.2	113	6.4
Dismissed or other	67	21.5	8	25.0	435	25.2	616	34.6
	312	100.0	32	100.0	1,725	100.0	1,779	100.0
Tried by court	3	1.0	0	0.0	42	2.4	55	3.1
Tried by jury	83	26.6	16	50.0	412	23.9	336	18.9
Not tried	226	72.4	16	50.0	1,271	73.7	1,388	78.0
	312	100.0	32	100.0	1,725	100.0	1,779	100.0

or more stories, to suggest a significant difference in results from the dispositions of all cases handled at the same period in the same Federal District Court. The fiscal years 1964 and 1965 (the years during which all the cases noted by the newspaper were processed) were taken for comparison in the accompanying table. There was a slightly higher ratio of findings of guilt for the cases given news attention, too small to indicate any significance in the difference. It may be noted that of the thirty-two cases given the most attention, there was no higher proportion found guilty (in fact, the proportion was a trifle lower, 75 per cent for the total cases covered to 72 per cent for the most covered cases). More interesting is the fact that among the most heavily covered cases (by definition, the more newsworthy and thus, by implication, the "worst" crimes in the sense of being the most serious or vivid), a larger proportion (50 per cent) of defendants chose to stand trial than among all the cases mentioned by the paper (27 per cent) or than among all the cases disposed of in the fiscal years 1964 and 1965 (24 and 19 per cent, respectively). From this statistically small number it may not be demonstrable that the heavier publicized defendants tended to *prefer* jury trials, but at least the data suggest that there was no greater reluctance among them than among the rest to face trial.

The second of our attempts to obtain information about the frequency of prejudicial publication was made through letters (written in the spring and summer of 1965) to all state attorneys general (the chief prosecutorial officials of the fifty states) and to the district attorneys of the fifty largest cities. The letters sought to elicit some objective measurement of the problem. The following request was made:

> Can you provide us with statistics showing how often prejudicial publicity is raised as a defense in criminal trials in your state and how often has it been dealt with on appeal?
>
> Is it possible to gather any comparable figures for earlier years in order to determine whether the problem is increasing?
>
> Can you provide us with any comments or thoughts or anecdotes about this general subject based upon your personal experience?

Forty of the fifty state attorneys general responded to our inquiry. Ten of these merely stated that no information was available.

Owing to the divisions of the legal structures of most states, most of the attorneys general were involved only in criminal appeals. And because of the special nature of the problem, none kept such statistics as would have definitively answered our questions. However, all these officials were obviously well aware of the trend of the law and the nature of the press and the trials in their states. Undoubtedly all were experienced lawyers whose personal estimates reflected accurately, if not precisely, the affairs of their states. Their separate responses were parallel, close to a consensus, so similar as to be persuasive and credible. The local district attorneys who responded corroborated the impressions of the office of the attorney general of their state.

A common theme is evident in all the responses. All these experienced trial lawyers had distinct impressions about the subject of prejudicial publication, based on their general experience. *None* reported high rates of frequency; all knew of a few examples in each place each year (sometimes over many years); all felt that these infrequent cases did receive wide comment. The general impression was that in recent years the subject was being discussed more, the defense was being raised more; but that this increase still reflected only several instances annually and actually indicated less a change in press practices than an increased awareness of the problem on the part of the public and especially the defense bar. The percentage of the over-all national caseload represented by these cases was miniscule, representing the unusual, local *cause célèbre*.

Usually, the defense of prejudicial publication was raised in the context of motions to change the venue or continue the time of the trial, and was coped with through the ordinary available procedures of the courts.

The comments of all these officials were variations on one theme. As they saw it, the issue of free press, fair trial in their states was "a minimal problem." It was raised in about "one case each year," or "only two cases," or "only two cases in the last two years." Others said that "the issue has not been a major one," it comes up in "only a few cases," or "only in extreme sensational cases," or "has come up in some isolated cases," or "only very rarely," or has been raised in "only two cases in the last five years." These separate approximations typify the sum of the responses, and there were no exceptions.[7]

[7] Condensations of these responses appear in Appendix A. The letters themselves are on file at the Freedom of Information Center, University of Missouri, Columbus, Missouri.

One conclusion is certain, despite the lack of statistical evidence, for it was pounded home in response after response: The case where press interference with trial justice is even claimed is extraordinary. Law officials throughout the United States thus testified that the problem, assumed to be commonplace and overwhelming by most critics of the press, actually arises very infrequently—and when it is raised, the contention is seldom accepted by the courts. Apparently, prejudicial publication has been a rare problem, although its consideration in some places, especially recently, has been significant.

Are the comments of the attorneys general and district attorneys colored by the fact that the respondents are principally engaged in seeking convictions and consequently are not worried about unfairness to defendants and tend to minimize its occurrence? No doubt subjective impressions from a similar number of attorneys engaged principally in representing defendants would have a different tone. Yet we cannot believe that the respondents would willfully misrepresent the numerical facts; and their conclusions are corroborated by other studies and surveys. Nor was there evidence of bias or lack of concern for fair play. To be sure, the majority agreed that the incidence of prejudicial publication was very low; but none, even by insinuation, suggested that he was indifferent to the problem or that as an issue and a principle he considered it inconsequential. Those who did go beyond the question of frequency to the substance of the problem were in fact unanimous in their conviction that it is grave and important.

In Kalven and Zeisel's *The American Jury,* referred to earlier in this chapter, there is much to substantiate and nothing to refute the conclusion that injury to a defendant from publicity is a very rare phenomenon, in either absolute or relative terms. The directors of that study sent questionnaires to judges for reports on 3,576 criminal trials over which they presided in the course of something over two years. Inasmuch as Professors Kalven and Zeisel estimate that about 60,000 criminal jury cases each year are tried through to a verdict, the sample reported on in *The American Jury* comes to almost 3 per cent of the total, an impressively high figure. In the total were 210 murder cases, 292 of aggravated assault, 106 of forcible rape, 229 of robbery, 298 of burglary, 128 of other grand larceny, and 39 of bribery and official misconduct—

all categories of high news interest and substantial press attention.

In not one case did a judge mention prejudicial publicity as a factor in the trial, the jury's verdict, or his own impressions. To be sure, the questionnaire used in the study did not contain a specific inquiry on this point; nevertheless, the fact that not one judge even alluded to the subject of publicity in the open-ended comments he was invited to make is significant and "cannot be argued around," in the opinion of Professor Kalven. In a conversation in September, 1966, Kalven said prejudicial publication seemed to him "enormously less of a problem than it was thought to be." He emphasized the significance of the fact that not one of the 555 judges who responded to the questionnaires thought prejudicial publicity was worth mentioning as a factor in the case. His own view of the issue parallels ours: Prejudicial publicity is a factor in the rare, sensational case; elsewhere it appears to be close to nonexistent.

From all this, unfortunately, no incisive demonstration can be made, on the one hand, that no problem exists at all or, on the other, that a vast toxic cloud smothers the administration of justice and contaminates every part. Instead, what emerges is a picture of occasional difficulty, too serious and too regular to be dismissed, but not on such a flood scale as to require that the temples be torn down for material to build the dikes.

In the first place, it appears with mathematical certainty that of all persons accused of crime only a rare few risk even the theoretical possibility of suffering from adverse publication, inasmuch as only a small fraction stand trial by jury.

Second, it is clear that even for this group, the real chance of facing prejudiced jurors is infinitely smaller: the press pays no attention whatsoever to most of them, and gives only a few sentences at the time of arrest or indictment (usually months before the trial) to the great majority of the rest. If Washington is a fair sample, only 2 per cent of those indicted face the amount of continued or repeated coverage even theoretically able to raise the possibility of leaving a residue of prejudice in the minds of potential jurors. And from the absence of a flood of appeals each year throughout the nation in which the ground of injurious publicity is raised, one must conclude that in only a miniscule fraction of these few does possibility become reality—or even alleged reality. There was no such "reality" in the 3,576 cases studied by Kalven and Zeisel.

The picture that emerges is of a very small number of cases a year on an average in each state where the problem of prejudicial publication is sufficiently grave to warrant serious attention by the trial court. If Cardwell's compilation of appellate cases throughout the nation (p. 58 above) is complete, the issue arises even less frequently on appeal. If one were to double or triple his figures, as a flamboyantly extravagant allowance for error, the incidence would still remain low.

Common sense and common experience corroborate these findings and lead us to the conclusion that the problem of adverse publication, pretrial and during trial, arises almost exclusively in the *causes célèbres,* the few but sensational crimes committed each year that—however the social critics may deplore it—capture the public attention. Lamentable as they are, the burglaries, robberies, knifings, assaults, mayhems, and even killings occurring in dreary succession in America each day, in the ratio of thousands to one of the sensational cases, are at least spared any press attention that could possibly result in a biased jury hearing the case.

The contention is sometimes heard that there are probably more instances where prejudicial publicity has denied defendants a fair trial than we have knowledge of.[8] But that is something like saying there are many more famous men in the world than we know about. Prejudicial publicity, almost by definition notorious and consequential, that is relatively unheard of is a contradiction in terms. As far as we can determine—and in the absence of any demonstration to the contrary—publication that has prejudicial potential is always noisy enough to make itself heard and to become widely known. It is hard to conceive of a situation even in a small or remote locality where a crime has been committed, a defendant has been tried, and publicity has ensued that was so sensational as to have adversely affected the objectivity of a jury while the case has not itself been the subject of publicity elsewhere and has failed to attract the notice of the rather vigilant members of the press and bar who are concerned with the "trial by newspaper" problem.

[8] See, for example, Telford Taylor, "Crime Reporting and Publicity of Criminal Procedure," *Columbia Law Review,* January, 1966, p. 53.

Even if there were such cases and knowledge of them were lost on the desert air, the bar would have cause for far greater concern about itself than about the press. For this would imply that counsel in such phantom cases was so irresponsible or incompetent as to have failed to complain at trial or to appeal an unfavorable verdict arising from prejudicial publication.

Surely, in terms of numbers alone, the menace of "trial by newspaper," of press pollution of the stream of justice, must rank well down in the hierarchy of ills that plague the administration of justice.

To repeat what was said at the beginning of this chapter, so to interpret this evidence is not to argue that infrequency dare be matched with indifference. There can be no ducking of the problem of the press prejudicing trials even if the occurrence is seldom and is almost solely confined to the *causes célèbres*. But the solutions that we seek must be appropriate to the difficulties, both to their nature and to their frequency. The question is not a matter of neglecting to find a remedy but to find one no more painful than the illness demands.

This attitude is reinforced by the Supreme Court doctrine that First Amendment rights must be treated preferentially and that any limitations upon these rights must be justified as the only alternative to demonstrable and urgent competing needs. The Supreme Court has said that in striking any balance in cases involving exercise of First Amendment rights recognition must be accorded

> . . . the preferred place given in our scheme to the great, the indispensable democratic freedoms secured by the First Amendment. . . . That priority gives these liberties a sanctity and a sanction not permitting dubious intrusions. . . . Any attempt to restrict those liberties must be justified by clear public interest, threatened not doubtfully or remotely, but by clear and present danger. The rational connection between the remedy provided and the evil to be curbed, which in other contexts might support legislation against the act on due process grounds, will not suffice. These rights rest on firmer foundation. Accordingly, whatever occasion would restrain orderly discussion and persuasion at appropriate time and place must have clear support in public danger, actual or impending. Only the gravest abuses, endangering paramount interests, give occasion for permissible limitation.[9]

As Justice Black said in the Bridges case about incursions on First

[9] *Thomas v. Collins*, 323 U.S. 516 (1945).

Amendment freedoms, the restriction itself must be confined within reasonable limits and must not go beyond the needs of the occasion.[10]

Need the house be burned to roast the pig? Conceivably, the pig that must be roasted may be so enormous, or there may be so many pigs that have to be roasted, that nothing short of the conflagration of a house will suffice for the cooking. Or the house may be of such little value that its destruction is no greater matter.

But some weighing of house and pig seems indicated before making the decision. An attempt has been made here to determine the number of pigs; we proceed next to put them on the scale, and later to see how much of a conflagration is being proposed and whether starting fires is truly the best way to proceed.

[10] *Bridges v. California,* 314 U.S. 252 (1941).

CHAPTER 4

FROM POTENTIAL

TO REAL

With few exceptions, potentially prejudicial publication becomes prejudicial in fact only in the sensational case. The statement comes close to being platitudinous, almost a piece of circular reasoning: if a criminal case is sensational it is likely to be highly publicized, and if it becomes the subject of voluminous publication it is thereby rendered sensational.

Yet the truism needs stating. Failure to take it into consideration in judging solutions to the problem of prejudicial publication leads to extravagant and needless complications. Unfortunately, many of those concerned about the problem appear to be convinced that (a) every publication about a crime that could in theory reduce the objectivity of someone who might some day be chosen as a juror in the case and (b) every piece of news containing material that might not be admissible in the trial will in fact prejudice the defendant's trial. If this were so, the necessary remedies would have to be Draconian indeed. But if the disease is localized to a few carriers and if they can be identified and treated individually, that course is surely preferable to quarantining or hospitalizing the entire community.

As any newspaper reader or television viewer can verify for himself, the daily grist in the crime mill contains from three or four to a dozen stories (depending on the city and the judgment of the news executives). Most of them—there is no way to establish a percentage, which in any event would vary from place to place and between one publication and another—will probably contain potentially prejudicial information as defined by the two criteria in the preceding paragraph. If a description of the circumstances of the arrest is not deemed prejudicial (public disclosure of that kind of information is sanctioned in the rules for Federal law-enforcement personnel promulgated by the Attorney General and in regulations proposed by the Reardon Committee (see pp. 131–138 below), the ratio drops considerably. If a full public description of the crime, given by the police when there has been no arrest, is also taken as nonprejudicial—and so far as we know, none of the currently proposed remedies for the problem suggests press silence in such cases[1] —then the proportion falls still further.

The routine story reads something like Example 1.[2]

EXAMPLE 1

Rockville Man, 38, Shot in Chest, Dies

A 38-year-old Rockville man died Saturday night after being shot in the chest.

Albert Lucas C_____, listed at 320 L_____ ave., was mortally wounded about 11 p.m. while at the home of Louise S_____, at 124 J_____ dr., Rockville.

Montgomery County Police arrested Carl H_____, 33, of D_____ Road, Rockville, and charged him with murder. H_____ is being held without bond for a preliminary hearing today in People's Court at Rockville, police said.

Clearly, this story raises no problems of prejudicial publicity. Nor does the next story, of a routine and frequent type, provided one concedes that a description of the circumstances of the arrest before an indictment has issued is unexceptionable.

[1] In a sense, this is illogical, however inescapable, because the information that may linger with real prejudicial effect in some future juror's memory will be the gory details of a sensational crime, published with mounting excitement day after day while the hunt for the fugitive is on. When he *is* arrested and brought to trial, the horror of the crime he stands accused of is likely to be all the more vivid, in the public mind, because of the pre-arrest repetition.

[2] All examples given here are taken from the Washington, D.C., press in the second half of 1965. The stories are reproduced in full except for some tampering with names; in Example 5 a short paragraph identifying the children in the family has been omitted.

EXAMPLE 2

Police Catch 4 in Cellar of Church

Four men caught by police in the basement of the Sacred Heart Catholic Church, 16th and Park Road nw., shortly after 2:30 a.m. yesterday were arrested and charged with housebreaking, police reported.

Tenth Precinct detectives called to the church by a passerby who heard noises inside, met three of the men, Alberto O____, 18, listed at 20 ____ st. n.w., Carlo E____, 18, listed at 2001 T____ st., Arlington, and Jose M____, of 1855 C____ st. n.w., as they were coming up the church's basement stairs.

A fourth man, Charles F. T____, of no fixed address, was found hiding in the basement by a Canine Corps dog, Pat I, police said. T____ was bitten by the dog on his arms and legs. He was treated at D.C. General Hospital.

The data reported in Example 2 are still confined to the circumstances of the crime and the arrest, but difficulties begin with a story like the third one, which is also typical and "routine."

EXAMPLE 3

Hit-and-Run Suspect Shot By Officer

A Hyattsville hit-and-run suspect was shot in the leg by a Prince Georges County policeman Monday night after he grabbed the officer's blackjack and attacked him, according to police.

Ronnie M. B____, 26, 5705 A____ rd., was reported yesterday in good condition at Prince Georges Hospital with a flesh wound in his left thigh. He was charged with hit-and-run, assaulting a policeman and resisting arrest.

The shooting happened at the B. & O. Railroad tracks near the Rte. 1 overpass, a block from the Hyattsville Police Substation, when B____ jumped from a scout car after being arrested on a count of leaving the scene of an accident.

As Pvt. Joe T. Wilson Jr. crossed the Rte. 1 viaduct on his way to the Hyattsville station, B____ jumped from the car. Wilson caught him and attempted to use his blackjack to subdue B____, according to Det. Capt. Earl Huber, but B____ took it from him and attacked him with it. Wilson then shot B____ in the leg.

According to Huber, several persons watched the scuffle. "As far as I can determine, no one attempted to help or call for help," Police Lt. Edward Gryskeiwicz said.

Here, potentially prejudicial information is present in more volume and variety: The newspaper printing the story has left scant doubt in the reader's mind about the accurate identification of the arrested man as the one who assaulted the policeman; other details of the episode add further unfavorable overtones.

The fair trial problem mounts, in theory at least, with the fourth story, intensely readable. If the police account to the reporter is true, and if his report was faithful in turn, then the case seems open and shut and the defendants have indeed undergone "trial by newspaper" in the court of public opinion.

EXAMPLE 4

PATIENT, HUNCH-PLAYING SLEUTH NETS THREE FLIMFLAM SUSPECTS

When Robbery Squad Det. William A. Best noticed the late model sedan parked on the lot of a Safeway Store at 14th Street and Park Road nw. at noon Friday he thought something was wrong.

The auto, with Pennsylvania tags, was empty when Best first saw it. But since it was parked across from the Riggs National Bank, he thought he might watch it for a while. After all, he reasoned, on Friday afternoons banks are natural targets for con men waiting to fleece customers.

Two hours later, Best was still watching the car. Then a man, looking over his shoulder as he walked, approached the car and got in. Three minutes later, another man, dressed the same way in ordinary street clothes and looking around nervously, got into the car.

At precise three minute intervals, a woman and then a third man, who Best says were forcing themselves to look nonchalant, walked to the car and joined the men inside.

The car and its four occupants pulled off, with Best following, drove to the 1300 block of U Street nw. and parked.

Best recorded the tag number and went to meet his partner, Det. Lester N. Crockett, who he knew was on the lookout for con men at another point nearby.

When the two policemen returned to U Street the car was gone.

But Best and Crockett, who are assigned to the Robbery Squad's Confidence Section, had another hunch. They drove to 8th and H Sts. ne., another known hangout for pickpockets and con men during rush hours. And that corner is also the site of a National Bank of Washington branch.

They were right. The same car was parked in the 700 block of H Street ne. Best parked in the next block and watched the car while Crockett walked to the corner to keep an eye on the three men and the woman.

About 5:30 p.m., all four converged at the car. Best pulled closer, parking a few car lengths away.

Soon one of the men got out and walked around the corner. He stopped an elderly woman on the street.

By now Best had left his car and followed. He edged closer, so he could overhear the conversation.

Almost right away he knew it was a flim flam variation know as "the drag," a variation of the envelope switch trick.

According to Best, here is what happened:

The first man struck up a conversation with the woman and soon a second man (who, Best said, was one of the four from the car), came up and asked the two whether they had lost an envelope.

He said the envelope contained almost $6000, which, according to a note in the envelope, was money that no one would report missing—the note said the money had belonged to a numbers backer—an illegal lottery financier.

The second man told the two he'd be glad to share the $6000 find with the two of

them if both would put up "good faith" money.

At that, the first man pulled a wad of bills from his pocket and gave it to the second man—proof of his "good faith."

So the woman took all the money she had—$20—from her pocketbook and handed it to the second man—her proof of her "good faith."

And then the first man handed each of them their "shares"—the woman got hers in the original envelope, and she could plainly see $2000 was in the envelope.

Then the two men walked off.

And Best walked in. He identified himself to the woman and told her to open the envelope, where she found one real bill and lots of play money.

The woman, Mattie Belle M____, 60, of 610 ____ st. nw., exclaimed:

"Thank the Lord you were watching. That was my last $20."

Meantime, Best's partner, Crockett, was following the two men back to the car in the 700 block of H Street, where the other two were waiting.

As they were about to drive off, Crockett arrested all four on charges of playing a confidence game.

The four were identified as Palmer S. W____, 60; James W____, 36; Winfred G____, 38, and Dorothy B____, 36, all of Philadelphia.

In General Sessions Court yesterday, Judge Dewitt S. Hyde held the three men on $500 bond each, while charges against Dorothy B____ were dropped by the U.S. Attorney's office on the grounds that she had not been a participant.

The fifth story provides a further turning of the screw, with "human interest"—almost "bleeding heart"—details. Yet it too is "routine" in the sense that, unhappily, many such homicides happen every year in a big city and are ordinarily the subject of a couple of stories at the time of the event, and a few more (barring startling intervening developments) during the ensuing trial. But Example 5 is not a "sensational" story if "sensational" is a function of the amount of publicity given it.

EXAMPLE 5

Bullets Beat Cupid

'I LOVE YOU ROSES' LATE, SLAYING ENDS MARITAL RIFT

A dozen red roses were delivered about 3:50 p.m. yesterday to a white-trimmed fieldstone bungalow on Alexandria's well-to-do R_____ Road.

But the man who had ordered them was dead and the woman to whom they were addressed was charged with murdering him.

Principals in the domestic tragedy, according to Alexandria Det. Capt. Francis Johnson, were William A____, 46, a prospering machinist, and his 44-year-old estranged wife, Aline.

A_____, Johnson said, was pronounced dead on arrival in Alexandria Hospital a few minutes after the shooting at 2:45 p.m. He had been struck several times by a fusillade of shots from a .22-caliber automatic held by Mrs. A____ in their home at 2215 R_____ rd., police said.

Investigators said the violence started heading for its climax with the issuance of two Domestic Relations Court warrants charging A_____ with using abusive language on Aug. 4 and with assault and battery on his wife the next day.

When the A____s appeared in court yesterday morning, police said, Judge Edwin Pierce reset the case for trial on Sept. 13, by which time it was believed a reconciliation could be worked out. In court, police said, A_____ agreed to stay away from his house unless he was invited to return.

Neighbors said A_____ parked his green Ford compact in front of his house, but that Mrs. A____ refused to admit him. He had broken through a window on the west side of the house, neighbors said, when the first of the shots rang out.

Police said two shots were fired through the broken window and the rest were fired as A____, already wounded, staggered out of the porch entrance. He collapsed on a green entrance mat on the front steps. Police said they retrieved the empty automatic from Mrs. A____'s purse.

The red roses arrived in a station wagon from Kirchner's Florists in Alexandria about an hour after the tragedy occurred.

J. Fred Kirchner, owner of

the florist shop, said A_____, an old high school school-mate, came into his place about 1 p.m. and said he needed a dozen red roses.

"My wife's a little mad at me," Kirchner said A_____ told him conversationally, "and the roses might help."

Kirchner said he asked A_____ if there was any special hurry about the delivery, explaining that his delivery-man would be going out towards A_____'s neighborhood "sometime later on this afternoon."

"Later on this afternoon," Kirchner said A_____ assured him, "ought to be just fine."

Kirchner said A_____ asked that the card accompanying the flowers be made to read, "I love you," above his name.

In this series of stories, potential injury to the defendants' chances for a trial by an unbiased jury mounts with increasing severity from the zero quantity in the first to the heavy freight in the last. (Mrs. A_____, incidentally, was acquitted.) Yet, in practice, the means to screen the prejudice out to prevent its entrance into the courtroom are neither complicated nor costly, at least in any metropolitan area.

Characteristically, the cases will not come to trial until several months after the arrest (and in any event, if the defense counsel believes the report of the incident is still too fresh in the public memory, he can ask for a postponement, to no one's great loss—assuming a decent bail system). To find through the voir dire examination of prospective jurors twelve men who—to go far beyond the requirement of the courts—have never even heard of the case, much less have an ineradicable opinion about it, presents no great problem. And this does not mean that the jury must be comprised of illiterates. The press might like to believe that its circulation extends to every last household, and that every last resident reads and remembers every last story; the fact is very different.

For the truth of the matter is, as hinted above, that stories of this sort are commonplaces; readable as some of them may be, few have that high drama (or have been invested with it by a press determined to synthesize a sensation) that causes the memory to linger.[3]

[3] The need for procedural remedies, such as change of venue, may be greater in a small community or a rural area, where the number of crimes is smaller and each one committed is a proportionately larger item for contemplation and conversation. Yet in those areas, the press is never the only vehicle by which prejudicial publicity is carried, and curbing the press will not cure the trouble. For even if there were no press publication, potential prejudice reaching the ears of the future jury would still be great; in a small town the job is done by word of mouth.

As is implicit in the statistics in the preceding chapter, as experience and common observation indicate, and as lack of contrary evidence validates, fear about prejudicial publicity in those cases that are not highly publicized has small factual basis. This is not to deny that there are exceptions, but for each exception we have knowledge of—or can imagine—a relatively simple remedy is at hand to prevent a miscarriage of justice. Seriously injurious publication in run-of-the-mill cases must be rare indeed. It is, in fact, hard to conceive how it might come about. Some possibilities can be considered.

Assume that in the pretrial period of some case a piece of prejudicial information is published. If it is slight enough to escape the attention of the defense counsel, so that he does not take pains to guard against it in the examination of the jury, the odds are high that it was slight enough to offer no threat of damage. If, on the other hand, it was so large as truly to reduce the objectivity of jurors, the defense counsel could scarcely avoid trying to deal with it. If he did not, or if he tried by examination of the talesmen to obtain an unbiased jury and failed, if the counsel failed to ask for change of venue or if the court refused to grant it, or to grant a postponement, and finally, on a guilty verdict, if counsel failed to appeal—in any of those circumstances, the legal profession would have far graver causes to worry about than the offenses of the press. And to try to rectify such a problem by punishing or silencing the press would be like attacking prostitution by forbidding the listing of massage parlors in the telephone book's yellow pages.

During the pending-trial period, however, the situation is quite different. Here, prejudicial publication may and does occur from time to time in nonsensational cases and in a form that truly jeopardizes the fairness of the trial: the jury has been chosen and is in the box; the trial is at hand; attention is focused on the particular case. But here the remedy is simple and straightforward, if costly: the declaration of a mistrial or the taking of an appeal. *Marshall v. U.S.*[4] was such a case. Published information, damaging to the defense, occurred in the course of a relatively routine, unsensational trial. The court in chambers examined jurors who had been exposed to the inadmissible material that had been published during the trial, accepted their assurances that they could disregard it, and let the trial proceed. The Supreme Court ruled that this decision had been wrong.

[4] 360 U.S. 310 (1959).

The lugubrious performance of the Raleigh, North Carolina, *News and Observer* which twice within seven months caused a mistrial for the identical sin in the identical case is worth recording as something of a track record. On December 16, 1964, one Harold Smith, an inmate of Raleigh's Central Prison, went on trial for the attempted murder of a fellow prisoner. As it happened, both the defendant and the man he assaulted had been convicted of murder three years before for a killing they committed together. The intramural falling-out and the ensuing assault were newsworthy, and the newspaper told the history in its report of the first day of the trial. Apparently, both the reporter and his copy desk editors were oblivious of the prejudicial aspects of what seemed to them necessary information to provide a complete and comprehensible story, that is, that the principals had been partners in the crime that originally put them in prison. It might have been argued that the locus of Smith's assault, which could scarcely *not* have been reported and which in any event had come to the jurors' attention in court, itself implied that Smith had a prior criminal record of some sort. Nevertheless, Judge Henry McKinnon of the Wake County Superior Court declared a mistrial. Retrial took place next July 21. The newspaper's report of the first day's proceeding repeated the identical prejudicial material and, to make the whole episode more wonderful, noted the previous mistrial and explained in detail just what the newspaper had done the preceding December to cause it. The despair of Judge Rudolph Mintz, presiding over the retrial, can only be imagined; his public comments, however, were doubtless tempered by the fact that both he and Judge McKinnon had apparently neglected to warn the jurors against reading newspapers or listening to broadcast accounts of the trial.

Many mistrials blamed on press publications could have been simply avoided by the court's taking the normal precautions designed just for that purpose. In November, 1965, for example, a mistrial was declared in Federal court in Alexandria, Virginia, because during the course of his trial a defendant was described by the *Washington Post* as having "a record of gambling convictions." The story was printed on page seven of the third section of the paper. Some of the jurors had read it. The story was brief, in no way sensational, and involved a defendant who had been widely known for many years as one of the leading gambling figures in the area (he was later retried and convicted). The prosecution was highly critical of the newspaper, but admitted that it had never requested that the jury be instructed against reading reports of the case. Nor had the judge, who later said he rarely instructs jurors to avoid reading newspaper accounts of trials they are hearing, made such an admonition on his own initiative.

Mistrials are deplorable, causing added expense to both sides and grief to the defendant in rehearings, and prolongation of the agony and uncertainty (and the lingering in jail if the prisoner cannot afford bail). Bar and bench, criticizing the press for its contribution to that evil, have often proposed the preventive step of requiring pending-trial publication to be confined without exception to the daily record.[5] But this preventive seems singularly severe and its absolutism likely to cause problems ranging from difficult to ludicrous. How, for example, could a sensible report be made of the trial of a member of the Ku Klux Klan on Federal charges of depriving an NAACP worker of his civil rights without mentioning that the case was a follow-up to the defendant's acquittal in a state court of the charge of murdering the man? Moreover, such a prohibition seems inconsistent with a willingness of the bar and the bench to resign itself to the device of retrial after mistrials caused by other errors. If a root-and-branch change in press procedures is commanded to prevent its conduct from causing mistrials, but the solution of retrial is deemed acceptable to cope with such situations as the court erring in its charge to the jury, witnesses' allusions to inadmissible information, counsels' careless or subtle extra-record references, bailiffs' too casual surveillance, or jurors' out-of-court conversations, then the press may be forgiven if it entertains a notion that it is being unfairly dealt with. We know of no statistics showing the relative frequency of the various causes of mistrial, but it appears unlikely that pending-trial press publication is a major or common one.

We return to the point made at the beginning of this chapter: The potential prejudice in pretrial and pending-trial publications relating to the nonsensational, routine, criminal case—to 999 cases out of 1,000—is a minor problem and susceptible of relatively simple and certain solution.

---

[5] Nothing less would be wholly efficient, for prejudice lurks in what the reporter might think were utterly innocent additions, as for example in damage suits, the fact that the defendant is insured, or that an out-of-court settlement had previously been offered, or even the amount sought. One such case was *Siegfried v. City of Charlottesville* (*Va.*), No. 5942, 6/14/65.

The real problem—and this is shown by the cases that the critics cite —arises with the sensational crimes, the ones freighted with "murder and mystery, society, sex and suspense," the ones that are gruesome or grotesque, heinous, bizarre, or enormous. It is with proposed solutions to that problem that the following chapters deal. First we examine the procedures governing juries and the means courts use to filter out potentially prejudicial publicity in those cases where the issue seems to be real.

CHAPTER 5

THE JURY AND
THE NEWS

Criminal jury trials are very special things. They occur relatively rarely, as we have noted. Their profiles vary widely. However, it is evident that almost without exception those cases causing the free press, fair trial problem are the ones that end in a jury trial, involving as they do the highly contested, more fractious issues of our time.

A criminal trial is, as we have suggested, an important dramatic incident carried out on the courtroom stage. It is governed by special, formal rituals as exacting as those controlling the movements in a Japanese Nō play; all steps in the process are carefully prescribed. The trial process has a special symmetry and logic of its own; it has its own set of rules, traditions, and rationales. And the accusatorial system that governs trials has even developed its own intramural myths and gamesmanship.

Some of the law's rules and procedures and the presuppositions on which they operate will be examined here and in the following chapter, not at all to question the validity of the jury trial system—something far beyond the purpose of this book—but rather as one way of assessing the inevitability of the free press, fair trial problem.

For the jury system is really the cause of the present dilemma. The key question in the present debate is not whether a free press is inherently inconsistent with a fair trial system but, rather, whether press coverage of crime and trial news prejudices juries. We do not treat the question whether the nature of the press should be changed in the abstract; we deal only with the question whether the press should be restricted in one particular category of its operations on the specific ground that it disturbs the impartiality of the jury.

All the legal rules of evidence presuppose that *judges* can, indeed must, be exposed to petentially prejudicial information about criminal cases and still decide those cases impartially. Thus, the only way that press publications about crime and trials provoke a legal issue is by intruding upon the trial process to a degree that seriously endangers or contaminates the Constitutionally required impartiality of *juries*.

In two ways, it is argued, press publications create prejudice and thus jeopardize the right to trial before an impartial jury: (a) when the press reports specific items of news that either do not make their way into evidence at the trial or that come to the attention of jurors before the trial, unconfronted and unexamined, and (b) when the amount and intensity of general press coverage of a case becomes so significant and so partisan that the whole community atmosphere is permeated with passion sufficient to preclude a fair, detached adjudication free from outside domination.

The latter situation is mercifully infrequent: it involves the truly extraordinary episodes where trials are surrounded by circus-minded crowds, the passionate partisan press, and unruly, injudicial courtroom scenes. Where the general environment subverts the processes of justice, the Supreme Court may reverse a decision even if specific non-judicial evidence did not come to the attention of the jury. Here, in the words of Justice Oliver Wendell Holmes, "the whole proceeding is a mask—counsel, jury, and judge . . . swept to the fatal end by an irresistible wave of public passion."[1] In such an atmosphere, it is bootless to argue whether the jury has been prejudiced. By definition, these are cases coming close to trial by mob. Nevertheless, and different as they are from the simpler situations where certain specific prejudicial information has come to a juror's attention, the ways to cope with them are doubtless similar.

The former situation is more common: it involves such things as pre-trial press reports of confessions and prior records and statements made out of the jury's presence. The problem here is to avoid what Lewis Carroll described in "The Barrister's Dream":[2] "The Jury had each formed a different view / Long before the indictment was read."

A jury trial is supposed to be a search for facts. The prosecution is

[1] *Moore v. Dempsey*, 261 U.S. 86 (1923); also see *Frank v. Mangum*, 237 U.S. 309 (1915).

[2] *The Hunting of the Snark*.

required to prove its charge against the defendant "beyond a reasonable doubt." It goes about this task by presenting evidence and the testimony of witnesses that adduce a conclusion which the court must decide as a matter of law is sufficient and which the jury must believe. The rules of evidence, articulated in statutes and developed through years of practice, govern what may be presented for the jury's consideration. They are based on theories of relevancy, guarantees of trustworthiness, and indices of veracity. Most make sense; some seem illogical. All combine to select and funnel the only information that is permissible for the jury to consider.

The main and most common problem arises when the press prints crime news which, however legitimate, may not be relevant by judicial standards and has not been subjected to the law's procedures to judge its truth and credibility. The press's criteria for publication are what is interesting, satisfies curiosity, tells a story, and, judged from *its* standards —which are not necessarily those of the court—what it *believes* to be true. If jurors learn from extra-judicial sources facts that are not brought out at trial, or if prospective jurors learn before trial facts that may or may not come out at trial, the way of the law is perverted.

Press evidence is unsworn, unconfronted, and uncontradicted, Judge Simon Rifkind has observed.[3] When the press comments about a case, other than simply reporting what transpired at a trial, it is, he argues, no different from someone privately sending a note commenting about a case to a juror.

Before we reach the question of the efficacy of trial procedures in keeping the minds of juries pure by keeping the evidence judicial, one key question needs to be raised. Just what is the effect of crime and trial news upon the jury? It is neither pedantic nor disingenuous to suggest that this question be explored. The assumption has been made peremptorily that *any* publication is dangerous and that a certain undefined quantity of publication per se renders a jury so partial that a fair trial presumably will be out of the question. A subsidiary question is whether or not juries are swayed more by press news than by their own past experiences and present predispositions. Is the press merely one of a multitude of forces and potentially prejudicial factors inter-

[3] "When the Press Collides with Justice," 34 *Journal of the American Judicature Society* 46 (1950).

acting upon the psyches of juries?[4] Little attention has been paid to these questions. And one reason may well be the difficult nature of any such inquiry and the impossibility of applying exact scientific methods to it.

The short answer to both questions is that nobody knows. But because the subject is basic to a consideration of the free press, fair trial issue, it seems useful to summarize some of the existing studies on how prejudicial information is deemed to create prejudice, even though no neat Q.E.D. can come as the finale.

What empirical data exist to measure the conclusion that press coverage, coming to the attention of juries, destroys their ability to decide cases fairly?

The *University of Chicago Law Review* recognized the importance of assessing the power of the communications media in forming public opinion, especially in this one area. "At the center of the analysis," it reported in a 1950 issue, "lie difficult sociological questions—to what extent do newspapers create community attitudes?—and psychological questions—to what extent do community attitudes affect the mind of the juror? The courts will have to rely on speculation from common experience to reach conclusions, until more reliable and specific studies are made than exist at the present time."[5] More specifically, the *Harvard Law Review* pointed out that "scientifically accumulated experience, dealing with isolated factors (like public opinion polls addressed at ascertaining a fair trial venue), will certainly be relevant to a judicial determination of probable influence; and such general data could properly be given even greater weight in formulating a legislative decision."[6]

Some social science studies have been made of the impact of the

---

[4] There is an interesting paradox about the nature of jury composition. Should a jury reflect the community's verdict about disputed issues and affairs? Although pretrial publicity may expose jurors to information that would not have come to their attention during trial, it is at least arguable that a community's general condemnation of certain specific practices should be reflected by the jurors' vote. In fact, the historical role of the jury was to bring to criminal proceedings the knowledge of the case as well as the attitudes of the community. Indeed, in the past, jurors were picked for their knowledge of the events to be considered. Today, of course, quite the opposite practice prevails; jurors are supposed to enter the box as blank slates to be written upon only by the hands of the law.

[5] 17 *University of Chicago Law Review* 540, 552 (1950).

[6] 63 *Harvard Law Review* 840, 842 (1950).

communications media upon the public. Paul Lazarsfeld has concluded in his book *Radio and the Printed Page* that while radio has a strong commercial effect it has little social impact. And, given what he concludes is the conservative tendency of radio broadcasting, radio should have a minimal effect upon mass audiences in large urban areas where most criminal trials take place. Dorwin Cartwright has concluded that readers tend to read only what they agree with, and are not swayed by conflicting opinions in the news. Readers read the newspapers that come closest to their own views, and the press would seem to cater to pre-formed ideas more than to set up new standards of belief.[7] An interesting study bearing out Cartwright's conclusion was conducted around the Baltimore Radio case (see Appendix B, pp. 292–298). Arthur C. Millspaugh studied the newspapers in Baltimore at the time of the crime and during the subsequent trial for murder. There were, he reported, four important newspapers in the area when the defendant, a Negro man, was charged with killing a white woman. Three newspapers, directed to the white community, favored conviction; the fourth, the *Afro-American,* which circulated almost wholly in the Negro community, stressed in its coverage the favorable facts about the background of the accused.[8] Another writer in this field, John Lofton, a Pittsburgh lawyer-editor, concludes: "Research on the effects of the mass media has indicated pretty clearly that persuasive communication is more often associated with attitude reinforcement than with conversion to new attitudes. The mass media are more effective in canalizing than in modifying basic attitudes."[9]

The Institute of Communications Research at the University of Illinois recently undertook a study to attempt an assessment of the influence of pretrial newspaper publicity on jurors' verdicts.[10] Two model jury panels were exposed to newspaper stories about a hypothetical case to be tried, one to conservative, restrained stories and the other to stories that were sensational and that contained prejudicial facts not to come out at trial (such as prior record). The panels were then asked to indi-

---

[7] "Some Principles of Mass Persuasion," 2 *Human Relations* 253 (1949).

[8] "Trial by Mass Media," *Public Opinion and Propaganda,* 113, 114 (1954).

[9] "Justice and the Press," 6 *St. Louis Law Journal* 449 (1961). See also Lofton's book *Justice and the Press* (Boston: Beacon Press, 1966).

[10] Rita Jane Simon, "The Influence of the Mass Media on the Verdicts of Potential Jurors" (1965).

cate their opinions about the defendant's guilt. Thereupon, mock trials were held according to the ordinary rules of evidence, and the jurors were instructed by the judge not to base their decisions on facts other than those developed at the trial. After the trial, the jurors again indicated their opinions of the defendant's guilt or innocence. Those who had been exposed to the sensational and prejudicial stories came to the trial more convinced than their counterpart group of the defendant's guilt (64 per cent as opposed to 36 per cent). But after the simulated trial the difference in conclusions between the two groups diminished almost to the vanishing point (of those with opinions, 25 per cent to 24 per cent voted "guilty"; 72 per cent to 76 per cent voted "not guilty").

The conclusion of the testers: publicity did not prejudice the juries' verdicts although the newspapers may well have influenced the readers' opinions initially. The study indicates that normal courtroom precautions can undo any pretrial damage done by press publication. Of course, the sample was small and the result far from conclusive. Moreover, the participants in the experiment were picked from volunteers chosen at random from the community; thus they might well have been a blue-ribbon group, especially interested in the experiment and anxious to be scrupulous models.

One conclusion that might follow from these findings, and one that may well form a part of the bar's distaste for published news of law enforcement affairs, is that the public's impression about a crime and the guilt of a defendant may, as a result of publicity about a case, be different from that of the ultimate jury that tries the case and makes the decision after considering a different set of facts. Thus, public confidence in the administration of justice may suffer as a result of the variant opinions about cases that are given coverage before, during, and after trials. The public may wonder why the villain who seems so guilty was not punished, what was wrong with the jury, and why the law let justice go undone.

Some relevant experiments by Goggin and Hanover[11] have attempted to test how man perceives, reasons, and comes to believe something

---

[11] Terrence P. Goggin and George M. Hanover, "Free Press v. Fair Trial: The Psychological Effect of Pre-Trial Publicity on the Juror's Ability to be Impartial; a Plea for Reform," 38 *South California Law Review* 672 (1965).

is true, and how those beliefs affect later decision-making capacities. One psychological experiment showed that first impressions about people's character will tend to refuse to yield or to change. Sometimes those impressions create barriers that exclude new and contrary data.[12] The study suggests that we tend to dismiss data that oppose beliefs we have formed and to remember facts that line up with our preconceptions. Furthermore, since people are not conscious of the mechanisms and processes with which they perceive and select and exclude, the authors concluded that press-stimulated impressions may be hard to dissolve.

But their conclusion that "the media's information is considered and weighed as independent evidence" and that beliefs thus adopted about the defendant's guilt "prompt[s] the selection, distortion and reinforcement of testimony" is, however plausible, still unproved. That their conclusion is, in fact, much to be doubted is suggested by Kalven and Zeisel's book, the most authoritative study of the American criminal jury made to date.[13] Professors Kalven and Zeisel studied 3,576 criminal trials that took place during a period of a little over two years. After making statistical adjustments for cases where the jury was hung, they concluded that judge and jury disagreed in their verdicts about 22 per cent of the time, and "massively in one direction": the jury was more lenient. Had the verdict been the judge's to make, he would have convicted in 19 per cent of the cases where the juries had acquitted; he would have acquitted in 3 per cent of the cases where the jury verdicts were guilty. One may conclude that in these cases either there was no publicity or at least no prejudicial publicity (or even that the publicity was favorable to the accused), or else that whatever publicity occurred did not exert its assumed evil effect of contaminating jurors' minds. The first supposition is highly improbable: among the cases where the "net leniency" of jury over judge ranged from 13 to 41 per cent were those of murder, robbery, grand larceny, rape and other sex offenses; in short, the most highly publicized cases and the ones where, if the complainants about press publicity are right, the publicity is more likely to be prejudicial to the defendant. The second supposition is the more believable:

---

[12] 18 *Journal of Personality* 431 (1950), cited in the same article.

[13] Harry Kalven and Hans Zeisel, *The American Jury* (Boston: Little, Brown, 1966).

publicity does not wreak its evil effects upon juries nearly to the degree commonly believed.

Moreover, the study supports the conviction that the jury is in fact what it is represented to be, an effective trier of the facts laid before it in the courtroom, and that trial procedures do indeed operate as they are supposed to, in practice screening out those nonjudicial elements which in theory are not allowed to enter into the jury's consideration. The authors found various reasons for the disagreements between judge and jury, one of which was that in some cases the judge knew something that the jury did not: mainly prior record, and the history of the defendant, but also the existence of a nonadmissible confession, withdrawal of an original guilty plea, refusal to take a blood test, etc. The interesting and to us persuasive kernel of the matter is that the jury did *not* know of those prejudicial circumstances. Somehow or other, effective screening *did* take place; whatever prejudicial publication there may have been about the case, pretrial and pending trial, it did not become part of the jury's knowledge.

There is a discomforting implication in this matter about traditional concepts of the sturdiness of the ability of judges, rather than of juries, to dismiss nonjudicial facts from their decision making. The number of cases where judge and jury disagreed because the judge knew facts that the jury did not was small, only about 2 per cent of the total disagreements. Nevertheless, here were cases where if the trials had been before a judge and not a jury the defendants would have been convicted for precisely those reasons which the law declares may *not* be part of the grounds for the guilty verdict.

This circumstance invites some perverse questions: Does it reinforce the argument for drastic suppression of prejudicial publicity, inasmuch as wherever the jury remains unaware of nonjudicial evidence it renders a verdict more in tune with the law's requirements for fair trial than the judge does? Does it indicate that the problem is not confined to juries since prejudicial publicity, it turns out, contrary to theory, also affects the judge, who may not be able to decide cases fairly when *he* is aware of prejudicial facts?

The present state of research indicates the need for much more scientific exploration of this area, and it suggests the value of such further study with the participation of the bar. How prior knowledge affects prospective jurors; whether jurors can in fact lay aside their preconceived impressions; whether prejudice operates on a conscious level; whether jurors recognize and admit prejudice, and similar questions ought to be considered. How efficient are our courtroom procedures and how could they be improved?

Otherwise we will never go beyond the present intraprofessional mottoes and myths about the effect of public information on the criminal trial process. Meanwhile, we must proceed with a situation about which observers on both sides of the dispute have strong intuitive opinions but few facts to back them up. As one writer put it: "If a tentative conclusion may be ventured at this point, it is that there is no empirical evidence to support the view that extensive or even irresponsible press coverage of a court case destroys the ability of jurors to decide the issue fairly. In the meantime the problem is ripe for study, and until scientifically accumulated data is available, courts and legislatures will have to act on little more than hunch and intuition."[14]

"The problem is ripe for study" has been a commonplace in the literature of the free press, fair trial dispute for the last quarter of a century. It is one of the few statements in the controversy with which both the bar and the press agree. But, except for a few experiments such as those mentioned above, no satisfying study of the effect of crime and trial news upon the jury has been made. We know of none even in preparation. Yet it should not be beyond the talents and resources of the press, the bar, and the academic communities to explore seriously this fundamental question.

We are obliged to proceed for the time being as best we can without an answer. Our assumptions for what follows are that press publications do influence jurors to some unknown extent, less than the amount ascribed by those who hold that publication is automatically prejudicial and more than the nil figure proclaimed by an occasional impassioned press partisan.

[14] Donald Gillmor, "Free Press v. Fair Trial: A Continuing Dialogue," 41 *North Dakota Law Review* 156, 172 (January, 1965).

CHAPTER 6

THE FILTERING

PROCEDURES

To block out whatever prejudicial effect published information about a criminal case might have on a jury, the law has developed a number of procedural filtering devices. They are intended to serve as a kind of screen to help keep the nonjudicial particles out of the carefully regulated clockwork of the jury trial system. If they were 100 per cent effective, there would be no free press, fair trial problem. The press could write anything, any time, and fair trials would nevertheless be assured, albeit with some added difficulty. Unfortunately, those techniques are not foolproof. Their operation and effectiveness need to be examined.

"The theory of our system," Justice Oliver Wendell Holmes said, "is that the conclusions to be reached in a case will be induced only by evidence and argument in open court, and not by any outside influence, whether of private talk or public print."[1] Specific nonjudicial evidence that could not later be allowed at trial must not come to the jury's attention through any other avenue. Moreover, general public pressure should not be brought to bear upon prospective jurors who are, again in Justice Holmes's words, "extremely likely to be impregnated by the envisioning atmosphere." Justice Felix Frankfurter put it this way: "Precisely because the feeling of the outside world cannot, with the utmost care, be kept wholly outside the courtroom, every endeavor must be taken in a civilized trial to keep it outside."[2]

In order to assure that appropriate conditions will prevail, the court-

[1] *Patterson v. Colorado,* 205 U.S. 454, 462 (1907).
[2] *Stroble v. California,* 343 U.S. 181 (1952).

room is made a very special place. It is thought that, no matter how life proceeds elsewhere, in the courtroom special requirements must be met to protect the lay decision-makers on the jury. The general purpose of this aspect of the law—to assure that jurors are not exposed to knowledge or influence about a case except that which emerges at trial—has been interpreted rigidly by most observers. One commentator, somewhat unrealistically, has said: "The minds of a jury may be likened to 12 test tubes"[3]; they are not to be used for important careful experiments when they are soiled by foreign elements.

There are four prime procedural devices used by the law to guarantee impartial juries: (1) the motion before trial to change the venue (location) of the case; (2) the motion before trial to continue the commencement time of the case to a later date; (3) the voir dire examination of prospective jurors at the beginning of the trial, a questioning by the judge and counsel to determine jurors' freedom from bias or prejudgment; and (4) the judge's instructions to the jury. Related to these are a number of other remedies, which will be discussed later in this chapter.

As evidenced by the very fact that it has set up these screening procedures, the law presupposes that jurors may be and often have been exposed to potentially prejudicial information. The law operates on the further assumption that these sanitizing devices will be effective in expelling from a jury's consideration what was nonjudicial and inadmissible information, so that the jurors may come to their verdict objectively and according to proper legal standards. But, whatever the law may presuppose, there is a body of opinion that holds that those measures do not adequately perform their described function.

Continuance and Change of Venue

The continuance and the change of venue are procedures developed in the common law and adopted everywhere in the United States by constitution, statute, or rule of court. The obvious and logical idea behind these two procedures is that the potentially adverse effects of community attitude and press publications may be abated by a delay (continuance) until things cool off, or by changing the place (venue) of the trial to a location where the presumed influence of the press and

---

[3] Harold Sullivan, *Contempt by Publication* (New Haven: 1940), p. 178.

public feeling would be less likely, if not totally absent. That a defendant is Constitutionally guaranteed a speedy trial in the place where the crime is supposed to have been committed has not been considered an objection to these two procedures which, however they alter those rights, are designed for the defendant's benefit. The rationale behind the continuance is that the right to delay for good reasons is part of the inherent power of courts to hear and determine cases. The rationale of the change of venue is that it is a means to a Constitutional end—trial by an impartial jury.[4]

The thought behind the change of venue procedure was articulated by a Minnesota court in a highly publicized romance-murder case:

> Courts can do little to restrain news media from printing or broadcasting what they claim is news, but when it appears that the public has been subjected to so much publicity about a case that it seems unlikely that a fair trial can be had in the locality in which the trial normally would be held, the court can and should see to it that the trial is transferred to another locality in which it is more probable that a fair trial can be had. . . . It is important that the constitutional guarantee of the freedom of the press not be curtailed if we are to exist as a free people. It is equally important, however, that, when the unrestrained exercise of this right clashes with the right of an accused person to be tried by an impartial jury having no preconceived opinions as to the guilt or innocence of the accused, the rights of such accused person must be protected by transferring the case to a locality where the public may not have been influenced as much by the publicity that has been given the case.[5]

In some places a defendant may move for a change of venire—that is, he may ask that a new panel of jurors be brought in from another area less under the influence of the adverse publicity. This procedure is designed to serve the same purpose as the change of venue without encountering the difficulty of removing the trial itself. It is felt that there is a public interest in trying cases in the community where the crime was committed in order that there be public confidence in the criminal law process—confidence based upon public surveillance.

The related but somewhat different idea behind the continuance has been described in these words:

[4] *Cockrell v. Dobbs*, 381 S.W. 2d 756 (S.C. Arkansas, 1964).
[5] *State v. Thompson*, 123 N.W. 2d 378 (S.C. Minnesota, 1963).

While a change of venue is designed to avoid local prejudice by transferring the case out of the community, and will therefore be of value only when the hostile feeling has not permeated the jurisdiction, continuance, which involves removal in time from the focus of the prejudice against the defendant, will be appropriate where this hostility exists throughout the jurisdiction but can be expected to fade within a reasonable time.[6]

As logical as these two techniques seem to be, they are not frequently used and in fact they are of questionable value in *causes célèbres*—those very cases where it is likely that they would be sought. The press is so ubiquitous nowadays that, given a case of strong public interest, it can follow the forum and rekindle interest in a case that has been moved or delayed. In the Roy Cohn case,[7] a Federal court in New York admitted: "Modern means of news communication have taken away many of the reasons for the transfer of the cause celebre which may have existed 50 years ago."

Whenever and wherever Teamster boss James Hoffa is tried, for example, the publicity is going to be great. In fact, in all celebrated cases where defendants might seek to escape the press through means like these, the remedy can be subverted by the press if it chooses to do so.

Moreover, once feelings are aroused, they may persist on their own momentum. Thus, the late Judge Learned Hand said in response to motions in the famous Communist trials in New York City:

> That such feeling did exist [heated public feeling against Communists] among many persons—probably a large majority—is indeed true; but there was no reason to suppose that it would subside by any delay which would not put off the trial indefinitely. The choice was between using the best means available to secure an impartial jury and letting the prosecution lapse. It was not as though the prejudice had been local, so that it could be cured by removal to another district; it was not as though it were temporary so that there was any reasonable hope that with a reasonable continuance it would fade. Certainly, we must spare no effort to secure an impartial panel; but those who may

[6] 60 *Columbia Law Review* 349, 368 (1960). *Delaney v. U.S.*, 199 F. 2d 107 (1st Cir. 1952) was a case where a verdict was reversed for failure to grant a continuance under what were considered appropriate circumstances. A prior legislative hearing regarding the same matter had saturated the community with comments about the case.

[7] 332 F. 2d 976 (2d Cir. 1964).

in fact have committed a crime cannot secure immunity because it is possible that the jurors who try them may not be exempt from the general feelings prevalent in the society in which they live; we must do as best we can with the means we have.[8]

The dilemma posed is that where these remedies may be most needed they are least likely as a practical matter to accomplish their aims. Court argument about invoking these procedures may compound the difficulty they set out to solve; publicity about the action ensues and spirals the problem.

Another difficulty with these two procedures is the hesitancy of courts to use them. Whether judges are skeptical about the potential prejudice of press publications (in other contexts they are not) or merely hesitant to pass their problems on to other judges, they frequently deny motions for continuances or changes of venue. Proof of more than a juror's exposure to publicity is required by most judges. But how can a defendant or his lawyer show more?

Judges have refused to grant continuances or changes of venue until it becomes clear that selection of an impartial jury is impossible, adopting a let's-wait-and-see approach to complaints about prejudicial publication. This is what happened in the Sheppard case described in Chapter 1. Once a jury is empaneled, why continue a case or change its site, it is argued; the fact that the jury has been empaneled is the best proof that an impartial jury *can* be empaneled. Other courts have indulged in a seesaw logic, denying a motion for change of venue on the ground that continuance was the appropriate remedy; and vice versa.

The courts do not grant these motions simply because there has been significant publicity about a case. Sometimes courts have reasoned (contravening the very core of the bar's argument in the free press, fair trial dispute) that press reports alone are not enough to make a juror decide contrary to the evidence and his oath.

Continuances, commonly granted for a multitude of different reasons, are infrequently allowed on the grounds of prejudicial publicity, and generally only when there are extraordinary circumstances. For example, continuances were ordered in a case where excessive pretrial publicity arose out of a prior legislative investigation and in another case where public interest was so intense that lynch mobs were formed,

[8] *U.S. v. Dennis,* 183 F. 2d 201 (2d Cir. 1950).

houses burned, and eventually the National Guard was needed to re-store order. Nevertheless, one bafflingly imaginative court denied a requested continuance on the theory that if jurors would perjure them-selves, or public officials would indulge in misconduct, they would do so without public pressures, too. Another court denied the remedy be-cause it feared that granting a continuance might create a greater harm by arousing the public about the lethargy of the judicial process.

The motion for a change of venue is based upon less subjective criteria than the continuance. Ordinarily the party seeking it must ac-company his request with affidavits attesting to his position that the climate of public opinion in that community precludes a fair trial. This practice often leads to a battle of affidavits between the prosecu-tion and defense, the former claiming the virginal virtue of the prospec-tive jury panel or that the defendant is shopping for a favorable forum, and the latter arguing the complete corruption of the prospective jury caused by public pressures of yellow journalism. Sometimes public-opinion polls are offered as proof of the need to remove a trial to an-other, less prejudiced community.

Both remedies are less than totally satisfactory even when they are granted, in that the defendant nonetheless has been caused delay, ex-pense, and inconvenience as well as the sacrifice of his Constitutional right to a speedy or a local trial.

But while in the extreme cases of sensationally publicized trials these two techniques may be ineffective in making the minds of the jurors into pure or even reasonably clean test tubes, this is not to say that the procedures have no value. Somewhere between the rare extreme of the sensational case of nationwide notoriety and the overwhelming majority of routine trials at the other end of the spectrum where prejudicial publicity is an almost nonexistent problem are a number of cases where continuance and change of venue could perform a real service.

An example is the case of Melvin Rees (see pp. 171–175), where pretrial publicity saturated a rural community in one part of a state but clearly impinged much less on a complex of industrial cities 150 miles away. In such a case a change of venue would surely be indicated and there is no reason to assume beforehand that it would not accom-plish its purpose.

In the Irvin case (Appendix B, pp. 304–306), a change of venue was granted, but it was almost meaningless inasmuch as it was to an adjacent county where public outrage over the series of murders for which Irvin was charged was as intense as at the locus of the killings. But this would not necessarily have been so, and surely a jury with fewer prejudices could have been empaneled in, say, the industrial community of Gary or the metropolis of Indianapolis rather than in the Evansville area. If the Rideau case (Appendix B, pp. 302–304) had been moved to New Orleans it surely would have been easier to empanel a jury that had not been exposed to Rideau's televised confession in jail in rural Lake Charles. In the Sheppard case, the court simply refused to grant either a continuance or a change of venue, and this in a city and at a time least likely to afford the defendant a fair trial. The Supreme Court was later to denounce the lower court's refusals.

Continuance would almost certainly be useful where there is to be a trial for a crime of the same species that for some preceding weeks or months has occupied local attention. Thus, if a city's fathers are pressing a special campaign for safe driving, a defendant charged with negligent homicide in an auto accident should be allowed to have his trial postponed until the campaign has been concluded.

The standard reluctance of the courts to grant continuances and changes of venue seems to us unjustified. There is a thoughtful rationale behind these procedures and they should be allowed to serve the purposes for which they were designed. Even in some highly publicized cases there are grounds for believing that initial community excitement and animus will be abated with the passage of time, and even with the modern-day pervasiveness of the news media, there are grounds for believing that some localities will be less absorbed and opinionated by news of crimes than the localities in which they occurred.

Failure to try available procedures such as continuance and change of venue has been central to many celebrated and problematical cases. And the Supreme Court itself has indicated in recent decisions that until the courts have used the devices available to them to cancel any impact on jurors that may have been caused by the press, verdicts will not be upheld and the press will not be restricted.

Voir Dire

Once past these pretrial procedures and at the beginning of the trial process, the next filtering technique of the law is the voir dire examina-

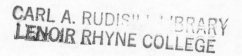

tion of prospective jurors. At this point, both sides may question jurors chosen at random from the jury rolls in an attempt to find an impartial panel to try the case (in theory, that is; actually, each side wants a favorable panel more than a totally impartial one).

If it can be established through the formal questioning of prospective jurors by the judge, the defense counsel, or the prosecuting attorney that pretrial publicity has caused a juror to form an unalterable opinion about the case, he can be challenged for cause. This right to challenge is available in all jurisdictions and is unlimited in number. If, for one reason or another, the challenge for cause is overruled, the juror may nonetheless be challenged peremptorily. Every jurisdiction allows some number of peremptory challenges, for which *no* cause need be proved. The number of peremptory challenges allowed usually is determined by the penalty for the particular crime in issue.

The Federal courts have varying procedures for challenges: some allow counsel to question the jurors during examination, the judge remaining passive (eleven states follow this procedure); others allow counsel to conduct pretrial questioning after the judge has questioned the prospective jurors (twenty-nine states); some provide only for questioning by the judge and allow none by counsel (ten states). In these latter cases, ordinarily counsel may submit questions for the judge to ask.

Here again, what seems like a logical answer is not necessarily a workable one. Here, too, the courts apply Judge Learned Hand's do-as-best-we-can approach. As the Supreme Court has said:

> The theory of the law is that a juror who has formed an opinion cannot be impartial. Every opinion which he may entertain need not necessarily have that effect. In these days of newspaper enterprise and universal education, every case of public interest is almost, as a matter of necessity, brought to the attention of all the intelligent people in the vicinity, and scarcely anyone can be found among those best fitted for jurors who has not read or heard of it, and who has not some impression or some opinion in respect to its merits. It is clear, therefore, that upon the trial of the issue of fact raised by a challenge for such cause the court will practically be called upon to determine whether the nature and strength of the opinion formed are such as in law necessarily to raise the presumption of partiality.[9]

[9] *Reynolds v. U.S.*, 98 U.S. 145 (1898).

In the Roy Cohn case, the Federal court took the position that *voir dire* is more than a charade and that a juror's word must be accepted at face value. "It must be assumed," the court held, "if we would continue to rely upon the jury system, that the talesmen will answer truthfully as to the prejudices or lack thereof. It would indeed be a cynical approach to believe that jurors, who give their assurance that they can fairly and impartially decide the fact issues before them, would deliberately conceal their prejudices. Despite the fact that every individual who enters the jury box of necessity must bring his own personality and point of view with him and may not be exempt from the general feelings prevalent in the society in which they [*sic*] live, such individuals once they take their oath must be trusted to act as honest and impartial fact judges."

"If there be human frailty," the court concluded, echoing Judge Hand, "we must do as best we can with the means we have."

Unfortunately, the subtle psychological question whether or not notoriety would affect the decision of the juror is for the most part left to the juror himself. It seems unlikely that a prejudiced juror would recognize his own personal prejudice—or, knowing it, would admit it. However, since there are no empirical data to contradict his declaration of detachment, his word is ordinarily the determining factor. What is more, the more prejudiced or bigoted the jurors, the less can they be expected to confess forthrightly and candidly their state of mind in open court. The more naïve or sincere juror, who might be likely to discard prior knowledge for the purpose of his decision-making duty, would probably be more ready to acknowledge his state of mind and thus be challenged.

There is a practical problem, too. The more publicized and notorious the crime and the more difficulty in securing an impartial jury, the more cumbersome and self-defeating becomes the examination of prospective jurors. Many members of the bench and experienced trial lawyers recognize that voir dire questioning in sensational cases may be suicide. As Justice Frankfurter said of this situation in one case:

> . . . it hardly seems necessary for the court to say to men who are experienced in the trial of jury cases, that every time defense counsel asked a prospective juror whether he had heard a radio broadcast to the effect that his client has confessed to this crime or that he has been

guilty of similar crimes, he would by that act be driving just one more nail into [the defendant's] coffin. We think, therefore, that remedy was useless.[10]

The risk of antagonizing the jury, or of bringing to its attention unfavorable facts about which it may have had no knowledge, is a vexation to even the most adroit and expert trial attorney.

The purpose of challenges is to allow each side to attempt to find a fair jury. Counsel question prospective jurors and make their choices on the basis of instinct and experience. Trial lawyers differ in their estimates of the efficiency of the examination. Some say it is a scientific probe and follow their pet formulas (minority religions are good, women are bad, government employees terrible, etc.); others feel it is a blind stab, a nonsensical procedure without rhyme or reason.

A Wisconsin court recently described the rather stilted ratiocination of this procedure:

> During the course of voir dire examination, one juror acknowledged that he had formed an opinion as to the guilt of the defendants. The court then instructed him that he was to disregard any information he received relating to the case, outside the evidence offered during the course of the trial. The court expressly explained to the prospective juror that out-of-court information was lacking in probative value because it was not offered under oath, and was not subject to test by cross examination. After this explanation and admonition by the court, the juror stated that he felt that he could predicate his verdict solely upon the evidence received during the course of the trial. A challenge for cause to this juror was denied and because the defense had exhausted their peremptory challenges, he subsequently became a member of the alternate panel.[11]

Different courts have placed varying degrees of confidence in this procedure. In the Sheppard case an appellate court said: ". . . our jury system is based upon the belief of jurors, and when jurors testify that they can discount influences of external factors and meet the standard imposed by the Fourteenth Amendment, that assumption is not lightly to be disregarded. . . ."[12]

[10] *State v. Baltimore Radio Show,* 338 U.S. 912 (1950).
[11] *State v. Nutley,* 129 N.W. 2d 155 (Wisconsin, 1964).
[12] *Sheppard v. Maxwell,* 231 F. Supp. 37 (D.C. Ohio, 1964).

One study of voir dire has been made based upon a series of jury cases in one Midwestern Federal district court over a year and a half period in the late 1950's.[13] Lawyers and jurors were interviewed with the permission of the court. The author concluded that voir dire examination generally is perfunctory and ineffective in weeding out unfavorable jurors or eliciting crucial data about prejudice. Jury panels resisted the procedure and displayed less than complete candor. However, the author concluded that voir dire, while not an effective screening vehicle, is useful as an indoctrinating gimmick to make points to a jury or to ingratiate oneself with a juror or jury.[14]

The juror's preconception of guilt will disqualify him if its source is direct and its strength is settled. Personal knowledge about a case is a basis for disqualification; rumor, general sentiment, or exposure to newspaper reports need not be. Aside from the practical problem with voir dire, there is a theoretical problem in that the line between these two areas is thin and unclear. There is no juror who can adjudge a case with no preconceptions. Moreover, if such a man existed he would not be an ideal juror, since the function of the jury is, in part, to apply the mores and sentiments of the community to the law. A juror cannot and should not come sterilized and untouched by human conditions. As one court said in the Baltimore Radio case: "Trials cannot be held in a vacuum hermetically sealed against rumor and report. If a mere disclosure of the general nature of the evidence relied on would vitiate a subsequent trial, few verdicts could stand."

But voir dire, for all its flaws and awkwardness, cannot be dismissed as a useless technique. In those cases where some prejudicial publicity may exist, but not in invincible superabundance, the examination of the

[13] Dale Broder, "Voir Dire Examinations: An Empirical Study," 38 *South California Law Review* 503 (1965).

[14] In the course of our own survey of the free press, fair trial problem in Washington, D.C. (Chapter 3), we collected impressions of local prosecutors about the efficacy of traditional filtering techniques. Most felt that pretrial publicity was a minimal problem because jurors forget what they have read a relatively long time in the past. Once on a jury, however, their now focused attention becomes underscored because they have a personal interest in the specific case. Therefore, the prosecutors concluded, publication of nonadmissible evidence *during* the trial can do the most damage. Most felt that voir dire was not effective because jurors who want to be on a jury will lie to avoid challenge; others will be too embarrassed to admit they are prejudiced.

talesmen may help weed out the obviously partial juror. If it is to do so, however, it must be conducted with considerably more care and seriousness than sometimes seems to be the case. Some defendants, we suspect, fail to receive from their counsel the careful attention to the possibilities that voir dire promises.

In the sensational cases, it may be impossible to screen out all jurors who have developed preconceptions from the news, but at least the questioning could serve as a guide in identifying the cases where change of venue, postponement, or careful instructions should be brought into play. In the Irvin case, for example, voir dire should have shown the judge that a change in venue to a distant part of the state was proper.

And even where it cannot block from the jury box every opinionated juror, the exercise may serve tactically to counterbalance prejudice if the attorney uses it to stress the point that the juror has a responsibility to try the case on evidence alone. Trial attorneys differ in their appraisal of its value, and its real efficacy may not be discoverable. But it is worth noting that some prosecutors see in the defense attorney's skillful use of the voir dire procedure an effective way to put the future juror on his mettle and on his honor to disregard the impressions he may have formed. The question of his objectivity and moral duty having been raised, the juror may well lean over backward to make his finding solely on the basis of what transpires in court.

Instructions

Where the filtering procedures of the criminal trial courts fail, the law provides a purification process—instructions by the court. The judge usually instructs the jurors at the outset of a trial not to expose themselves during the trial to press comments about pending cases. And at the conclusion of the trial the judge will ordinarily tell the jury what it may consider in reaching its verdict, and what it must ignore. W. S. Gilbert described this procedure less prosaically in *Trial by Jury:*

> Now, Jurymen, hear my advice—
> All kinds of vulgar prejudice
>   I pray you set aside:
> With stern judicial frame of mind,
> From bias free of every kind,
>   This trial must be tried.

The idea behind instructions about prejudicial publicity is that whatever deleterious effect the press may have had upon a jury's impartiality will be cured by the court's admonition. Thus, in theory, the judge is supposed to be able to wipe out any effects of press or personal comments about a case and the knowledge of facts never received in evidence.

There is reason to be skeptical about the efficacy of instructions. The late Judge Jerome Frank equated the practice with Mark Twain's anecdote of the young boy who was told to stand in the corner and not to think about a white elephant. He called reliance on such "ritualistic admonitions" an unrealistic way to cure defects in the composition of a jury. "The futility of that sort of exorcism is notorious," he said. And Justice Robert Jackson wrote: "The naïve assumption that prejudicial effects can be overcome by instructions to the jury . . . all practicing lawyers know to be unmitigated fiction."

Nevertheless, courts regularly allow the question of fair trial to turn on this ritual, arguing or pretending that the judge's instructions vitiate the effect of any improper knowledge that may have come to the attention of the jury. Great deference is given to the trial judge's discretion by the appellate courts, which have upheld verdicts with rationales such as that the jury could not have come in with any other decision, or that only the actual prejudice and not mere susceptibility to it should determine the propriety of the juror's extra-judicial knowledge.

Furthermore, in long and complicated cases, juries are sometimes confused, sometimes annoyed by the court's instructions. It is also questionable whether juries are scrupulous in heeding the court's instructions. One study of instructions in general by Professor Harry Kalven, Jr., of the Chicago Law School, showed that jurors find it difficult to cope with them, and that attempts by the court to sift evidence are unrealistic.[15] Nevertheless, Kalven remarked about his study, "We do . . . have evidence that the jurors take with surprising seriousness the admonition not to read the paper or to discuss the case. . . . the jury is a pretty stubborn, healthy institution not likely to be overwhelmed . . . by . . . a remark in the press."[16] And the central point of his great work,

---

[15] "A Report on the Jury Project of the University of Chicago Law School," *Insurance Counsel Journal*, October, 1957.

[16] Donald Gillmor, "Trial by Newspaper," 41 *North Dakota Law Review* 156, at 167 cites a letter from Kalven to the Director of the American Law Institute.

The American Jury,[17] done with Professor Zeisel, is this if nothing else.

Recognizing the futility of instructing jurors to put something out of their minds, Judge Matthew Magruder admitted that the average juror is not capable of excluding the "unconscious influence of his preconceptions as to probable guilt." Yet in many cases where jurors had read articles about the trial they were hearing, it has been held that the judge's instructions to them to decide the case strictly on the evidence presented in court, and their assurances that they would, were sufficient. In the famous Barbara Graham murder case, in California, the court ignored the potential effect on the jury of sensational press coverage by indulging the reasoning that the prosecution had not caused the publicity, and since the jury was instructed by the court, there arose a presumption that they obeyed.

But courts cannot simply give up when there has been pretrial publicity about a case. As Judge Charles Clark once wrote: "Trial by newspaper may be unfortunate, but it is not new and, unless the court accepts the standard judicial hypothesis that cautioning instructions are effective, criminal trials in large metropolitan cities may well prove impossible."[18] Indeed, this condition is not a new phenomenon. Years before, Justice Holmes pointed out that if the mere opportunity for prejudice or corruption was enough to raise a presumption that they existed, it would be hard to maintain jury trials under conditions even then. And one judge recently pointed out: "The mere fact of unfavorable publicity does not of itself raise a presumption of prejudice. The prejudice must have manifested itself so as to corrupt due process."[19]

Yet the reasoning of the courts does raise some questions. In one place a juror may be allowed to decide a case where he has been exposed before trial to a prejudicial publication when he assures the court that he will not allow this exposure to affect his judgment; elsewhere it was considered a reversible error for a judge to instruct a jury that it might follow the case in the press so long as it did not consider extrajudicial information as evidence, or for a juror to do this against the court's order not to.

[17] Boston: Little, Brown, 1966.

[18] *U.S. v. Leviton,* 193 F. 2d 848, 857 (2d Cir. 1951).

[19] *Editor and Publisher,* August 14, 1965, quoting Federal Judge William J. Neelon.

As a general rule, in the average case where trial publicity is minimal and the temptation to ignore admonitions to abstain from exposure to the press are not great, juries no doubt are true to their oaths, and a judge can avoid the problems of prejudicial publicity by instructing the jury not to read or listen to nonjudicial accounts of the case. At least this much caution should be required of the courts before the bench and bar criticize the press for interfering with fair trial.

During the year and a half when this book was being written we learned of several instances where mistrials were declared because, while the trial was going on, jurors read newspaper articles containing potentially prejudicial facts that did not come out at the trial. The press was criticized in these instances for callously obstructing justice. Yet in each case the judge had failed to instruct the jury *not* to read press accounts of the case during the trial.

We believe, along with the do-as-best-we-can school, that the instruction technique, despite its flaws, should be utilized more extensively and more earnestly. The cynical supposition that juries are in no way affected by the court's instructions to disregard nonjudicial information and to avoid seeing or hearing reports of the case outside the courtroom remains unproved. Until the supposition to the contrary, which is the presumption of American law, is disproved it deserves to be honored.

At the very least, courts should attempt to use their own means to reach the desired goals of fair trial. The judge's instructions may not be powerful enough to overcome all the latent prejudice created by the news media in sensational cases, but where prejudicial publicity has not been excessive there is no reason to suppose that instructions cannot often be powerful enough to disarm it.

There are a number of other available procedures to prevent or correct interference by the press with fair trials.

Blue ribbon juries, special panels usually composed of a more sophisticated, educated class than the ordinary jury, are used sometimes to ensure that the careful rules of the court control the trial of an unusually complicated or controversial case.

A suggestion also has been made that a defendant who fears a prejudiced jury be allowed to elect to be tried by a judge or by a panel of judges.[20] This is predicated on the viewpoint that judges can be exposed to outside pressures and nevertheless try cases fairly. Sometimes the law does allow a defendant to waive his Constitutional right to trial by jury, but only if the court and prosecution agree. We believe this right should be unqualified; that a Constitutional right may be waived where it might work to the disadvantage of the defendant. Here, the Constitutional right to trial by jury would be sacrificed, voluntarily of course, to assure the vitality of two others, freedom of the press and the right to a fair trial.

Recently, courts have resorted increasingly to sequestration of juries to avoid their exposure to publications during trials. This procedure is expensive, annoyingly disruptive, and takes its toll on jurors. Whether juries resent the government for putting them to this inconvenience or whether they become hostile to the defendant because of it is beyond proof. But one thing is sure: no one likes the practice and it is at best a device to be saved for the unusual case.

In cases where extraordinary public pressure surrounding a case has injected outside influences into the trial atmosphere, a defendant jailed as a result may seek habeas corpus relief where all else fails. However, this remedy is technical, cumbersome, prolonged, and used only infrequently—in flagrant situations. It is nevertheless a useful last resort, and can be used (as it was in the Sheppard case) to allow the Supreme Court to scrutinize the atmosphere surrounding state court trials and assure that Constitutional standards of due process have been met.

Sometimes courts declare mistrials, reverse a conviction, and order a new trial on the ground that press influence deprived defendants of fair trials in the first instance. New trials have been granted for such incidents as mob dominance during trial, unfair atmosphere at the court itself, misconduct on the part of jurors. Courts are more likely to grant new trials where the government contributed to the publicity. Of course, these procedures are not cures; they are merely devices to undo injustices already done. None of these latter methods is an answer to the free press, fair trial problem. In a sense, all are a surrender to the press—an admission that prejudice could not be avoided or erased. But at least they are an accommodation by the courts to the world outside and an

---

[20] Ronald L. Goldfarb, "Public Information, Criminal Trials, and the Cause Célèbre," 36 *New York University Law Review* 810 (1961).

attempt to adjust to competing Constitutional and social demands. Inherent in all these steps is an ultimate fairness, but also a frustration.

If its techniques for filtering trial prejudice from the courtroom are not always effective, American law is not as helpless as some arguments suggest. In essence, American law does not guarantee that it will always be possible to find an impartial jury. Indeed, such a goal might be unattainable. However, it does guarantee at least that no defendant's conviction will be upheld if the jury was not impartial.

We conclude that for the average criminal case the law's filtering procedures are logically conceived and are no doubt useful in most situations. In the sensational case with special problems of publication that undermine fair trial procedures, the efficacy of these procedures is often questionable. This fear is reduced by the hunch that the cases where they might not work are few; and that in some they might suffice if they were tried. But in any event, because we concluded in Chapter 5 that it is likely that publication surely impregnates some trials, and because we conclude here that the law's filtering devices are not the complete answer in those cases, we must look further. In Chapter 8 we will examine the proposals that have been made in recent years to cope in other ways with the free press, fair trial problem. First, however, we must look at how the law itself has been applied to the issue over the course of this country's history.

CHAPTER 7

THE COURSE OF
THE LAW

It was natural that solutions to the free press, fair trial problem were first sought through means of the law. For whether acts by the press that seem to jeopardize the administration of justice are considered merely as forms of community misbehavior or, more sharply, as infringements on the rights of a single person, they stand as obvious breaches of the sort that the law exists to correct or punish. Precisely this category of wrong affronts the law's very purpose.

It is a curious fact of American jurisprudence, however, that in this area the law has not been a notably successful weapon for its own defense, that is to say, in defending its own needs for assuring fair trials. In more than a century of wrestling with the problem in the United States, a series of judicial decisions has emerged that has significantly reduced the ambit within which legal prohibitions against crime and trial reporting can be applied. Although the potential remains—for the door is neither closed nor locked by these precedents, nor is it likely to remain jammed where it is—under today's interpretations by the Supreme Court the law does not punish the kind of press treatment of crime and trials that causes the chief complaint.

For the most part, the law has dealt with the free press, fair trial problem by devising, as we saw in the preceding chapter, a maze of filtering procedures calculated to keep the stream of justice pure, as it flows into courts and before juries, of the corruptions of press publication. Additionally, two substantial legal doctrines have been used in an effort to stop or render harmless the current of pretrial prejudice: punishment of publications as contempt of court and reversal of convictions on the ground that publicity deprived the defendant of due

113

process of law. This latter technique is an obvious stopgap, almost a symbol of frustration, but it has nevertheless been resorted to recently. Principally, until about 1830 and again from 1917 until 1941, use of the contempt power, treating publication of prejudicial material as an interference with the administration of justice, was relied upon. But over the last two decades, the Supreme Court has so consistently reversed contempt convictions in this area on the ground that they violate the First Amendment that today the press is little deterred by the threat of being held contemptuous. Nevertheless, with mounting pressure against what is increasingly argued to be press mischief in the judicial process, some invigoration of the contempt law could be in prospect; the law is not static. Moreover, it may be noted when plotting the force of past decisions that the majority have dealt with nonjury cases. Most of them involved criticism of judges, as opposed to the kind of cases that have provoked the recent criticism of the press—assaults on the character of defendants and publication of damaging, nonjudicial evidence in jury cases.

A long look at the course of the law is, accordingly, more than an academic exercise or a footnote to legal history. A view of where we have been and how we got to where we are is essential for determining where we will go in the future. It provides the perspective necessary for the view ahead and for judging and measuring alternate paths. It happens also to be an interesting and provocative story.

In Appendix B we present a detailed analysis of the development of the law and a description of all the key cases (with their citations). For purposes of this chapter, the history may be briefly summarized.

Attempts to prevent press injury to the administration of justice by prior restraint of publication have had little success in the United States. The idea of prior restraint was abhorred even before the American Revolution, and the Constitutional fathers made certain by the First Amendment that it would gain no foothold here. The landmark decision of *Near v. Minnesota*, in 1930, made the doctrine crystal clear and should banish whatever lingering temptations remain to apply prior restraints on publication. Nevertheless, lower-court judges from time to time seek to prevent the press from reporting on some matter before them, and generally have been promptly rebuffed when the press takes the matter on appeal to the next higher court.

With prior restraint outlawed from the beginning, contempt of court was the principal device used over long periods to prevent or punish press assaults on fair trial procedures. The reasoning was that if the press cannot be restrained before the fact, it can be punished after it.

The application of the contempt power to trial news was not made easy by the inherent conflict between the First Amendment, "Congress shall make no law . . . abridging the freedom of the press," and the Fifth Amendment with its requirement of due process and the Sixth Amendment with its guarantee of trial by an "impartial jury." Nevertheless, the severe and rigorous doctrine of contempt that is the British law (any comment beyond a report of a judicial proceeding is punishable as a contempt for polluting the stream of justice) was also the pattern for the new Republic in its early days. The Judiciary Act of 1789 gave Federal courts power to punish "all contempts of authority in any case or hearing"; and the words "all contempts" were understood as all that the common law and British precedent considered them to be.

But although British contempt law has continued to this day on a consistently strict line,[1] American law has veered away sharply from the much more limiting British pattern. The first change came in 1831, when the Congress, in a new law that resulted from strong reactions against the inclusivity of the 1789 statute's interpretation, defined contempt as "any misbehavior in the presence of the court or so near thereto as to obstruct the administration of justice."

For almost ninety years, interpretation of the law was clear and consistent. The "so near thereto" phrase was taken in a literal, spatial sense. Misbehavior that was punishable was deemed to be only that which, like noise and interruptive disturbance, took place so near the court that its effect was the same as if it had occurred in the presence of the court itself. Obviously, that interpretation could not and did not include what was printed in some newspaper, however much a judge might feel that the publication interfered with the administration of justice or affronted his dignity.

In 1917, the law took a sudden 180-degree change of direction, back to the route of the British contempt philosophy, with the Supreme Court's decision in *Toledo Newspaper Company v. United States*. In an opinion written by Chief Justice Edward D. White, the Court held that in interpreting the "so near thereto" clause, the test was whether the

[1] Its operation is considered in Chapter 9.

character of the acts tended to prevent and obstruct justice. The spatial concept gave way to a causal one that could well include press publication. Justice Oliver Wendell Holmes dissented vigorously. He argued that the use of summary contempt power by a judge must be confined to situations where it is essential to prevent actual interference with the court proceedings, that is, in its physical presence or near enough to amount to the same thing.

The reversal in the interpretation of the 1831 law was soon adopted by other Federal courts and by all but a few state courts. Scholars referred to what happened as a twentieth-century subversion of a Constitutional rule that had been settled in the nineteenth century.

The rule continued for twenty-four years, until it was reversed in *Nye v. United States* in 1941 and again set on the earlier path. The case had nothing to do with freedom of the press, but rather with the action of an attorney that a lower court had found contemptuous. The Supreme Court in effect made Justice Holmes's dissent in the Toledo case the majority opinion. The Court specifically denounced the Toledo opinion as inaccurate: it ruled that the words of the 1831 act had only a geographic, not a causal, application. Reprehensible conduct that is exempted from punishment for contempt can nevertheless be penalized by other laws, the Court pointed out.

The Nye case settled the construction of the language in the contempt statute, but a series of cases was to follow on another issue, about the meaning and application to the press of the clear and present danger test in contempt cases. It was a doctrine that the Court—again through an opinion of Justice Holmes—had framed in 1918 in a different context, one relating to the free speech guarantee. That ruling, in *Schenck v. United States*, in effect protected freedom of speech against punishment unless the words uttered were "used in such circumstances and are of such a nature as to create a clear and present danger that they will bring about the substantive evils."

The issue arose in three cases: *Bridges v. California* and *Times-Mirror Company v. Supreme Court of California* (considered together by the Supreme Court in 1941), and in 1946 in *Pennekamp v. Florida*, and *Craig v. Harney*. The common denominator of all three was the question whether newspaper comment and criticism of courts and judges presented a punishable and "clear and present" threat to the administration of justice. The Supreme Court ruled that they did not. In all cases, the

Court weighed the desideratum of free discussion and free press against that of fair and public trial, and decided that unless the language constituted an imminent—not just a likely—threat with immediate peril, the balance must come down in favor of the First Amendment guarantees. The fortitude of judges, it was felt, should be great enough to withstand press comments about their cases, their courts, and the law itself.

In 1950, the issue arose again in even sharper form in *State v. Baltimore Radio Show*. Radio broadcasts following the arrest of a suspect of a particularly horrible murder were deemed contemptuous by a Baltimore trial court. The Maryland appellate court ruled otherwise. The defendant had waived a jury trial—his counsel had indicated that he believed it impossible to empanel an unbiased jury in the light of the preceding publicity—and the conviction had been made by a judge. The appellate decision held that the broadcasts had not made a fair trial impossible. There was no direct evidence of specific prejudice and therefore no clear or present danger to the administration of justice. The Supreme Court declined to grant certiorari (i.e., a review), but Justice Felix Frankfurter filed an angry opinion nonetheless, pointing out that the refusal to grant certiorari meant only that fewer than four members of the Court wanted to review the state court decision. Of his own view he left no doubt: he clearly felt that the broadcasts had denied the defendant a fair trial, and implied strongly that a rule more like the British, under which the broadcaster would have been punished for contempt, was very much in order.

Thus, by 1946, the Supreme Court's treatment of contempt by publication seemed to have settled into a position that gave the press something close to immunity from punishment so long as its misconduct did not take place in the courtroom itself, or at most in the corridor outside, the last places where it was likely to occur.

But beginning with a series of new cases six years later, the Court struck upon a different method of protecting defendants from damaging publicity without at the same time encroaching on the First Amendment guarantees to the press that it had so carefully conserved and given preference to in earlier decisions. The device was simply the reversal on due process grounds of convictions that were reached in prejudiced or inflammatory environments, where the jury may well have been influenced by prejudicial publication.

The doctrine was enunciated first by Justice Tom Clark in *Stroble v.*

California (he was later to develop it further), where, as it happened, the Supreme Court chose to uphold a state conviction for murder in a highly publicized case. Justice Clark said that "we are not faced with any question as to the permissible scope of newspaper comment regarding pending litigation . . . but with the question whether newspaper accounts aroused such prejudice in the community that petitioner's trial was fatally infected with an absence of that fundamental fairness essential to the very concept of justice."

Justice Robert Jackson found precisely such deprivation the same year, 1952, in *Shepherd v. Florida,* where Negro defendants had been tried and convicted for rape of a white girl in a Florida community seething with hostility and where the local press had published large amounts of inflammatory material. "The verdict was dictated by the press and the public opinion," Justice Jackson said, concurring in an opinion that reversed the conviction. Marking a new path for court consideration of the free press, fair trial problem, Justice Jackson declared that in the exercise of their First Amendment freedoms, newspapers will not be allowed to deprive defendants of a fair trial. If convictions do not meet civilized standards of fairness, they will be reversed, he said.

In several landmark cases that followed, *Irvin v. Dowd* (1961), *Rideau v. Louisiana* (1962), and *Estes v. Texas* (1965), convictions were reversed on grounds that the pretrial publication had been such that defendants could not possibly have enjoyed a fair trial by an unbiased jury in that environment. In each of the cases, the state courts had failed to use available procedural devices to filter out any effects of prejudicial publication (see Chapter 6 and Appendix B), so that the trials had been "fatally injected" by outside opinion or press excesses. Proof of the probability of unfairness is enough to warrant reversal, the Court held, and in cases of unduly dangerous publicity it is not necessary for the defendant to prove specific prejudice.

To the end of his term on the Court, Justice Frankfurter expressed his dissatisfaction with a policy which merely reversed a conviction obtained under the influence of hostile and prejudicial publicity and did not proceed from there to prevent such publication or punish the publishers. He insisted, in a concurring opinion in *Irvin v. Dowd,* that the Court's failure so far to do more than reverse what it felt was a miscarriage of justice caused by the press's having "poisoned" the minds of jurors or potential jurors in no way implied that the Court thereby ruled that "the poisoner is constitutionally protected in plying his trade."

The Supreme Court's opinion in the Sheppard case (1966) made it clear that the primary responsibility for assuring the proper judicial requisites of a fair trial lies with the sources of prejudicial publication. Recognizing that the press is the "handmaiden of effective judicial administration," the Court declared that the way to avoid excesses that cause a prejudiced trial is for public officials—prosecutors, judges, police, lawyers, and their associates—to conduct themselves according to their professional pledges and responsibilities; in particular to withhold comment on pending cases. The Court pointed to available procedures for securing impartial jurors—procedures neglected in this case—and to existing professional controls, equally neglected, over police, prosecutors, and lawyers. Before moving to punish the press, the Court admonished, the trial courts should bring the sources of prejudicial information under control. It was clear that the Court felt that the key to fair trial was to cut off unbridled comment by officials—a habitual misconduct that the Court called "highly censurable and worthy of disciplinary measures."

Today's position, accordingly, is that for the defendant's protection, the Supreme Court stands ready to review criminal trials to assure that publicity has not created an unfair trial atmosphere. Where it has, a resulting conviction will be reversed as a denial of due process of law.

But with respect to punishment of the press, Justice Frankfurter's bitter comment remains accurate. Since the Nye decision, the Court has not sanctioned the punishment of a news medium for contempt of court through prejudicial publication. But it has not had before it a contempt citation in a situation where the press was alleged to have prejudiced a jury, and, in principle, no prior decision stands in the Court's way if it chooses at some future date to confirm a contempt judgment against a medium that had "poisoned" the minds of jurors.

But it seems to us that the solution to the free press, fair trial problem is not likely to be found through the return to the pre-1831 or English contempt doctrine. In the first place, the Court has shown itself remarkably loath to sanction its use; for two decades, in which Justice Frankfurter remained always in the minority, the Court majority showed a clear preference in all constructive contempt cases for free discussion and unencumbered publication—the essential promise of the First Amendment.

Second, except for the special case where a news medium may have set about deliberately to stack the deck and create a biased environment,[2] prevention of prejudicial publication by fear of punishment for contempt seems an awkward and uncertain device and one not likely to work or to win the kind of acceptance necessary for effectiveness. Unless there were a reversion to the British doctrine, something hard to conceive of as long as the First Amendment stands, application of the contempt power would tend to remain so imprecise and so dependent on individual and varying circumstances of each case, and on the mood and interpretation of each judge, as to provide no clear guide for press action and no assurance for a defendant. In the past, it has been used by judges piqued by criticism—and not to punish the press for prejudging juries.

Indeed, here as in almost all other situations where one Constitutional provision appears to stand in conflict with another, a solution is unlikely through a ruling that one always takes precedence over the other. The argument that one Constitutional amendment should prevail over another is useless, being entirely too simplistic, especially when both concern vital institutional, libertarian values.

The Supreme Court has refused to say that one part of the Bill of Rights may overpower another. The First Amendment continues to stand, therefore, as protection for the press against punishment for prejudicial publication, while the due process clause will be used to redeem defendants who have been prejudiced. The implication in the Supreme Court's opinion in the Sheppard case is that punishment of the press, if applied at all, will come only as a last resort, when all other possibilities have been tried and have failed. Only then, it can be assumed, will consideration be given to revitalizing the contempt power.

But to conclude that the solution to the free press, fair trial dilemma will not come via the contempt power is not to proclaim defeatism or to be resigned to having unbridled publication forever to inflict injury on criminal defendants. There are a multitude of other approaches, varying in promise and problems. They will be considered in the chapters to follow.

[2] The idea is discussed more fully in Chapter 13.

CHAPTER 8

NEW PRESCRIPTIONS

FOR OLD AILMENTS

Legal attempts to curb the press, whether by prior restraint or by punishment for contempt, have largely been rejected by the courts, as we have seen. And when procedural techniques to blockade potential prejudice have been unavailing (see Chapter 6), the remaining remedy that courts have so far granted, retrial, has left a large segment of the bar and the public unsatisfied.

Accordingly, in the period following President John F. Kennedy's murder and the Warren Report, many other proposals have been offered and new life has been infused into some that were dormant.

The measures fall into three categories: (1) a return to the use of some version of the contempt power; (2) the voluntary adoption by the press of codes of conduct that would curb publication of potential injury to fair trial; and (3) the devising of methods to limit the dissemination of injurious information by law enforcement officers and others involved in the administration of justice.

The "British Approach"

Despite the consistent Supreme Court position in the last few decades denying the use of the contempt power to curb press publication, there has been a great deal of wistful argument for the need to return to the British contempt rule, which strictly punishes publication deemed a threat to fair trial.[1] Some law review writers and critics of press extrava-

[1] The "British system" and its theoretical applicability to problems of criminal news coverage in the United States are more fully discussed in the following chapter.

gances feel that the courts should take control of the problem; they have proposed new contempt statutes that would, they predict, pass Supreme Court and Constitutional muster.

Of these, the most all-embracing is that embodied in the 1965 American Bar Association Ross Prize essay.[2] If it reflects the most extreme bar view, it clearly does not reflect modern Constitutional doctrine. It would prohibit publication of: the fact of existence or the contents of confessions at any time before their admission at trial; prior records of bad conduct or any other evidence that could later influence a juror; tangible evidence that might not later be admitted in court and that connects the accused with the crime; facts bearing on the merits of a pending case; matters at trial not brought to the jury's attention; out-of-court statements by witnesses tending to incriminate the accused or discredit his defense; opinions of the accused's guilt; comments about evidence or witnesses, and any other inflammatory or prejudicial feelings about the case. All these constitute such "prejudicial publicity" that, the author believes, they would fall within the clear and present danger test of the Bridges case (see Appendix B, pp. 282–287). The proposal appears to be almost equivalent to saying that on the asserted commission of a crime, the press could print little more than the name of the person accused, and thereafter nothing other than what emerged at the trial in the presence of the jury, with a rule of silence on all else until the last appeal is made and the ultimate legal proceedings have come to an end.

A few other suggestions, less sweepingly inclusive, have been made to prohibit publications during a certain prescribed time (usually from arrest to verdict), or of certain categories of news (prior criminal record, alleged existence of a confession, etc.). Some others have proposed making a distinction between evidentiary facts, which would be prohibited, and editorial opinions, which would not.[3]

A restrictive statutory solution has been suggested in some states. For example, in Massachusetts a bill[4] was proposed making it a crime

[2] Jerome Martin LeWine, "What Constitutes Prejudicial Publicity in Pending Cases?"

[3] For example: Richard Donnelly and Ronald L. Goldfarb, "Contempt by Publication in the U.S.," 24 *Modern Law Review* 239 (1961); Louis Jaffe, "Trial by Newspaper," Speech to American Political Science Association, 1965.

[4] House, No. 2504 (1965).

for a reporter or editor from any press medium or for a police or court official to publish confessions, prior records, incriminating evidence or opinions, or information given the court out of the jury's presence before it is admitted at trial. Truth or absence of intent to prejudice would be no defense. Prearrest or postjudgment comments would be exempted from the ban.

Voluntary Restraint by the Press

The report of the Warren Commission revived consideration of an older but semidormant idea: codes of press ethics and behavior, to be embraced voluntarily by individual publications or by regional or national groups of news media, unilaterally or with corresponding groups of lawyers and law enforcement organizations. The Commission noted that while press coverage of the aftermath of the assassination performed an obvious and necessary public service, it also "endangered Oswald's Constitutional rights to a trial by an impartial jury." The Commission called on the press for "promulgation of a code of professional conduct governing representatives of all news media" and for some action on the part of "state and local governments, the bar, and ultimately the public" to ensure "that appropriate action is taken to establish ethical standards of conduct for the news media."

Voluntarism is fundamental to press codes. While press codes avoid the First Amendment problem of legal enforcement from outside the craft, they raise tough practical problems of realistic enforcement from within. Moreover, as members of the press who have tried to devise and work with them can testify, they incline to be so restrictive that their frequent breaching is seen by editors as imperative or else so general as to amount to little more than a pious statement in favor of virtue. One of the best-known examples of a voluntary code is the Massachusetts *Guide for the Bar and News Media*. It is difficult to know into which category it should be placed, inasmuch as the prescription itself is considerably less than forceful. It was approved by the Massachusetts and Boston bar associations, and was adopted in 1963 by the Massachusetts Broadcasters' Association and by twenty-six daily newspapers and thirty-six weeklies in the state (the major big-city dailies, with one exception, refused to join).

The preamble restates the basic principles: the presumption of innocence, the fundamental imperatives for a free press and for fair trials, the important need to inform the public as well as the need to be responsible in doing it. The *Guide* then lists the following categories of information about crimes, defendants, and criminal procedure, the publication and broadcasting of which "should be avoided": postindictment interviews with witnesses, criminal records, confessions, stricken testimony, leaks or conclusions of participants, names of juveniles, and editorial comment before or during trial "tending to influence judge or jury."[5] To preserve the control of criminal trials by courts, "news stories of crime should contain only a factual statement of the arrest and attending circumstances."

On its side, the bar is advised that a factual statement of the arrest and its circumstances and incidents is permissible, but that statements or conclusions about the guilt or innocence, the nature of the evidence, the expectations of what will be proved, what witnesses will be called, remarks about admissions or confessions, and statements whose source is undisclosed also "should be avoided."

A reading of the *Guide* leads to the assumption that its drafters wrestled with the problem but could not pin its shoulders to the mat. The categories of tabooed publication and utterances are so loosely worded as to serve only as broad indicators rather than as operable definitions of what may be inimical to fair trial. But the instruction that these categories should be "avoided" rather than prohibited evidences a conclusion that a tight and enforceable rule is impossible.

Somewhat similar is a "code of guide lines" adopted on their own initiative by the Toledo *Blade* and Toledo *Times,* in August, 1966. "Unless very special circumstances dictate otherwise," the papers will not publish prior criminal records, "confessions" (although they may note the fact that the accused has made a "statement"), any statements by officials, attorneys, or anyone else "construed as detrimental or beneficial to the accused," names of jurors, and court arguments not heard by the jury.

But after marching to the top of the hill, the papers' announcement of the guide lines goes on to say that in pursuance of their responsibility

[5] If this phrase means what it says, it constitutes an extraordinarily far-reaching and restrictive concession by the press. For very little of what is reported about a trial would be *without* a potential that "tended" to influence a judge or a juror.

to monitor public affairs they may be required to report beyond the limitations of the new rules. They would have to be modified or suspended temporarily, the announcement declared, if a wave of violent crimes had stirred community apprehension and reassurance was thus made necessary, or if there were a breakdown of law enforcement, or a lapse of conduct by a public official, or a failure of a proper investigation of alleged official misconduct, or finally "if other sources of information so aroused the public through sensational reports—particularly from out of town—[that] newspapers could not maintain credibility without taking account of information or misinformation spread by others."[6]

The conclusion is hard to resist that what the Toledo papers are saying is that in routine cases where prejudicial publicity is a rare or minor factor they will avoid publication of categories of crime and trial news generally believed to produce the most prejudicial results, but that they reserve the right to print all the news in sensational cases, in which, almost exclusively, the real free press, fair trial problem is found.

In a somewhat similar way, a study of the 1965 *Kentucky Press Statement of Principles for Pre-Trial Reporting* suggests that high hopes for universal principles had to be tempered by difficulties of practical day-to-day news operations.

Restraint is suggested in the publication of confessions: "It is recommended that all law enforcement officers and all journalists refrain from using the term 'confession' to describe a statement attributed to a person under arrest"; corroboration from the accused should be sought and the reporting should in any event "be couched in such dispassionate terms as to not impair the accused person's right to a trial free from prejudice." Restraint is also proposed in the publishing of prior records ("unless there be clear and overpowering reasons dictated by the public interest"). The *Statement* urges that general pretrial reporting be "fair, factual, and impartial," and that reports about the trial itself avoid publication of proceedings out of the jury's presence. Equal time is urged for the reporting of acquittals, clearances, and corrections. At the same time, the press is encouraged to continue investigations and exposure of wrongdoing and corruption.

The difficulties as we see them in codes, guide lines, or statements of

---

[6] As reported by *Editor & Publisher*, August 27, 1966.

the Massachusetts, Toledo, and Kentucky types is that they raise false expectations of press forbearance and by implication condemn as sinful certain acts that all participants know they cannot avoid committing.

More general in its terms, and accordingly less awkward in trying to accommodate the ideal with the possible, is the joint statement of principles adopted in 1962 in Oregon by the State Bar Association, the Newspaper Publishers Association, and the Association of Broadcasters. Its call for decency and restraint is commendable, but it is no more enforceable than the other codes.

The statement acknowledges the values of free press and fair trial as means to the ends of individual freedom and public information and expresses a joint desire to accommodate any conflicts that would jeopardize either of these "fundamental precepts." It therefore avows that:

1. The news media have the right and the responsibility to print and to broadcast the truth.
2. However, the demands of accuracy and objectivity in news reporting should be balanced with the demands of fair play. The public has a right to be informed. The accused has the right to be judged in an atmosphere free from undue prejudice.
3. Good taste should prevail in the selection, printing and broadcasting of the news. Morbid or sensational details of criminal behavior should not be exploited.
4. The right of decision about the news rests with the editor or news director. In the exercise of judgment he should consider that:
    (a) an accused person is presumed innocent until proved guilty;
    (b) readers and listeners are potential jurors;
    (c) no person's reputation should be injured needlessly.

Restraint by Attorneys and Law Enforcement Officers

The category of proposals that would appear to have the best current chance of adoption contains strictures that are directed not to the actions of the press but at its sources of crime news: lawyers, prosecutors, police and other government employees. A significant number of measures of this sort have been suggested, and some adopted, since the Kennedy assassination and the Warren Report.

They appear to reflect a conviction that voluntary restraint by the press is chimerical and regulation of it by law is barred by present interpretations of the First Amendment. Accordingly, the solution is sought by a policy of silence, or at least restraint of utterance, by those who are the initial source of most of the material that could undermine the objectivity of a future jury.

The concept of professional self-control by the bar is, of course, not new. The American Bar Association has long had Canon 20 in its rules of ethics. It reads:

> Newspaper publications by a lawyer as to pending or anticipated litigation may interfere with a fair trial in the Courts and otherwise prejudice the due administration of justice. Generally they are to be condemned. If the extreme circumstances of a particular case justify a statement to the public, it is unprofessional to make it anonymously. An *ex parte* reference to the actual facts should not go beyond quotation from the records and papers on file in the court; but even in extreme cases it is better to avoid any *ex parte* statement.

The language is less than muscular and its enforcement through the years has been nil. Although it is conceivable that Canon 20 could be invigorated so as to result in a kind of adherence to its spirit if not its words, in fact it has remained a dead letter since its birth.[7]

Invigoration and rigid enforcement of Canon 20 has been urged. Erwin N. Griswold, dean of the Harvard Law School and long a critic of press crime reporting, has admitted that "lawyers cannot criticize the news media very seriously if they publish the information that lawyers give them or if they present radio or television programs in which lawyers participate." A way to cleanse the house of the law of this fault would be to amend the Canon "to include an absolute prohibition against the release by any lawyer, either for the prosecution or for the defense, of any material relating to a trial, either before the trial or while the trial is going on." Then, in Dean Griswold's words, "the American Bar Association, the state bar associations and their grievance committees, and the courts should enforce this requirement." And law enforcement officials who are not subject to the built-in pro-

---

[7] Inasmuch as there is no known case where an attorney, a member of a licensed profession, has been punished under this Canon, reactions of members of the press tend to range from skepticism to scorn when judges and lawyers propose, as they often have done, that the press adopt codes of ethics "with real teeth in them" and expel violators.

fessional controls which may bind lawyers should be prevented from
making any statements or releases about cases "through the rule-making
and contempt powers of the courts."[8]

Another of the American Bar Association's Canons of Professional
Ethics, Number 5, has been raised as a possible answer to control of the
bar in the free press, fair trial dispute. This Canon affirms the high purpose of defense lawyers to defend criminal cases "by all fair and honorable means," and of prosecutors to see that justice is done and not
merely to convict. In 1964, it was proposed to amend Canon 5 to make
it much more specific. The amendment under consideration would
place upon attorneys, prosecutors, and defense lawyers alike a duty to
refrain from remarks that would interfere with the right of a defendant
(or the government) to a fair trial. Opinions about cases, predictions
about projected outcomes, discussion about guilt, the evidence, or the
likelihood of conviction are all discouraged. Dean Griswold praised this
amendment but indicated that it does not go far enough. Reflecting the
traditional strict bar view, he called for the prohibition of "any sort of
statement whatever about any pending criminal case . . . from the
moment of the arrest until the ultimate completion of the trial." In his
view, upon arrest an iron curtain should quickly fall between the legal
process and the public and not be lifted until a criminal case is complete.[9]

In the period between the first proposals of the American Bar Association, following the assassination of President Kennedy, and the issuance of the report of the Reardon Committee (discussed below), the
concept of curbing the flow of information from counsel, police, and
prosecutors was widely debated, and varying proposals were considered
by several state and city bar associations. One that provoked much comment was the Philadelphia Bar Association's proposed code. Critical of
pretrial publicity engendered by prosecutors and police, the Philadelphia Bar Association called for regulations to control public statements
by prosecutors, police, and judges.

Its specific proposals: Releases should be limited to the facts of the
case. Details about victims or suspects should be avoided. Prearrest

---

[8] *Saturday Review,* October 24, 1964.

[9] Speech to American Bar Association Section on Judicial Administration, August
11, 1964.

publicity is to be discouraged unless necessary to the investigation of the case. Information that would be inadmissible at trial should not be released or remarked upon. After arrest, the warrant, nature of the charges, and possible penalties may be publicized. Judges and prosecutors and defense lawyers should refrain from public remarks about the evidence or the case. Public records and information, of course, may be disclosed as at present. Once the trial begins, only evidence presented to the jury in open court should be publicized.

An earlier, more restrictive version of this proposed code came under heavy fire from the organized press and even from some members of the bar as an unwarranted choking-off of legitimate sources of legitimate news. The revised version was approved by the Philadelphia Bar Association on December 29, 1964.

There has been one attempt to put a statewide curb on the flow of pretrial and pending-trial information from counsel and law enforcement personnel. Its objective is similar but it would carry far greater authority than the Philadelphia Bar Association proposal. Because it would be backed by the power of the state through its court system, its application both to members of the bar and to police officials would be more realistic and effective. The ruling, standing as a prospect for the future, came on November 16, 1964, as dictum in the opinion of Judge John J. Francis of the New Jersey Supreme Court. In *State v. Van Duyne*,[10] Judge Francis affirmed a murder conviction and life sentence. Refusing to overrule the conviction on the ground of prejudicial publicity, he nevertheless seized the opportunity to set out a prospective publication rule for New Jersey lawyers and police which has drawn extensive national comment and raised much concern among the press and public officials, as well.

He wrote:

> In our view Canons 5 and 20 of the Canons of Professional Ethics require a broader and more stringent rule. We interpret these canons, particularly Canon 20, to ban statements to news media by prosecutors, assistant prosecutors and their lawyer staff members, as to alleged confessions or inculpatory admissions by the accused, or to the effect that the case is "open and shut" against the defendant, and the like, or with reference to the defendant's prior criminal record,

[10] 43 N.J. 369, 204 A.2d 841 (1964).

either of convictions or arrests. Such statements have the capacity to interfere with a fair trial and cannot be countenanced. With respect to prosecutors, detectives and members of local police departments who are not members of the bar, statements of the type described are an improper interference with the due administration of criminal justice and constitute conduct unbecoming a police officer. As such they warrant discipline at the hands of the proper authorities.

The ban on statements by the prosecutor and his aides applies as well to defense counsel. The right of the State to a fair trial cannot be impeded or diluted by out-of-court assertions by him to news media on the subject of his client's innocence. The court room is the place to settle the issue and comments before or during the trial which have the capacity to influence potential or actual jurors to the possible prejudice of the State are impermissible.

The opinion concluded that these inhibiting rules would not impinge upon freedom of the press. The implication of the opinion was clear: the bar and the police had better clean their own houses through intramural controls or the courts will do it for them, through their judicial powers of contempt, and of control over the bar through the power to censure and conceivably to disbar attorneys.

The United States Supreme Court referred to the Van Duyne case in its opinion reversing Dr. Samuel Sheppard's conviction, and indicated its agreement with the proposition that *all* trial courts must use all available means to avoid the adverse effects of trial publicity. The power to apply rules and regulations to this problem area exists and ought to be implemented, Justice Tom Clark admonished.

One step in the direction of self-control was taken by the Federal prosecutive fraternity. In an address to the American Society of Newspaper Editors in April, 1965, Attorney General Nicholas deB. Katzenbach outlined the practices relating to public pronouncements about criminal cases, which he said were long standard but which he was newly ordering all Federal prosecutors to follow. Candidly admitting that lawyers "are hardly the exclusive keepers of the keys to the kingdom of justice" and pointing out that "many of our differences of opinion exist not because of principle but because of timing," he then divided pretrial information into two categories, one of which would be made available to the press, and the other, which was prejudicial, would not.

Pursuant to this directive, the following information will be made available by Federal prosecutors and investigators: identification of a defendant (name, address, marital status, and similar statistical information), the substance or text of the charge (a public record), the identity of the arresting agency and the length of the investigation, information needed to enlist public assistance in apprehending fugitives, and prior Federal convictions and descriptions of arrest (these latter two the Attorney General acknowledged could be prejudicial, but in his opinion they were official records which could not be kept secret and he was therefore obliged, as their official keeper, to make them public on demand).

The following will not be provided: information about confessions or admissions, editorial comments by prosecutors, and references to evidentially investigative procedures (fingerprints, polygraphs, ballistics, etc.).

Thus, with one administrative directive, the practices of all Federal prosecutors and investigators throughout the country were brought under uniform control.

By every standard, the most important and potentially consequential set of recommendations in this area to have emerged from the legal profession in recent years is that of the Reardon Committee. One of the American Bar Association's several advisory groups on minimum standards of criminal justice, the group on Fair Trial and Free Press was created in 1964 as an aftermath of the Warren Report's discussion of press treatment at Dallas. Composed of prominent attorneys and jurists, and chaired by Justice Paul C. Reardon of the Supreme Judicial Court of Massachusetts, the Committee and its staff conducted a twenty-month study of the problem. They met with representatives of the media, law enforcement agencies, and the bar; they reviewed the relevant literature here and abroad, conducted surveys of press practices in a number of cities, made deeper content analyses of some others, and gathered facts through questionnaires to police, prosecuting and defense attorneys, judges, and educators. In the fall of 1966 the Committee issued a tentative draft of proposals, to be placed before the American Bar Association Convention in August, 1967, for adoption and for ultimate recommendation to the states.

The Reardon Report is one of the more responsible and prestigious scholarly efforts in this area and of all such bar committee efforts it is surely the best balanced. We agree with its general thrust, although we have serious reservations about certain major specifics.

The Report began by calling for accommodations "principally in the adoption of limitations—carefully defined as to content and timing—on the release of information bearing on the apprehension and trial of criminal defendants by members of the bar and by law enforcement agencies, with appropriate remedies available when there is a showing that a fair trial has been jeopardized." More specifically, it placed "the primary burden for ensuring fair trial on the legal branch and the agencies which serve and minister to it." In doing so, the Report moved in the opposite direction from past bar-press committees: It did not place the blame for unfair trials on the press, but, consistent with recent court rulings, upon the bar and law enforcement agencies themselves—the source of most crime news—as the Committee repeatedly emphasized.

The Committee's recommendations fall into three categories: (1) proposed rules for attorneys and public officials enforced through bar and court disciplining proceedings; (2) improvement of existing court filtering procedures; and (3) a "limited" contempt rule against deliberate press interferences with jury trial.

The general approach of the Reardon Report, at least in the first two main categories, follows closely the direction marked by the Supreme Court in the Sheppard decision. The Committee's bill of particulars on the sins of the press is severe, even as the Court's was with respect to the Cleveland newspapers; but, like the Court, the Committee turned to find a remedy, not by restricting press freedom (except for one narrow measure), but in cutting down the flow of potentially prejudicial news at its source, before it reaches the press.

The first category of proposals, and the most far-reaching, concerns comments by all attorneys and members of the law enforcement establishment—judges, prosecutors, defense attorneys, court officials, and police—while criminal procedures are pending. From the time of arrest until the completion of trial, the Report proposes, no mention should be made of prior records, confessions, tests, interviews, the defendant's guilt, or about the case generally where such a publication would be likely to prejudice a jury.

The Report proposes that lawyers and law enforcement personnel confine their disclosures to a brief description of the offense charged, the circumstances of arrest, the identity of the defendant, and, at the time of seizure, the evidence seized. When the defendant or suspect is a fugitive, additional information could be made public to the extent necessary to aid in his apprehension or to warn the public of any danger he may present.

The guide lines follow the 1965 Justice Department strictures except that disclosures of prior records, though they are public records, are forbidden by the Reardon Committee but not by the Justice Department rules.

The proposal calls for enforcement against lawyers through the canons of ethics and against police through departmental regulations; and against both by court rules backed up by the contempt power.

We have two major objections to the Reardon Committee's first category of proposals, one general, one specific.

The first relates to what seems to be a pervasive, underlying notion that the less said about crime news, the better will justice be served. To be sure, the Report firmly supports the need for the watchdog role of the press, but its discussion of that thesis is close to cursory; the overwhelming burden of the argument was premised on the view that concern with the administration of criminal justice is a monopoly of the legal profession, that no loss to society will ensue from suppressing or postponing publication of crime news, and that if left alone, the bar and bench will move effectively and irresistibly toward providing justic and completely meeting the objectives of the community. It was this tone, more than any precise single provision, we believe, that produced a furious reaction, almost without exception, from prominent figures in the press and from the nation's several press organizations when the Report was made public in October, 1966. The common denominator of the complaints was that the Report was an invitation to the secret administration of justice.

While proposing that certain categories of information be withheld by law enforcement agencies, the Reardon Report failed to contain a positive command for the release of permissible news, particularly the details of criminal events. Consequently, the press saw the Report as tending to encourage secrecy, to sanction the maintenance of silence even about the basic facts of the offense, the arrest, and the person accused. Its wording is unclear about just how much information describing the crime itself may properly be made public. Our own view is that in all cases there must be complete and immediate revelation of details about the crime itself.

Almost unanimously, press critics of the Reardon Report hit at its implicit—perhaps subconscious—praise of silence, and saw the Report as providing an excuse to law enforcement bodies to withhold all information. It may be unfair to accuse a proposal for sins it does not propose. But there is no little justice to the charge that the Report's failure to call for full disclosure of certain facts of a crime in effect sanctions and even invites intolerable secrecy, highly dangerous to the society.

That the Report had precisely that effect was evidenced by a rash of complaints within the first few weeks of its issuance about official news blackouts in criminal cases in many different localities. A dramatic example came in mid-October, 1966, in the small town of Luray, Virginia, where a young man, deranged and attempting suicide, was slain by police bullets. A local policeman was later arrested on charges of manslaughter. Within twenty-four hours of the slaying, news of the episode, in its broad outlines, was universal in Luray and, according to later investigation by newspaper reporters, gossip and speculation were rife. But the police officers involved, the mayor and other town officials, and, in particular, the Commonwealth Attorney, refused all comment. To reporters who called him, the Commonwealth Attorney cited the Reardon Report as the prime reason for his silence, according to the *Washington Star,* which investigated the situation and published its findings on October 23. The newspaper reported that two days after the shooting, "there was no one to confirm there had been a shooting, let alone who had done it or why it had happened. . . ."

The newspaper account continued:

> And so the whispers built up. With no official source available, the questioning of the press became more persistent, and news stories said plainly that the shooting was wrapped in mystery. What might have passed as a minor item mushroomed into a major story.
>
> A big question remains: Was the shooting necessary? Was [the victim] on a rampage and the shooting a matter of self-defense or was this a case of a country cop who panicked with little or no excuse to do so?

On this point the people of Luray are up in the air. The shooting is still the No. 1 topic of conversation and a visitor hears widely differing versions of what actually happened.

But an even more important question is: Why the cover-up of a case that involved a police shooting? . . .

On Thursday, a reporter asked [the local policeman] if he would tell what happened Sunday night. . . . [He] answered in a troubled voice:

"I can't talk. I wish I could. People are saying all sorts of things, and it's worrying my wife and daughter to death. . . .

"I'd like to get this out in the open but the Supreme Court and those new bar regulations won't let us do it."

The grotesque situation was, of course, the result of a misreading of the Sheppard decision and of a misunderstanding of the Reardon Committee proposals. But it demonstrates that the news media fears were in no way fictitious.

Our second and more specific disagreement with this first category of the Reardon Report's recommendations has to do with its strictures on disclosure by defense counsel. They are in all but one respect equal to those on prosecutors and police. Defense may "announce without further comment that the client denies the charges made against him." The prohibitions, lying equally on both sides, may seem at first even-handed, and the argument may sound plausible that if certain restrictions against prosecutors are necessary to prevent "trial by newspaper" they must logically be applied to the defense as well. But the mere facts of arrest and publication of an indictment, accompanied by the accusatory comments allowed even under the Reardon proposals—the whole disproportionate weight of the state arrayed against an accused criminal—require in the interest of fairness and balance something more than a spare exculpatory denial.

The objection may be seen at its clearest in today's civil rights situations. Community prejudice, police anger, fervor for heavy punishments, frustration at the intractability of America's most anguished single problem can all combine to invite denial of due process—in a word, a frame-up—to an integration activist. We have alluded to the problem in Chapter 2. We are convinced that the Reardon Committee dismisses the danger much too cavalierly, and we hope that there will be a reconsideration of the tentative Report before its final submission to the American Bar Association. The proposals could be subverted to a weapon of suppression and a shield for injustice in civil rights cases and others where corruption or hostile community pressure is present; they could dangerously limit the press in performing its most useful and admirable service in aiding the cause of justice.

In any event, the prohibition against defense counsel offering argument and opinion outside of court is subject to frustration because the Report lays no restraints (nor should it) on the defendant himself. If he is literate and articulate he can fight for himself when he needs to. The difficulty is that someone not able to tell about his plight would be at a disadvantage.

In general, there is cause for worry about the Report's proposals for punishing offenders of the nondisclosure provisions. Not only in civil rights situations but elsewhere the temptation runs high to harass, silence, and even take revenge against the man who offends the Establishment. The court-police complex in most jurisdictions is more often than not, and understandably, self-protective. It is usually highly political and its disinterest in fact falls far short of its theoretical ideal. It is hard to picture such a local court cracking down on a prosecutor or police chief for talking out of school; it is easy to picture the vengeful prosecution of an unpopular counsel defending an unpopular client in an unpopular cause.

The second category of the Reardon proposals is the soundest. The Committee is most persuasive in its own arena—the reform and refinement of courtroom procedures. Its proposals would encourage, liberalize, and intensify the cure of present procedural techniques for ameliorating or dissipating the impact of potentially prejudicial publicity on juries. The Committee dealt with voir dire (proposing broader, more general grounds for challenging jurors exposed to publicity), venue change and continuances (to be more liberally granted), instructions to be given more attention by courts (the Committtee even recommended a standard charge on this point), sequestration, limited *in camera* hearings and waiver of jury trial (at defendants' request or consent), and stricter control in courtrooms by judges. Here the Committee is on solid ground, ground already plotted by the Supreme Court in its Sheppard decision, and all its suggestions ought to be carefully considered.

In its final area, the Committee recommended a limited contempt power to cover cases of deliberate and serious interferences with fair trial by the press. It would confine contempt action to cases when the offense is committed while a jury is in the process of being selected or a trial is actually in progress, to situations where the publication goes to matters beyond the court record and where it is both calculated and reasonably likely to affect the outcome of the trial, and where the statement is made "with the expectation that it will be so disseminated." Contempt is also provided for violations of court orders not to disseminate specific items of information. The Committee also suggested that any fines be used to reimburse the defendant for additional costs arising out of mistrials, or changes of venue attributable to these contempts, and that all criminal procedural guarantees apply to these contempt proceedings.

Contempt action against the press for its own deliberate attempts to influence a jury will be extremely rare under any such provision, we believe. Whatever stage-setting or climate-creating a publication might attempt for or against a defendant—and there have been only two or three such to our knowledge in the last several years—will almost certainly be done in advance of a trial; once the process of selecting a jury begins, it is hard to think that any journalist would be so stupid or audacious as to try it.

Nevertheless, there is a real danger that news media might find themselves the target of contempt proceedings as an indirect result of a court process to punish someone else for disclosure of information forbidden by the Report. In effect, the press might well be the victim of an end-run.

If the Report's proposals were put into effect, it is easy to visualize a situation where a news medium published a piece of information that should not have been released and where the indications were that it was leaked by someone connected with the case. In a contempt action against the persons suspected of leaking, an editor or a reporter from the publication might be subpoenaed and called on to disclose from whom the leak came. The newsman has no recognized privilege in most jurisdictions to maintain silence and could be charged with contempt for refusing to speak. Yet his standing and his very livelihood are threatened if he breaches that sort of confidence. In attempting to force him, the court might be acting in all good faith to uphold the Reardon regulations. Or it could be using a subtle means offered by the proposed regulations to punish a publication against which the local Law Establishment is hostile.

It is worth noting that in an interview[11] anticipating some of the conclusions of a forthcoming report of the New York City Bar Association prepared under his chairmanship, Judge Harold R. Medina of the U.S. Court of Appeals attacked the Reardon Committee proposals for pretrial restraint on the press and police officers. He stated his belief that any such restraint would be unconstitutional.

Describing the theme of his own future report, Judge Medina said:

> . . . We are now of the opinion that the First Amendment guarantee of free speech and free press, and the critical importance of the concept of freedom of communication that underlies this guarantee, preclude, on both constitutional and policy grounds, direct controls of the news media by a governmental scheme of legislative or judicial regulation.

By implication, he cast doubt on the court's power to control police utterances, indicating that his report would recommend a code of regulations for law enforcement agencies to be adopted voluntarily, not imposed by the courts.

An extensive survey of chiefs of police and law enforcement administrators in thirty-eight major cities to determine police practices and regulations of the release of crime news to radio and television was conducted by a special committee of the New York City Bar Association under the chairmanship of Judge Medina.[12] Generally, the results show that there are few places where set rules govern the police; usually, custom and practice substitute for rules and regulations. Historically, the survey reported, most police stations were open to the media, which could photograph and broadcast from the jail; in some places a distinction was drawn between public premises such as outside rooms, which could be covered, and inside offices and cells, which could not; in some places the media were completely barred from police premises; in some all coverage was at the control of the chief, who decided in an ad hoc fashion when and where to allow reporting, interviews, and the disclosure of nonpublic records.

Since the Kennedy assassination, however, we have observed a noticeable tightening of regulations governing the access and actions of

[11] *New York Times,* October 7, 1966.

[12] *Radio, Television, and the Administration of Justice: A Documented Survey of Materials* (New York: Columbia University Press, 1966).

reporters and photographers generally. Heightened concern by the courts themselves has stimulated this process. A number of recent decisions reversing criminal convictions and necessitating retrials were occasioned by press interviews of suspects as they were arrested and booked, out of which incriminating information emerged. Police have responded by adopting more stringent regulations on press access.

A number of state and local prosecutors have instituted rules similar to those of the Federal system, some even considerably more restrictive. There have also been several instances of judges, police, and prosecutors enforcing silence upon law officers in some notorious or potentially notorious criminal cases. Typical was the order by a Maryland State's Attorney in late 1965 that police not disclose to the press information about confessions or incriminating statements, prior records or speculation based on evidence—under threat of contempt for disobedience. At about the same time, an Arizona judge issued an injunction prohibiting local police and prosecutors from discussing details of one notorious criminal case being investigated. In 1964, the California Attorney General asked local law enforcement agencies to control the interviewing and photographing of prisoners. The National Conference of State Trial Judges has drafted a set of guide lines that would prohibit comments about pending criminal cases. The Wisconsin Attorney General advised state district attorneys in 1965 to evaluate critically any information released to news media concerning pending criminal cases; and the Wisconsin House of Representatives sent the state Senate a bill forbidding police or attorneys to make public statements about evidence or opinions of guilt under penalty of criminal contempt.[13]

There has been only one recent attempt to obtain by law the goal of stopping the flow of potentially prejudicial comment from counsel and officials. In January, 1965, Senator Wayne Morse, of Oregon, introduced S.290, a bill that reads:

> It shall constitute a contempt of court for any employee of the United States, or for any defendant or his attorney or the agent of either, to furnish or make available for publication *information* not already properly filed with the court which *might affect the outcome of*

---

[13] In listing these and other current restrictive developments, the Freedom of Information Center of the University of Missouri also noted a general trend throughout the nation by prosecutors and police toward a policy of curbing official disclosures to the press.

any pending criminal litigation, except evidence that has already been
admitted at the trial. Such contempt shall be punished by a fine of not
more than $1,000. [Emphasis added.]

Although the bill enjoyed the support of the Judicial Conference of
the United States (composed of the chief judges of all the Federal
courts), it was pummeled heavily in hearings before a subcommittee of
the Senate Judiciary Committee, and has been shelved with little apparent chance of revival.

Adverse testimony on the Morse bill at the legislative hearings
stressed these points of law and policy: The statute's absolutism invites
the cliché that enjoins throwing away the baby with the bath water;
prohibited by its broad mandate would be such unexceptionable publications as explanatory or exculpatory remarks of a defendant or his
counsel (the public denial of charges) as well as the most innocent and
necessary comments of government officials. The statute could well be
considered violative of the Constitutional guarantee of the right to
counsel because it prohibits any statements about a case by defense attorneys; to be so vague and uncertain as to deny due process of law in its
prohibition of publications "which might affect the outcome of any pending criminal litigation"; and even to cross into areas of free expression
protected from incursion by the First Amendment. The uncertain criminal procedures of such an inclusive contempt statute as this compound
the legal questions that could be raised about such a law. Moreover, as
a matter of policy or even good judgment, the bill aborts. Government
investigating officials would not be able publicly to call for assistance
in pursuing fugitives. Even the Congress and the highest executive officials would be banned from any general comment about, or public
investigation of, matters of great national moment where there is a
specific criminal case pending in any jurisdiction, for whatever they said
would violate the statute's rule of silence.[14]

The general concepts embodied in these several proposals, the consequences of their application to daily coverage of crime news, their usefulness, and their acceptability are discussed in the chapters that follow.

---

[14] Hearings of August 17–20, 1965, before the Subcommittee on Improvement in
Judicial Machinery of the Judiciary Committee, United States Senate, published in
two parts, with appendix.

CHAPTER 9

DO AS THE

BRITISH SAY

At the heart of almost all the proposed remedies for prejudicial publicity discussed in the previous chapter is the concept of postponement—postponement of publication of certain news until it is made public at trial or, if it is not, until after the trial is completed. The response of the press has been that a policy of news postponement will be largely unworkable, usually needless, generally futile, and will hurt more than it helps. In turn, the proponents of reform have a seemingly irrefutable and pat answer: The solution of postponement, backed by the contempt power, works in Britain.

The British system derives from venerable precedent. It is interesting, full of intricacies and not a few seemingly perverse aspects.[1] But for our purposes, it may be stated simply. Anthony Lewis, a highly respected newspaperman who has specialized in writing about the law, has provided a clear description:

> In Britain the general rule is that nothing that might conceivably affect the attitude of a potential juror may be published unless and until it is formally disclosed in court. This interdiction begins with a suspect's arrest—perhaps even before an arrest—and runs on until all possible appeals are concluded.
>
> A newspaper may not, therefore, publish material that may be used in evidence at the trial. It is totally against the rules to quote from a suspect's confession before the trial, or even to indicate that a confession exists.

[1] For a complete discussion, see Ronald L. Goldfarb, *The Contempt Power* (New York: Columbia University Press, 1963), pp. 77 ff. Also see Chapter 7 above and Appendix B.

It is equally improper to publish material that cannot be admitted in evidence. Outstanding examples are a defendant's criminal record—that familiar feature of almost any American newspaper account of an important arrest—or such characteristic descriptions as "Mad Dog Killer."

For a newspaper to carry on its own investigation of a crime after there has been an arrest, and to publish the results of its inquiry, is forbidden. It is dangerous to interview witnesses or to publish any but the most innocuous hand-wringing quotes from, say, the defendant's mother.

All of these strictures are enforced by the swiftest and most certain of weapons, the judges' contempt power. Any publication in violation of accepted standards is sure to be followed immediately by a contempt proceeding in the court that has jurisdiction over the criminal case.

There is no jury, and until a very few years ago there was not even any appeal from a contempt conviction or sentence.[2]

This formula, it is argued, (1) leaves the British press as free as the American, (2) preserves a fair and proper trial for the defendants, and (3) can operate just as well in the United States. In progressively increasing magnitude, the three statements are in error.

1. The British press is manifestly less free than the American, if only to the extent of the very existence of the limitations on the British press in reporting crime. It takes a rather remarkable piece of logical legerdemain to contend that if the American press can report certain aspects of criminal procedure at will and the British press cannot, there is no difference in the relative freedom that each enjoys.

The difference between the legal status of the English and the American press is, actually, very great. In England, the press operated from the beginning under royal licensing grants; the classic documents of English freedom, the Magna Charta and the English Bill of Rights, do not even mention freedom of the press. Indeed, freedom of the press in England has been considered merely freedom from prior restraint. In contrast, the press's freedom in the United States is Constitutionally guaranteed, and derives from a historical tradition preferring freewheeling and uninhibited publication.

The reduction in press freedom in Britain is not confined only to practices of criminal coverage. British libel laws are notoriously more restrictive than American. And most important, the flow of information

[2] "British Verdict on Trial-by-Press," *New York Times Magazine,* June 20, 1965, © 1965 by The New York Times Company; extracts used by permission.

from official sources to the press is vastly more restricted in Britain than in the United States, as any reporter who has worked in both countries can bear witness to. In strictly legal terms, that diminution may not be taken as a limitation of the "freedom" of the press to publish what it discovers, but in every real sense it means that the flow of information to the public is markedly less "free."

The British reporter or news executive is rare who doubts the difference in relative freedom between the American and British press, and who does not feel that the limitations have a consequence much greater than the simple withholding for a time of details about some criminal action.

Speaking particularly of the stringent British libel laws, and more generally on press freedom itself, Britain's former Attorney General, Lord Shawcross, declared:

> The strange thing is that the law does not recognize that the Press has any duty to communicate: any duty to disclose. To my mind, there is no doubt that one of the primary duties of a free Press is to disclose without fear or favour that which it believes to be true and to be of public concern. The business of Government, of public professional and commercial life would be in danger, and politics would become utterly corrupted were it not for the fact that ordinary people recognize that the Press has this duty to disclose and, moreover, expect it to discharge the duty. Unfortunately, the Press is gravely inhibited in this necessary task by the fact that if in the event it turns out to be impossible to prove beyond doubt the truth of that which has been alleged, however carefully it had inquired into the matter in the first instance, it may be mulcted in extortionate damages. The defence of qualified privilege, which recognizes the duty to communicate within a limited circle or in special relationships, has not hitherto in practice been available to the newspapers.[3]

Lord Shawcross has also noted that the severe limitations on the British press inhibit its performance in monitoring the administration of justice itself. He wrote:

> In the law relating to contempt of court, the notion that some matter was *sub judice*, or that criticism of the Court might be regarded as contempt, has undoubtedly led to the stifling of comment in a number of cases where public interest required that comment should be made.[4]

[3] Speech to International Press Institute, London, May 25, 1965.
[4] *Grassroots Editor*, January, 1966.

A small example of how the strictures on coverage of criminal proceedings can result in a temporary blackout of somewhat more significant information is provided by an episode in February, 1950, when
Anglo-American relations were at one of their rare bad moments. The
Washington correspondent of the important national newspaper, the
Financial Times, was besieged by his London office to explain and comment on the situation. He responded, but his paper was unable to publish that part of his dispatches pointing out that one of the major causes
was anger and dismay, especially in the Congress, at the betrayal of
American atomic secrets to the Soviets by the British scientist Klaus
Fuchs. For Fuchs was under arrest at the time, and until the trial was
over no mention could be made of the American reaction to the affair.
Thanks to the speedy pace of British justice—Fuchs was arrested, tried,
convicted, and sentenced in less than four weeks—the period of silence
was brief.

This is not to argue that the prohibition against publication of extra-
record material commanded in British practice while proceedings are
pending is wrong; it is merely to point out that it is accomplished at
the expense of a certain amount of information flowing to the public.
In this case, the intelligence offered by the Washington reporter may
have been less than cosmic—England seems to have muddled through
without it—but it is the kind of news of which useful diplomatic correspondence is constructed.

2. That the British system serves the goal of fair trial by assuring a
jury untainted with preconceptions about the crime is a durable but
inaccurate piece of folklore. It operates to achieve its proclaimed end
in those cases where the potential danger from pretrial and pending-trial
publication is the least, and fails in precisely those sensational cases
where the menace of prejudicial publicity is the greatest; the results
leave Britain with as troublesome problems as those in the United
States. The prevailing myth derives from the fact that the plausible
logic of the British system has been accepted as reality without having
been put to an examination of how it works.

As a matter of fact, the British contempt rule fails to resolve three
crucial problems in this area: It does not assure stable verdicts for
society, because, whatever punishment is subsequently meted out to
the offending publication, its offense can cause a mistrial or reversal;
it does not serve as a deterrent to miscreant newspapers, as will be
shown later; and it does not save the defendant the ordeal of trial by

newspaper or provide him solace in knowing that the paper that injured him was later obliged to pay a fine for the deed.

3. Before devoting most of this chapter to the preceding subject, we set down a few words on the thesis that the British system could work in the United States. The central consideration here is the differences in the legal systems, especially the judicial atmospheres and processes, in the two nations. No matter how many hundred differences in detail, the laws and the principles of criminal justice of Great Britain and the United States are closely related; the various parts of the machinery of justice, the jury, the public prosecutor, the trial and appellate judge, have similar sources. But in almost every other important aspect—except perhaps the identical gruesomeness of the crimes and the sensational press treatment accorded them—the environments in which justice is administered in the two countries are remarkably dissimilar.

The greatest difference and the one most crucial in the free press, fair trial context is the almost complete quarantine of British justice from politics and, as a corollary, the higher quality of judges and trial counsel in the lower courts (and of the personnel in the police agencies). Lord Bryce long ago noted the dismaying difference arising from the American system of electing most local and state judges; he praised public and press scrutiny of the trial process as the indispensable preventive of the evils that would otherwise grow out of the political nature of this major part of the American judiciary (see p. 45).

From the fresh outlook of his new assignment as head of the *New York Times* London bureau, Anthony Lewis wrote, in the article already cited:

> In Britain, politics scarcely intrudes into the courtroom. The bar is a small and cosy group whose members may be appearing for the prosecution one day, the defense the next. There is no band of aggressive young prosecutors trying to climb the political ladder by making big cases. There are no judges trying to ascend the judicial ladder on spectacular criminal trials.
>
> There are only 2,100 barristers in England, and they are a much clubbier and less political little group than the American bar. In court the observer immediately notes the absence of that edgy competitiveness so often sensed between American lawyers, and since there are no publicized prosecuting jobs, that is not a path to political fame.
>
> The contrast with the American situation does not need to be elaborated. . . .

The second difference, evidenced in the example of the Fuchs trial, has to do with the speed of the criminal process in Britain. Although British critics are given to complaining of delays, the magnitude of the justice-delayed-is-justice-denied problem they must cope with is comfortably small compared to America's. The difference is critical in the matter of tolerating temporary postponement of the publication of extra-record information. Press silence about certain facts over a brief period does not bring in its wake the harmful consequences noted in earlier chapters; for reasons of practicality and because of the psychological attitudes of the press, a policy of restraint is much more likely to be accepted and lived with if the period of restraint is short and is seen to be accompanied by brisk progress in disposing of the case. The average criminal case in England is tried within a month and the appeal completed two weeks later. In the United States, according to a recent survey (1963) the median time interval between indictment and ultimate disposition of Federal criminal cases where there was a jury trial was 4.8 months. In state cases, the time is even more protracted.

A third, and enormous, difference is the criminal climate in the two countries. A comparison of a few 1965 statistics on crime in London and New York, cities of almost identical size, illustrates the point. The New York data, incidentally, are thought to understate the total by anywhere from 25 to 90 per cent.[5]

	London	New York
Murders	37	631
Rapes	202	1,154
Assaults	4,021	16,325
Robberies	1,609	8,004

Here is such a difference of degree as to be a difference of kind. If the means of detecting crime, trying the accused, and punishing the guilty may be similar, surely the atmosphere of public opinion, the interest, and the impact on the community are so divergent that what has value and relevance in one community would be incongruous in the other.

As a fourth difference, one should remember that in the United States the press has a special role of monitoring the process of justice.

[5] See *New York Times,* April 5, 1966, p. 1.

That function of the press is by no means superfluous in Britain, but the nation does not stand in such need of it and does not have to rely on the press to the extent the United States does as its principal agent for that purpose.

In this connection, and also with reference to a kind of qualitative difference in the crime of the two countries, Anthony Lewis wrote, again in his article of June 20, 1965:

> Britain is a small and relatively homogeneous nation with strong and generally accepted traditions, among them that of a Parliament that is sensitive to abuses by judges or prosecutors or policemen. Police corruption is virtually unknown, and indeed there is comparatively little organized crime.
>
> By contrast, the United States is a large and diverse country with a vast organized criminal element that bought and sold many policemen. Even judges are not immune from corruption, as the recent impeachment of Oklahoma's Chief Justice reminds us. Regionalism is also a problem: racial prejudice in the South has often prompted those who are supposed to enforce the law to help those who brutally violate it.

The final, and perhaps the greatest, difference is the operation of the preliminary hearing. In the United States, the institution is almost neglected. It stands as a procedural way-station between arrest and indictment, and in most jurisdictions it is paid scant regard by the press. A good part of the time, the defendant waives the hearings; where proceedings take place they consist usually of a pro forma statement by the prosecution sketching the complaint against the person arrested. The accused, almost invariably and as a matter of tactics, reserves his defense for the trial. In some places, if the case is inherently sensational, what transpires receives intense coverage; but this is rare and usually the proceeding remains unreported.

The public preliminary hearing is a major part of the English trial process, with results that will soon be evident. But in the United States, it is all but replaced by the grand jury (which we adopted from Britain, but which Britain has now eliminated), which operates in secret, so much so that it is a criminal offense for jurors and officials to divulge what takes place in the grand jury room.

In England, the preliminary hearing is a major source of crime news. It provides the press with its single reportable bundle of information about a crime between the arrest and the trial. The prosecution lays out its case in detail and the press is free to report it in its entirety. It is an open judicial proceeding and, therefore, it is uninhibited under the British rule. In a juicy case, the ensuing reports in the mass publications—every word of them before trial and before a jury is chosen—often make the wildest excursions of America's sensationalist press look stolid. The cases of Dr. J. Bodkin Adams, Stephen Ward, and Christine Keeler are among the most recent examples.

It is precisely because the preliminary hearing provides such a gaping but impeccably lawful hole in the protection against prejudicial pretrial publication that the defendant is supposed to enjoy that there has been intense soul-searching about it in Britain for almost a decade.

The procedures of the institution became formalized as inquisitional affairs more than four centuries ago and were normally held *in camera*. By the middle of the nineteenth century, however, the accused was given the right to be present, and once that was granted, a principal reason for the secret hearing was removed and proceedings began to be held routinely in open court. But the consequence was extensive press coverage which led jurists to wonder whether the defendant might not have lost from the publicity that ensued more than he had gained.[6]

It was the murder charge against Dr. J. Bodkin Adams in 1957 that revived British debate about the problem. Dr. Adams was suspected of causing the deaths of a number of his patients. Details of those deaths, offered in preliminary hearings to show a pattern of criminal action, gave the British press a field day of sensationalism (Adams's counsel had asked for, but was refused, closed hearings). At his trial, however, Adams was prosecuted for only one slaying and no evidence was offered on the two other deaths that had been discussed at the committal hearings. Thus, as an observer noted at the outset of the trial, "Everybody knows a bit too much and no one knows quite enough; there is a most disturbing element in this case, extra-mural half-knowledge that cannot be admitted and cannot be kept out."[7]

Lord Justice Devlin, who presided, was deeply disturbed by what had happened and did what he could in his summation to the jury to dis-

---

[6] A summary of pertinent British and American history is contained in Gilbert Geis, "Preliminary Hearings and the Press," *UCLA Law Review*, March, 1961.

[7] Sybille Bedford, *The Trial of Dr. Adams* (New York: Simon & Schuster, 1958).

arm such preconceptions as the jurors may have had. In passing, he observed that "it might have been wiser in this case if these preliminary hearings before the Magistrates had been held in private." Dr. Adams was acquitted.

Later the same year, Devlin pointed out[8] that pretrial publication in notorious cases can have two adverse effects: It can (1) "stimulate public discussion and the formulation of opinion perhaps adverse to the defense, one side only having been put forward, and so create an undesirable atmosphere for the trial"; and (2) it can allow publication of evidence admitted in the preliminary hearings that the defense may succeed in keeping out of the later trial, but only after the harm has already been done.

It is, of course, the same harm—potential or real—that results from publication in America; the difference is merely that in Britain it arises from a single specific and official (and no doubt more credible) stage in the pretrial proceedings. But whatever its locus, it seems to us that the result is in every respect the same there as here: an ex parte accusation against the defendant accompanied by a mass of tendentious evidence is made public and a future jury is exposed to it to the same degree as in the United States. Ironically, the speed of British criminal procedures, admirable in every other respect, may serve to inflict even greater injury on the accused than he sustains in America (where justice usually comes more slowly, egregiously so in celebrated cases), because the defamatory material is that much fresher in the jury's mind.

Nor does the defendant have much to hope for from self-restraint by the British press. The "class" publications, to be sure, are models of decency. Perhaps in consequence—according to some natural or unnatural law—the British "mass" press is a model of horror, not matched on this side of the Atlantic since Bernarr MacFadden's *New York Graphic*. And the circulation of the quality journals is terrifyingly small in Britain; that of the sensational press correspondingly great.

The ignorance of American press critics of the nature of British crime coverage is enormous. The probable explanation is that the average educated American, or at least the person to whom this debate would be of intellectual interest, has had contact with or will read when he visits Britain, the *Times,* the *Guardian,* or the *Telegraph,* and on Sundays, the

---

[8] In the Sherrill Lectures at the Yale Law School.

Sunday Times, the *Observer,* and the *Sunday Telegraph,* all of which
reach a smaller percentage of readers, all very upper class, than do even
the *New York Times* or the *Christian Science Monitor.* Yet the American
reader will contrast the British class papers with the American mass
papers of his home town and draw generalized conclusions about the
total press of both countries—to the disadvantage of the American. As an
antidote, a reading of the British papers *News of the World* or *People*
on Sunday (each of more than five million circulation), and on week-
days, the *Daily Mirror,* the *Sketch,* and from time to time the *Express*
is recommended. It is also worth noting that the British pattern of crime
reporting produces more offensive and lurid results than the American,
and its adoption here would not seem to promise any abatement of that
evil. Possibly because the British mass press has only two opportunities
for crime coverage, the preliminary hearing and the trial itself, when
the chances come it behaves like a sailor on a long-postponed shore
leave. As contended in Chapter 2, this has to do with a question of taste,
and insofar as the trial coverage is concerned does not necessarily have
to do with prejudicing a defendant. But it is no prettier in England than
in the United States.[9]

Principally because of the concern that the publicity of the Adams
hearings created, the Home Secretary set up an investigative committee
under the chairmanship of a former High Court Judge, Lord Tucker.
It favored preliminary hearings (except for cases involving delicate
matters of state or taste), but recommended that they should not be
publishable. If the accused was not bound over for trial, what took
place in the hearings would thereupon become public information, and
in any event the proceedings at the committal hearings would be publishable after the ensuing trial was completed. Periodically bills have
been offered in Parliament to convert the Tucker Committee recommendations of "public but not publishable" into law, but they have so
far been unsuccessful. At present writing, however, the British government is supporting the proposal and the Home Secretary has introduced
appropriate legislation in Parliament.

---

[9] In his *New York Times Magazine* article of June 20, 1965, Anthony Lewis reflected the consensus of American and British reporters in quoting these words of
an American newspaperman, an old hand in London: "The British popular press
is more scurrilous and more scandalous and more prurient than anything published
in this country. The British newspaper reader has to wait, but in the end he gets
his four-penny-worth of thrills."

What is remarkable about the Tucker Report is that it made *any* recommendation about publication in view of its finding that the question of jury prejudice from publication of the preliminary hearings proceedings was "incapable of proof either way." But the belief that injury ensued was said to be so widely held that "the continuance of the evidence at the preliminary hearing before examining justices can be justified only if it can be shown to have some overriding merit." The possibility that the freedom of the press amounted to an overriding merit apparently did not occur to the Tucker Committee. British journalists together with a great many lawyers, politicians, and others would put the matter quite differently: "The continuance of the existing law is justified unless it can be shown to have some overriding *de*merit."

However, opinions on the subject are still expressed with total conviction. For example, in the weekly *Spectator* of January 21, 1966, the following appeared over the signature of the editor:

> The Tucker Committee's recommendation, which the Government has accepted, that press reports of committal proceedings should be severely limited, is clearly a step in the right direction. But the real truth of the matter is that there is no need for public committal proceedings at all, and their effect can only be to inflame prejudice and reduce the chances of a fair trial. *Vide* the recent Moors case.

This might appear to settle the matter. But as Charles Fenby,[10] a director of Westminster Press Provincial Newspapers, points out, what the editor of the *Spectator* sees as "clearly" a step in the right direction is clearly a step in the wrong direction to Lord Shawcross, former Attorney General, and to the Law Society (the professional organization of the solicitors) and the British Press Council (a prestigious group organized to play watchdog for the press, comprised of representatives of the newspaper owners, editors, and journalists, and public representatives, and chaired by Lord Devlin[11]). In addition, the Lord Chief Justice, apparently unable to accept the guidance of the *Spectator,* said a few weeks later: "I strongly dislike the idea of judicial proceedings in private or in public with a muzzle on the press. I do not think the case

[10] We are indebted to correspondence from Mr. Fenby for much of the material reported here on the Moors murder case and its press treatment.

[11] If Lord Devlin shares the majority view of the Council, he would seem to have changed his attitude from the days of the Adams case and the Sherrill Lectures.

has been made out for preventing press reports; neither has the case been made out that jurors are influenced by reading reports of committal proceedings."[12]

So the controversy is by no means closed; and since the Moors case has become the newest focus for the reheated debate, it is worth considering in some detail. It also offers a recent and flamboyant example of just how effectively the British system permits the press to manufacture enormous potential prejudice. And the disclosure that the *News of the World* was paying a fee to the principal prosecution witness in the Moors case suggests that the British press procedures in criminal cases occasionally fall short of their idealized picture abroad.

The Moors case was so called because the bodies of three murder victims, two boys of twelve and seventeen and a ten-year-old girl, were found on a Cheshire moor, near Manchester. The girl, Lesley Ann Downey, had been reported missing in December, 1964, when the police put out six thousand posters plus five thousand handbills in an effort to trace her. Ten months later, in October 1965, newspapers carried stories suggesting multiple murder. The following passage was typical: "Eight may be victims of a mass killer: Search today of a Cheshire moor for eight missing people believed to have been victims. . . ."

The search went on, more police took part, new devices were used to probe the moor, and public expectation grew. The public was not disappointed. The first discovery was a boy's body; then the girl's body was found in the grave, naked except for shoes and socks. Another youth's remains were found nearby, and according to rumor in the neighborhood (and indeed far afield), more graves would be uncovered at any moment. The state of local opinion was by this time in such a ferment that, according to a statement made in court at the subsequent hearings, a petition for the restoration of capital punishment was signed by 24,000 people in and around the nearby town of Hyde (population 31,000) before anybody had been arrested, let alone charged (similar petitions were organized in the Midlands a few weeks later when mass murder of children was again alleged).

Eventually a store clerk named Ian Brady and a woman typist, Myra Hindley, were arrested. Public excitement was intense. On the morn-

[12] Lord Parker, reported in U.K. *Press Gazette*, February 14, 1966.

ing when they were due to appear in the local magistrates' court a crowd of women queued up for two and a half hours in driving rain in the hope of getting in. There were fifty newspapermen in court. The occasion was to prove even more historic because of a decision that the magistrates were immediately called upon to make.

Applying for the hearing to be held *in camera,* counsel for Brady said: "In this case the matters to be investigated will inevitably arouse powerful emotional reactions. . . . I don't think I am putting it too highly when I say that probably never before has there been more need for an approach by the jury to such a grave issue to be unbiased and unprejudiced, and above all unhampered by preconceived issue."

Counsel referred to the Tucker Committee's recommendations, mentioned that Parliament was expected to pass legislation to forbid reports of preliminary hearings, and invited the local magistrates to anticipate the House of Commons. But they were in obvious difficulty. How could they be expected to agree with counsel on the nature of the evidence before they heard it? Accordingly, they decided to begin proceedings in private, and spent a day listening to the prosecution case. Then they announced that the hearing would be in open court, and the prosecution started all over again. The result was not merely an acute stimulus to newspaper circulations but an opportunity to judge what sort of evidence a local bench of magistrates thought fit for public consumption.

The allegations were as follows:

Brady's favorite author was de Sade and he was also alleged to have a whole library of books on torture and perversion, the titles being withheld by the court in order not to advertise them. His collection of photographs was said to include "a number of a young girl in the nude in various pornographic poses," and the girl was identified as Lesley Ann Downey, the ten-year-old victim. The court went into closed session again in order to hear tape recordings of the voices of a man and a woman and the young girl. It was alleged that when these recordings were played in the presence of the accused woman "she did not speak but sobbed quietly with her head bowed, in a quiet voice said 'I am ashamed' and began to cry." Counsel alleged that "after what these two had done to that little girl they could not afford to let her go home without putting themselves in danger." Photographs of the child's body were produced but counsel advised the chairman (a woman) not to look at them. There were suggestions that the boy victims had been sexually assaulted.

The seventeen-year-old brother-in-law of the accused woman gave the following evidence: One evening the woman asked him to walk her home, and when they arrived at the house, he was invited in to collect some miniature wine bottles. After being admitted by Brady he went into the kitchen, heard a scream from another room, went in, and saw Brady striking a boy with an ax. Counsel asked questions as to how this weapon was used and how often. The witness alleged that the victim crawled round the floor and was finished off with a cord round the neck, at which Brady said, "That's it, the messiest yet." The witness was asked to describe the noises made by the victim, the state of the room ("blood everywhere, all over the floor, walls, door, everywhere"), the mopping-up operations, trussing of the body, disposal upstairs. All this with a frail grandmother in another room of the house, against the background of that moor where the accused man and woman were alleged to have held wine-drinking parties sometimes attended by a small girl from the town.

What was reported of this hearing was, of course, allegation, not necessarily fact, and whether it would be received in evidence, and if so whether substantiated or refuted, would not be known until the trial, several months ahead. The way in which it was reported made an unusually interesting study because it varied from extreme exploitation to total silence. There was no mention of the case in the BBC's evening television bulletin; this may have been prompted by fear of giving offense, of being accused of sensationalism, or by a doubt as to whether a short bulletin could give an adequate summary of such evidence. It is interesting, and bears on the argument in Chapter 11, that the decision invited debate on the credibility of BBC news.

The print press went to the other extreme, reporting the allegations at length, including the most grisly details of the exhumations. It was a story for the afternoon papers, of which there are seventy in England. The competition affected the editorial outlook; for instance, one North Country editor, when reviewing his paper's performance on this case, said, "My sub-editors don't have much time to think about ethics." Some editors gave the instruction, "Give every word." Others started off discreetly, even modestly, but where they came into competition with less inhibited publications threw off restraint. This happened with several papers in the West Country, which allowed only a brief summary of the first day's hearing on the front page, but changed policy on seeing what London was doing. In London's two afternoon papers the coverage was extreme; the spectacle of one story running to many columns spread over several pages has a compulsive effect.

One London paper reported the appearance of the girl victim's mother under the headline " 'I WILL KILL YOU,' CRIES LESLEY'S MOTHER," followed by the paragraph:

> Her voice shaking and sobbing, Mrs. Gertrude Ann Downey, mother of Lesley Ann Downey, faced accused Myra Hindley across the tense courtroom here today and shouted: "I will kill you, I will kill you—an innocent baby."

The other London paper carried a similar heading and its description of the scene included a passage quoting Mrs. Downey as saying: "She sits staring at me and she has taken a little baby's life. The beast."

Should Parliament finally translate the Tucker Committee recommendations into law, no doubt a great deal of what is now prejudicial publicity in its potential will be ended in Great Britain. No more than in the United States, however, will that action eliminate the totality of news that might predispose a jury with extra-record information. One need only recall that when the notorious Christine Keeler was ultimately tried and convicted for perjured testimony, her jury (and all of Britain) had been subjected to months of sensationally reported news deriving from the immediately preceding news stories and trial of Dr. Stephen Ward, in which she had been a principal figure. A total solution in Britain, in the United States, or anywhere else where some unfettered news is still allowed to flow, is an impossibility.

The First Amendment and the history of Supreme Court decisions on the free press, fair trial issue would seem to make American adoption of the British system a purely academic speculation. But the question posed in this chapter is somewhat different and warrants an answer: Would some system patterned on the British approach, but depending on sanctions that somehow could be squared with the American Constitution, operate successfully in this country to end the abuses complained of?

Once again we quote Anthony Lewis, not merely because he enjoys the highest esteem among the press as well as among the legal profession, but because a bare eight months before he ventured his conclusions on the British system, he was echoing Justice Felix Frankfurter in castigating the American press for its sins against criminal justice. Writing in the *New York Times Magazine* on October 18, 1964, Lewis spoke highly of the "clean-cut way" in which the British dealt with the problem, and seemed to endorse a restrictive proposal of Justice Bernard S. Meyer of the Supreme Court of Nassau County, New York, one of the most redoubtable critics of American press coverage of criminal procedure. Like many of the other more extreme current proposals summarized in Chapter 8, it would have state or Federal law forbid any disclosure of a confession, of the accused's prior record, or any expression or opinion on the defendant's guilt or the credibility of evidence or witnesses. It would go on to list other practices which, while not automatically barred, could be punished if a jury found that they had threatened substantial injury to justice.

His locus of reporting having moved from Washington to London, Lewis's views seemed to have undergone a sea change. In his article of June 20, 1965, quoted earlier, Lewis described the British system and its acceptance in England and asked:

> Does this acceptance suggest that the United States should adopt the British approach to control of public comment on pending criminal cases? Certainly not.
> The British system, however satisfactory it seems here, is not suited to the United States—indeed it would not be possible simply to move it whole across the Atlantic. For there are basic differences between the two societies and their traditions.

In a tone very different from the one of his earlier excoriation of the press, Lewis concluded:

> Britain can teach us fidelity to the ideal of impartial justice. She should also remind us that a nation's system of criminal justice is indivisible, that a question such as fair trial and free press cannot be considered apart from other aspects of criminal procedure.

In short, to assure fairer criminal trials the United States needs to attack problems other than the surface one of press comment. It should worry about police corruption, political prosecutors, incompetent judges, regional bias and many other deficiencies in American criminal justice.

And Lord Shawcross himself summed up the answer to those who want to import the English rule:

The laws and institutions of each country depend upon circumstances of history, of tradition, of the character of its people, infinitely variable, and no one would suggest that what may be appropriate for one country would necessarily provide an apt pattern for another.[13]

[13] Speech to the International Press Institute, London, May 25, 1965.

CHAPTER 10

THE CURE

THAT FAILS

Proposals for curing trial by newspaper have taken it as axiomatic that the threat posed by the press to fair trial would be eliminated if only, once a defendant is arrested, the press would publish nothing about the case except what was in the official record until the trial is finished and the judgment rendered. But is it true? The axiom has not been examined.

Regardless of the methods suggested to accomplish the postponement—whether by statute directly prohibiting extra-record publication, or by regulation forbidding law enforcement personnel from disclosure, or by voluntary agreement among the press itself—all of the solutions currently being considered contain as their core the concept of postponement: postponement of publication of material that might prejudice the decision of a future jury. Some advocates of this corrective may agree with the argument in earlier chapters that it is not needed except for the extraordinary, sensational situation; others hold it is necessary for all criminal cases. Some will concede that its imposition will entail the payment of a high price in terms of the denial of information to the public; others assert that the loss is minimal and temporary. Some acknowledge a certain quota of danger in the method; others see none. All of these are interesting and important contentions, but for the moment we choose to leave them aside. Instead—whatever the methods and whether the remedy should be universal or selective, whether it will be difficult to administer or easy, costly or cheap, dangerous or without hazard—we propose to look now at a single question: Is it likely to be effective? All other considerations and difficulties aside, will it accomplish what is intended?

159

Let us begin the examination by considering the dangerous cases, those where the potential of prejudice is strongest, that is to say, the extraordinary, highly publicized instances. If the solution operates so as to disarm the menace latent in them, it will surely be fully as efficient in coping with less troublesome cases.

In the illustrations that follow, as throughout this book, we avoid hypothetical examples and the one-in-a-million exceptions. By postulating some unlikely concatenation of events, it is easy enough to construct an unreal but conceivable situation to prove one side of an argument or the other, but it is not very convincing. Neither do we hark back to some historical or obscure case to validate an argument. Instead, there are offered below fifteen cases where the crime took place or the proceedings were active during the period when this book was being written—in 1965 and 1966. Some cases were of national interest; others were notorious in only a single area. The situations are, paradoxically, both sensational and typical: sensational in that all were highly publicized, either nationally or in the community where they occurred and where they would be tried and where the potential prejudice in the publication was high; and typical in the sense that they illustrate problems that are real and recurring. As nearly as we can select them, these situations exemplify a large portion—we believe the major portion—of the cases that engender the free press, fair trial dilemma.

The cases cannot be neatly classified, because most of them illustrate difficulties arising from more than one cause; the equations contain too many variables. But in general, we begin with a set of situations where none of the solutions of postponement could have helped in any way to eliminate the potentially prejudicial publication—because it emerged from prearrest reports of crime or posttrial reports affecting a future case; we proceed to others where it is politically unrealistic to expect any of the solutions to be applied; the potential prejudice of a third group arises principally from the circumstances of the arrest, the publication of which almost none of the proposals would prohibit; we conclude with others where, in theory, the potentially damaging data might have been withheld—but with uncertain results.

Potential Prejudice from Nonsuppressible Sources

1. A wildly sensational story began in Oregon late in June, 1965, and ended two weeks later in Nevada, by which time the two men involved

were the subject of a prodigious volume of what must be taken to be prejudicial publication. What was prejudicial—and there is small doubt that it was anything but—was the consequence of the current reports of what happened before the two men were apprehended. Short of a flat prohibition on publication about a crime once it happened—or in this case, prohibition of publication even that the crime was committed—it is hard to imagine how all but a fraction of the prejudice could have been avoided.

On June 28, Carl Cletis Bowles, twenty-four years of age, burglar, robber, and car thief, who began his criminal career at the age of fifteen, was released from the Oregon State Prison, at Salem, after serving a six-year term for burglary. Three days later, on July 1, another inmate, Wilfred M. Gray, thirty, was freed from the same prison, after a four-year sentence for assault and robbery in a motel near Portland, where he had threatened Isabelle Goodnight, fifty-eight, with rape. The two men joined forces. On Monday, July 5, Mrs. Goodnight told police, two men walked into her motel. She recognized one as Gray. She said they beat her, stole $28, tied her up, and that Gray thereupon made good his threat of four years before.

Next day, two men walked into the 42d and Going branch of the National Bank of Oregon in Portland at 1:20 P.M., threatened employees with an automatic pistol and a sawed-off shotgun, and made off with $13,400.

That evening, the two men were seen at the Elsner Motor Company in Salem. They bought a sports car. At 11:10 that night, Lane County Deputy Sheriff Carlton E. Smith, a rookie on his first night patrol, stopped the car for speeding. He was thereupon shot once in the back with a shotgun and six times with a pistol. Before he died he used his police radio to say he had been shot, and gave the license number of the assailants' car.

Within less than an hour, at Springfield, Oregon, the two men knocked at the door of Mrs. Shirley Corbin, a housewife, and at gunpoint abducted her and her twelve-year-old son. Having abandoned their sports car, they drove off with their prisoners in Mrs. Corbin's Thunderbird.

An hour later, now in the early morning hours of Wednesday, July 7, they knocked at the window of a camper truck parked beside U.S. Highway 20. Asleep inside were Uldis Riekstins, his wife, their fourteen-year-old son, and a family friend. After threatening the group, the two men commandeered the camper. Bowles drove off with it and its passengers,

Gray following in Mrs. Corbin's automobile. A few hours later, they abandoned the Thunderbird, packed everyone into the camper, and continued driving.

At 8:30 Wednesday evening, by which time police had found Mrs. Corbin's abandoned car but knew nothing of the camper truck, the two men and their victims had reached Sacramento, California. At an intersection near the state capitol, Bowles and Gray simply jumped out, leaving six stunned passengers in the truck.

About two miles from where they got out, the two men spied the house of Hale Champion, State Finance Director of California and a close political adviser of the Governor, Edmund G. Brown. At pistol point, they abducted him, his wife and eighteen-month-old daughter. The five of them set out in Champion's Ford Galaxie.

They drove for twenty-four hours. The hue and cry and the police search in Oregon and California were by this time enormous, and the story was front-page news in the area, and indeed, throughout the nation. By now, Thursday, July 8, presumably what is meant by the Morse bill's term "pending criminal litigation" (pp. 139–140) had begun. For on that day a Federal grand jury in Portland indicted Bowles and Gray for bank robbery and kidnaping, and state courts issued warrants charging the pair with assault, robbery, and murder. Gray was also charged with rape.

To leave the story for a moment, one may pause to speculate on what newspapers and broadcasting stations would have been allowed to publish at this point in the case and from that time on had one or another of the currently proposed measures to prevent prejudicial publication been in effect. What emerges from such an attempt is something manifestly unreal. Under one or another of the measures patterned on the British rule (see Chapter 9), it would appear that from some time Thursday until, one supposes, the ultimate arrest of the two men on Friday, publications could relate only that the Champions had been abducted, without any reference to the fact that the two kidnapers were suspects or defendants of the earlier crimes, and, of course, with no references at all to those crimes themselves, inasmuch as indictments had been issued. Thereafter, with a view to keeping extra-record influence out of the future trial on the Champion abductions, no news story could refer to the commission of the other crimes; and the future trial or trials of the earlier crimes would be contaminated by mention of the Champion abduction. Alternately, under some of the measures aimed at cutting off comment from law enforcement officers, police and prosecutors would have been reduced to saying almost nothing once the indictments issued; it is a nice question whether they would have been in violation of some of the proposed regulations had they spoken even on the progress of the chase of the now-indicted fugitives.

Under some of the proposed codes of behavior for newspapers, such as that in Massachusetts, news media would have been enjoined to "avoid" mention of the fact that the fugitives were ex-convicts, since that would imply prior criminal record.

And had the proposals of the essay that the American Bar Association Ross Prize jury thought sufficiently highly of to reward with a liberal prize in 1965 (p. 122) found their way into law, it is hard to see how any news medium could do much more from July 5 until all trials and appeals were concluded than to mention, without linking one to the other, that each crime was committed—or was asserted to have been committed—and that warrants and indictments had issued.

To return to the chase: While hundreds of police and sheriffs were searching, the trail grew warm at 7:30 Thursday evening, at Luning, in western Nevada, where the car stopped for gas and was recognized by a service station attendant. Shortly thereafter, the police chief of Tonopah, Nevada, in company with a deputy sheriff, found the car parked with a flat tire. The fugitives threatened to kill the Champions if the officers fired. They ordered the policemen to surrender their car and took it over, piling into it with their hostages. They drove into Tonopah, parked in front of a casino-restaurant and demanded over the sheriff's radio that deputies get them sandwiches and ammunition.

When no such action was forthcoming, the pair fired six shots into the casino marquee. Inside, a card dealer fired three shots at the car. One hit Champion in the hip, inflicting only a superficial wound.

Warning police on their radio that the Champions would be shot if any attempt at arrest were made, the car sped out of town. Ten miles away, the pair released Champion by the side of the road. Bowles and Gray then radioed police that they would release Mrs. Champion and the baby at a point near the California border. They kept their word: police found the two hostages in the car; the abductors had left it and hitched a ride in a truck. A short time later, about 2:30 A.M. Friday, they were found walking along a highway and they surrendered meekly.

They are now serving two life sentences each, one handed down by a Federal District Court in California for the kidnaping of the Champions, and the second by an Oregon court for the killing of the deputy sheriff. Other criminal charges against them were dismissed.

Initially, their attorneys talked of the need for change of venue and of the problem of prejudicial publicity, but pleas of guilty were soon entered, thus rendering those considerations irrelevant.

2. On Friday, June 5, 1965, a gunman walked into the Farmers State Bank of Big Springs, Nebraska, a town of some five hundred people, and shot dead three of the four persons there—the president, the cashier, and the bookkeeper—and seriously wounded a fourth employee. The scene when police arrived indicated that the bandit had ordered the victims to lie face down on the floor, and had thereupon shot them. Within two days, the event became, like the Oregon-California rape-murder-abductions, one of the most highly publicized crime stories of the year.

By Sunday, a suspect was charged and the search for him began. He was Duane Pope, a twenty-two-year-old Kansas farm boy who had graduated just a week before from McPherson (Kansas) College. He was put on the FBI's "Ten Most Wanted" list, and hundreds of law enforcement officers, including FBI men, took up the chase. Three days later an automobile Pope was known to have bought was found in Wichita, a rifle inside.

Details of the search, of which there were many, were widely published. So also was extensive information about the fugitive, his interest in guns, and views about him (mostly neutral when not favorable) of those who knew him.

On June 11, he surrendered in Kansas City to police, who quoted him as saying, "I'm tired of running." By this time, the man who survived the attack on the Nebraska bank had sufficiently recovered to relate the harrowing details of his experience. In addition, the president of McPherson College, Dr. D. W. Bittinger, had broadcast an appeal to Pope, asking him to give himself up; immediately after the arrest, Bittinger related that Pope, hearing the radioed appeal, had telephoned him. Bittinger was quoted as saying, "He wanted to know if I could call his parents and how they were reacting to all the publicity."

At the trial, six months later, Pope confessed to the shootings but pleaded innocent by reason of insanity. He was found guilty and sentenced to death. At this writing, Pope is appealing the verdict; prejudicial publication is not raised as an issue.

To speculate once again on what might not have been publishable under one or another of the postponement formulas: We may grant that Pope's alleged statement to the Kansas City police would have been barred and possibly also Bittinger's account of the phone call. But almost certainly, everything else—that is, developments in the case while Pope was a fugitive—that was published up to the point of his surrender would have been sanctioned. But it was the "everything else" that made the impact.

If Pope went to trial burdened with the handicap of prejudicial publicity from press accounts—and what was published was about as damning as could be imagined—the prejudice surely sprang from the account of the horrible crime itself (even though the reports in the large and small papers nearest the scene and in the national wire services were written with a minimum of sensationalism) and the positive identification of him as the killer that was implicit in the specificity of the six-day search. No variation on the "solution by postponement" theme that we are aware of would have abated, much less eliminated, the potential prejudice thus generated.

To turn from theory back to fact, Pope's trial was conducted with scrupulous care. Although the government proposed trial at North Platte, the nearest Federal court to the scene of the crime, defense lawyers argued that too many people in the area knew the victims. The judge asked Pope for his preference. He said he wanted the trial in Lincoln, and it was accordingly held there.

Neither during the trial nor later did the defense contend that jurors had been prejudiced by any news coverage. The examination of the jury appears to have been carefully conducted. All jurors were asked if they had read one or more of the three or four accounts of the crime reported in national magazines; only a few had, and those who said they had not formed impressions that would require evidence to remove were accepted; in their examination there was no special emphasis on pretrial publication.

During the pretrial hearing, a defense motion to suppress Pope's statements to FBI officers at the time of his surrender was offered and argued in open court, but the judge forbade all mention of it outside the courtroom, a command which the press heeded. Later, during the trial, the statements were admitted into evidence.

3. In July, 1966, eight student nurses were murdered in their apartment in Chicago. The enormity of the crime created a news story so sensational and widespread that its circumstances need no restatement here. What is important for our consideration is that within a matter of a day or so, fingerprints of a ne'er-do-well named Richard Speck, with a considerable prior record of law violations, were found in the nurses' dormitory. Amid a fanfare of furious publicity, a search was begun for him; Chicago's chief of police declared that Speck was beyond doubt "the killer." A great deal of his background was made public, along with the fact that he carried on his arm a tattoo reading: "Born to Raise Hell." It was this tattoo that a young doctor observed two days after the crime as he was washing off the arm of an unconscious drunk who had attempted suicide and had been brought by unknowing police from his skid row flophouse to Cook County Hospital in Chicago. The doctor asked a nurse to bring him the newspapers, where he recalled having read that the fugitive sought for the atrocious crime carried such a marking. Thus was Speck captured. No clearer demonstration can be found for the necessity of disclosure, prearrest, of what might ultimately be prejudicial and not proper to disclose after arrest.

What was the prejudicial material that, under some of the various proposals to eliminate prejudice, might not have been made public? None of those proposals calls for suppression of the identification of a suspect who is a fugitive; almost none would suppress the circumstances of the crime. Accordingly, under almost any of the proposed rules, the fact of Speck's fingerprints being found, the identification of him as the suspect (although certainly not the police chief's characterization of him, prearrest, as "the killer"), enough of his background to help in finding him, and the wording of the tattoo, bespeaking a less-than-savory fellow, would have been issued.

If Speck is tried before a jury (at this writing, no determination of trial procedure has been made), he will suffer, in theory, from prejudicial publicity. It is hard to conceive that any jury in Illinois will not have known something about the case. But whatever prejudice may exist will have come from the facts of the case that almost no one would propose should *not* have been made public. Those facts, and the necessary information issued to accomplish his capture, as compared to the objectionable characterization of the police chief, must weigh in the ratio of 99 to 1.[1] And what is proper prearrest news and is allowed by most proposals like the Reardon Committee's as a way to catch fugitives is devastatingly prejudicial after arrest—even if there is restraint at that point in time (as there was *not* in the Speck case).

4. The advocates of postponement of publication as a means to spare defendants prejudicial publicity rarely address themselves to its effectiveness and applicability in criminal cases that grow from prior press and/or public investigations. Perhaps this is because the problems are insoluble: every variation of the postponement method is here both vain and impracticable. Prevention of potential prejudice is achievable in this kind of case only by preventing the investigation.

The matter is most generously illustrated by the Maryland savings and loan company scandals of 1961–65, in the course of which nearly twenty individuals have been indicted. If their trials were or will be prejudiced it was because of a cry of alarm issued from the floor of the U.S. Senate by Senator J. Glenn Beall of Maryland, in 1958, the investigative and legislative bulldogging of Joseph D. Tydings (then a member of the Maryland House of Delegates, later United States Attorney

---

[1] Much less justifiable are other pieces of officially released news in the Speck case. After the arrest, the police chief and the prosecutor appeared to maintain a policy of strict nondisclosure, but subordinates clearly did not, for the Chicago press was able to report with appalling detail over the next week every conceivable fact about Speck's life and activities. Full details were published about his acquisition of a knife that may have been the murder weapon, along with a detailed chronicle of his acts—many unsavory—in the several days preceding the murder. The press referred to the murder as "the crime of the century." Lawyers, psychologists, and psychiatrists debated in a dozen public forums about the problems of Speck's future trial and the state of his mental health, and propounded a new psychoanalysis of him each day. Members of the Chicago bar were no less loath to enter into public discussion of how Speck's trial might, or should, or possibly would be conducted. Police executives from other jurisdictions as far away as Australia announced their desire to question Speck about unsolved rape-murders on their books, with descriptions of those crimes promptly published in detail in the Chicago press.

Finally, reporters chivvied a young minister sent to visit Speck in jail by members of his family into the revelation that Speck was "remorseful." The episode suggests that man's foresight can never be sufficient to devise 100 per cent protection. Who would have dreamed that in specifying persons who should be barred from disclosing information in a criminal case, in order to prevent prejudicial publicity, the clergy would have to be included?

for Maryland, and subsequently U.S. Senator—elected in no small part because of what he did in that affair), and relentless pressure by the Washington and Baltimore newspapers.

Until 1961, Maryland was the only state in the Union with no controls over the phenomenally swelling savings and loan business. The large majority of the companies in the state were honestly and prudently administered, but a handful came into being under the care of some veteran embezzlers whom increasing controls had forced out of Tangier and other theretofore congenial bases of operation. Before the laws that Tydings succeeded in forcing on a reluctant Maryland legislature caught up with them, and before the prosecutions that other public and press disclosures made possible, the proprietors of twenty savings and loan associations fleeced some 43,000 members. With luck, they may recover about half of the $40 million they deposited.

The ties between the operators and the state legislators and political bosses were as close as they were intricate. Among those convicted and jailed were the speaker of the Maryland House of Representatives and one other Delegate. Also convicted, fined, and placed on probation was Representative Frank W. Boykin of Alabama. He was ultimately pardoned by President Lyndon B. Johnson. Found guilty with him on charges of conspiracy and fraud was Representative Thomas F. Johnson of Maryland. The two Congressmen had sought to save one of the most notorious of the embezzlers from prosecution and were found guilty of bringing improper pressure to bear on the Justice Department in the process. The course of public exposure extended over the years. Intense publicity—surely justifiable, but no less "prejudicial" for that—preceded the indictments.[2]

Congressman Johnson was also convicted on another charge: taking a bribe for making a speech on the House floor defending certain of the savings and loan institutions in his state. The conviction on this count was reversed on September 16, 1964, by the Fourth U.S. Court of Appeals, on grounds that Johnson was Constitutionally protected from challenge about actions he performed in Congress. The Supreme Court sustained that ruling, rejecting the Justice Department's appeal, on

[2] When four of the most crucial indictments were returned, including those of Boykin and Johnson, the Attorney General of the United States said the investigation that led to the charges "stemmed from outstanding efforts by postal inspectors and reporters for the *Washington Post.*"

February 24, 1966. But in doing so, the Supreme Court left standing the ruling by the Court of Appeals that Johnson should be retried on the other seven counts of which he was previously found guilty.

This last ruling, however, came on a 4–3 vote, with Chief Justice Earl Warren and Justices William O. Douglas and William J. Brennan, Jr., dissenting. Chief Justice Warren, who wrote the dissent, referred to Johnson's previous sentence—six months' imprisonment and a $5,000 fine—characterized it as lenient, and argued that the convictions on the other seven counts were valid, that they remained so, being separable and thus unaffected by reversal of the eighth count, and were the result of an eminently fair trial.

As of this writing, the Justice Department remains undecided whether to reinstitute prosecution of Johnson. But if it does, the former Congressman may be justified in feeling that when he enters the courtroom next time, he will have been the target of one of the largest, albeit inevitable, barrages of prejudicial publication ever laid down—and not one line of it avoidable by any solution of "restraint" or "postponement," or caused by any act of the press that could be criticized as thoughtless, malicious, unfair, or even superfluous. The potential prejudice against him came in three stages: the press and state investigatory prearrest reports of his actions and those of the savings and loan tycoons that led to the indictment; the much publicized account of the trial that found him guilty; and the opinion of the Chief Justice of the United States and two other Justices that he was fairly tried and correctly found guilty of the seven charges that presumably will be reinstated for the prospective retrial.

The plight in any future trials of such men as Billie Sol Estes, Bobby Baker, James R. Hoffa—the plight of all who come to the bar following publicized investigations by executive and legislative governmental bodies, by the press, and as a result of published complaints by other groups—parallels that of Johnson in the matter of pretrial publicity. In none of these cases would a postponement rule cure the problem.

5. In a somewhat similar fashion, publication of what was perfectly legitimate to report, that is, the proceedings of previous trials, produced what would seem to be most of the potential prejudice (but not all of it) in a California case.

In March, 1965, a Seabee with $296 in mustering-out pay in his pocket was robbed and killed in Ventura County, California. Three people were indicted for murder and after charges against one were dismissed two were left to stand trial. One was Dorman F. Talbot, Jr., twenty-five, unemployed. The other was Albert R. Randall, twenty, a Seabee.

Randall went to trial first and separately. The news media faithfully reported the events in the court, with story after story about what Talbot, still to be tried, was asserted to have done. The district attorney attempted to show that Randall had handed the murder knife to Talbot and had shared with him the murdered man's money. Randall was found guilty of first-degree murder but on the basis of an account that the fatal blow was struck by another man who had not yet come to trial.

The news accounts were privileged, of course, and would be prohibited under none of the proposed postponement-of-publication formulas. But the effect, surely, was "trial by newspaper" of Talbot before he had trial by law. Granted, the content of the trial stories had emerged under the rules of the court: no hearsay, no heady stuff from the cops, no gossip from irresponsible or unconfronted witnesses. But even so, the complaint against pretrial publication is that it *is* pretrial, not that it is inaccurate. And news of the proceedings about Randall was surely, from Talbot's viewpoint, pretrial.

In most matters, life is never willing to provide researchers with tidy, clean-cut examples on which to make a telling point, and so it was with the Randall-Talbot story. The local paper, the *Oxnard Press-Courier,* did not merely report what happened at the Randall trial. Before the trial, it published two stories based on a presumably bootlegged transcript of the grand jury hearings, not a public record in Ventura County. The transcript was of course an ex parte presentation of the prosecution and so, consequently, were the newspaper reports of it. Curiously, defense attorneys never contended the stories prejudiced their clients' cases.

And just as Talbot's trial began, the *Press-Courier* published an article containing the sentence: "Sources close to the court have disclosed that before the trial began, Talbot's attorney . . . offered the District Attorney a guilty plea to murder on the condition that Talbot escape death in the gas chamber."

Next day a motion for mistrial was granted because of an accidental procedural error in empaneling prospective jurors. But Talbot's counsel said he would not have made the motion had it not been for the report (not denied) of the attempted deal. He also asked for change of venue, which was granted.

The new trial was held in Santa Barbara County, where the *News*

Press noted that the case had come there on a change of venue but, sensibly, gave no details, thus avoiding the kind of mistake that was made by the Raleigh *News and Observer* (p. 81). Talbot was found guilty and sentenced to death. If pretrial publicity was an issue, no postponement rule would have made a difference.

6. In the immediate area of Washington, D.C., the most recent sensational case, by anyone's definition, arose from the murder of a Virginia family of four in January, 1959 (with proceedings still continuing as of this writing). The episode is so replete with what defense counsel described as highly inflammatory and prejudicial publicity that this ground is one of the two on which a currently pending petition to the Supreme Court for a writ of certiorari is based; at the same time, it illustrates a situation like that of the preceding case where much of the most damaging publication derived directly from the verdict of a prior trial, the reporting of which no one can suggest barring or postponing.

The victims of the murder, Carroll Vernon Jackson, Jr., his wife Mildred, and their young children, Susan and baby Janet, left the house of Mrs. Jackson's mother in Louisa County, Virginia, during the late evening of January 11, 1959, to drive to their home a few miles away. Next morning, their car was found about midway on the journey by the side of the road, unoccupied. Not until March 4 were the bodies of Jackson and the baby found in adjoining Spotsylvania County. The baby had been killed by blows on the head; the father was severely beaten and fatally shot through the head. A little more than two weeks later, on March 31, the bodies of Mildred Jackson and Susan were found in Maryland, both cruelly clubbed on the head.

Press coverage of the ghastly murders was, not unnaturally, intense; it began with the two-months' disappearance of the family before the first two bodies were found, and grew with the discovery of the remaining two. It persisted while authorities sought to identify and locate the killer.

Some fifteen months later, on June 24, 1960, FBI agents arrested an itinerant musician, Melvin Davis Rees, Jr., in West Memphis, Arkansas, for unlawful flight to avoid prosecution for another murder in Maryland. For various reasons, he was also a prime suspect as the Jacksons' murderer.

On notification of Rees's arrest, FBI agents went to the home of his parents in Hyattsville, Maryland, a suburb of Washington, and obtained their permission to search their house including the belongings of their son, who used the residence from time to time.[3] In an accordion case, the FBI agents found what was identified as the murder pistol. Also in the box was a large sheaf of lewd writings, apparently in Rees's hand, including what the press was soon to call the "death diary," an obscene and explicit account of the abduction and molestation of Mrs. Jackson and of the murders.

On the day after the arrest in Arkansas, an FBI agent appeared before a United States Commissioner in Maryland and obtained a warrant for Rees's arrest on a charge of kidnaping. He informed the Commissioner of the handwritten account. Next day, the Commissioner made a statement to the press about the existence and nature of that document, which the press reported. Two days later, the news media began to print and broadcast actual quotations from the account, said to have been released by the Baltimore police.[4]

Rees was brought from Arkansas to Baltimore and tried in the United States District Court for kidnaping Mildred Jackson and Susan. He was convicted on February 23, 1961 and, on recommendation of the jury, given life imprisonment. No appeal was sought. The pistol was admitted into evidence; the handwritten account was not.

The press coverage was, of course, extensive. It continued even beyond the trial. In March, several weeks after the verdict but on the eve of the scheduled sentencing, a Baltimore television station broadcast a program in which nine of the jurors who convicted Rees re-enacted their deliberations. (The three jurors who had been an initial minority and ultimately succeeded in fighting off the majority's demand for the death sentence did not participate.)

Apparently feeling the sentence was insufficiently punitive, the State

[3] The legality of that search, the means the FBI agents used to obtain permission, the admission into evidence of a pistol thus discovered, and related factors constitute the second ground on which Rees's counsel appealed to the Supreme Court.

[4] An amicus brief filed by the National Capital Area Civil Liberties Union in the Supreme Court supporting Rees's appeal makes its argument on the question of "Whether this Court should exercise its supervisory authority over the administration of criminal justice in the Federal courts *to prevent persons within its control from making prejudicial pretrial statements* which deprive the accused of his constitutional right to a fair trial." (Emphasis supplied.) It cites *Irvin v. Dowd* (pp. 304–306), the Attorney General's April, 1965, instructions (pp. 130–131) and those of Judge Francis of the New Jersey Supreme Court (pp. 129–130).

of Virginia almost at once began considering whether to bring Rees to trial for the murder of the father. An indictment was issued in June, 1961, in Spotsylvania County, where the bodies of Jackson and the baby had been found.

At this point, the problem of prejudicial publicity was present in an excruciatingly difficult form, and a rare one, inasmuch as the identical and presumably legitimate pending-trial publication of the Maryland events was transformed into a virulent pretrial species with respect to the forthcoming Virginia proceedings.

The dilemma was in large part caused, first, by the fact that Spotsylvania is a small town—the whole county from which the talesmen were assembled contains only 13,800 persons—and second, by the fact that, in communication terms, it is "near" the site of the Maryland trial. Almost midway between Washington and Richmond, it is within the circulation areas of the newspapers of those cities and some of their radio stations. It is within a few miles of Fredericksburg, with its newspaper, radio, and television stations. All of them, and the Baltimore media as well, had covered and would continue to cover the matter heavily. The initial interest of the inhabitants of rural Spotsylvania County, which generates almost no enthralling news items of its own, must be presumed to have been overwhelming throughout the case from the moment the Jackson family, residents of the adjoining county, were known to be missing, and continuing with the discovery of the two bodies in their own county and lasting until the end of the Baltimore trial.

The press did nothing to ease the situation thereafter. On the contrary. By the start of the Virginia trial, according to Rees's pending appeal brief, "news media serving Spotsylvania County had made at least 120 separate references to the inadmissible handwritten account of the Jackson deaths which had been found in [Rees's] accordion case. . . . The Fredericksburg paper had already printed eighty pictures concerning the case. . . . Three days before selection of the jury, at a time when it was known that the [Virginia] court had excluded the document from evidence [on a pretrial motion], a front page newspaper headline referred to it as a 'death diary.'[5] . . . At least twenty-three references

---

[5] The offending paper was the *Washington Post*, of which I was then managing editor. A. F.

were made to the document by news media in the ten days immediately preceding the start of the trial."[6]

Rees's attorneys sought a change in venue, which was denied. (Their current appeal argues that a move to far southwestern Virginia, deep in Appalachia, to one or another of Virginia's more metropolitan, industrial areas would have helped, since the future talesmen might have been less contaminated with knowledge about the case, or had other things to occupy their attention and provide subject matter for gossip. Both Virginia and Federal appellate courts through which the case was appealed rejected that contention.) In the voir dire, twenty-nine prospective jurors declared their opinions were fixed, and they were accordingly disqualified. Members of the panel who said their opinion was not fixed were accepted. The defense exhausted all its peremptory challenges and the final jury contained at least two persons who admitted before trial having already formed opinions about Rees's guilt.

Rees was found guilty and sentenced to death. He appealed in the Virginia courts, which sustained the conviction. The Supreme Court denied certiorari. Thereupon the United States District Court denied an application for a writ of habeas corpus and was again sustained by the Court of Appeals. The pending petition to the Supreme Court for a writ of certiorari is for a review of that last decision.

Whatever emerges from future court decisions, and whatever each observer's personal view on the effect of the publicity on Rees's Virginia trial, a theoretical question remains to be considered in the context of the argument in this chapter.

Assume that no public allusion had ever been made to Rees's handwritten account; assume that at the conclusion of the Baltimore trial the press thenceforth conducted itself with utter silence, and resumed its chronicling only after the Spotsylvania trial began seven months later, in September, 1961. Even so, every Spotsylvania juror would have known on entering the jury box one single, gigantically prejudicial piece of what by then had become inadmissible evidence: that another jury

---

[6] These figures may somewhat overstate the presumed impact, since many of the references, especially in the first tally, derived from the Maryland trial and appeared months before the Virginia hearing; others may have appeared in media with meager or minimal circulation in Spotsylvania County. But even if some of the numbers are discounted, the remainder is devastating enough.

had found Rees guilty of murdering two members of the Jackson family. What percentage of the totality of prejudicial information that fact constituted, what its relative weight was compared to the knowledge of the "death diary" and the remainder of the pretrial news about the case (including reports that Rees was wanted for eight or nine other murders) no one can know. But surely it must have been great. It could have been eliminated only if there had been no trial in Maryland or if the proceedings and verdict of that trial had been kept secret.

Yet, like the presumed prejudicial publicity that emerged in the other cases recited here, that particular piece of prejudicial, inadmissible information derived from events that no "postponement" solutions to the free press, fair trial problem—or any other solution that can be taken seriously—would have blockaded.

Potential Prejudice from Officialdom

Those concerned with keeping the stream of justice unpolluted condemn —and rightly—the stacking of the deck against a defendant by high governmental officials in the executive, legislative, and even by the judicial branches. The practice should be ended, but it is not within the realm of practical and political feasibility that it will be ended by any of the measures currently under consideration. One may doubt even if the Morse bill (pp. 139–140) were enacted that charges would be brought against the President of the United States or a chairman of a Congressional committee for commenting on a criminal case before trial.

7. On July 16, 1965, Representative Wright Patman of Texas, chairman of the House Committee on Banking and Currency, announced that its Subcommittee on Domestic Finance, which he also chaired, would shortly begin hearings "to inquire into the infiltration of banks and financial institutions by undesirable elements." The first hearing, he said, would consider the Crown Savings Bank of Newport News, Virginia. Investigation by his committee, Patman said, "has revealed that Crown Savings Bank, through its dealings with Peter D'Agostino, Andrew 'Dukie' Goldberg, Alvin D. Townsend, Robert Strauss and others, was involved in amounts of more than $2 million with loan sharks, gambling, numbers racket activities, fraudulent money order sales, worthless security sales, the passing of forged securities, embez-

zling, and possibly other criminal activities along the East Coast from New York to Georgia. . . ."

Patman continued: "In our crime investigations, we will be dealing with a new type of criminal, far removed from the mask and gun variety. The new criminal type establishes a respectable front and, by using the respectability of a bank, is able to loot that institution without firing a shot or conking someone in the head."

Many of the witnesses who were called were under indictment at the time of their appearances. Most declined to respond to questions, invoking their right under the Fifth Amendment; they were treated to a reading by committee staff of memoranda accusing them in elaborate detail of illegal acts. One of those under indictment, Townsend, was advised by Patman that his money-order enterprises performed "one of the most vicious deeds ever perpetrated on the public."

Counsel for several of the witnesses raised furious objections to the whole investigation, and particularly the public sessions. Patman's response was that if his subcommittee had to await the completion of criminal proceedings in the courts, it would have no way to remove criminal elements from the banking world. Reporters covered the hearings faithfully and the results were duly published, particularly in the areas where the Crown Savings Bank operated and where the trials were scheduled to take place.

Of the prejudicial nature of the material there can be no doubt: Besides the accounts of the alleged crimes committed, the Congressional group made extensive references to the criminal careers of most of the witnesses and a number of their associates, also facing trial.

Under various of the postponement rules, presumably, the Committee would have been in violation for prejudicing a case in the most egregious imaginable fashion and the press would be compounding the wrong if it printed news of the hearings. Even the Public Printer might be in something of a dilemma when the time came to print the transcript.

In the spirit of Senator Wayne Morse's bill, the hearing could never have taken place, at least in public, and were they not Constitutionally immune Patman and his associates could be punished for criminal contempt, because he, and each of them, is surely, in the words of the bill, "an employee of the United States." And under all of the voluntary press codes of ethics in effect or under consideration, the news executive in charge of a newspaper or television or radio station could make a choice either to leave a major Congressional hearing uncovered, or breach the principles of the code.

The solution to the problem raised here, of course, would be for Congress—and other governmental investigatory bodies—to forgo public investigation wherever the chance exists of prejudicing a prospective trial.

Insofar as trials of future defendants are potentially prejudiced by Congressional (and perhaps also state legislative) investigations, the various "solutions by postponement" are futile. Constitutionally immune from prosecution, Congress could ignore them and continue to generate prejudice as in this example; Congress could not abide by the proposals without giving up even legitimate investigations of all situations in which the law has been breached—for somewhere, somehow, some defendant could contend that what happened on Capitol Hill in the investigation damaged his case, even though his name was never mentioned. Presumably a Congressional study of labor racketeering would theoretically hurt some obscure defendant in a pending Hobbs Act case and thus might violate the terms of all of the currently proposed solutions by postponement.

We may abandon this speculation on grounds that it draws too long a bow. The practical, realistic fact is that there is nothing on the horizon to suggest that Congress is going to change its ways, and none of the proposed solutions is likely to bring about any modification of its practices for a long time to come. Here again, postponement regulations would not work in practice, no matter how good they sound in theory.

In the following two cases the element of potential prejudice against defendants deriving from pretrial comments of high officials is also present—although, in view of the Deep South locus of the crimes and their racial aspect, the thought that the comments may have helped rather than injured the accused may be just as good a hypothesis. The cases also illustrate the core problem of many of the examples that follow: preconceptions unfavorable to the accused that arise, inescapably and even before arrest, as in the Speck case (pp. 166–167), from the heinous nature of the crimes themselves, the circumstances of which we take to be publishable without any question.

8. The murder of a prominent and respected Negro, Lemuel A. Penn, a high official in the Washington, D.C., public school system, was such a case. A lieutenant colonel in the Army reserves, Penn was returning by car with two other Negro officers from a tour of active duty in the South when he was killed by a shotgun blast fired in the night from an overtaking car on a Georgia highway. The date was July 11, 1964.

On August 6, the FBI announced the arrest of four men in Athens, Georgia. They were charged by Federal officials with conspiracy to deny Penn his civil rights and were served with murder warrants by a county deputy sheriff. Later, two more men were indicted.

FBI director J. Edgar Hoover announced at the time of the arrest that the men were members of the Ku Klux Klan, and that one of them had been arrested at a Klavern headquarters, that two others had just attended a meeting there, and that the fourth was on his way. Either Hoover or a United States Commissioner—press reports are conflicting— stated that one of the four confessed and implicated the others. Georgia Governor Carl Sanders congratulated the FBI and said that "if" those arrested were responsible, he sympathized with their families "who will have to bear the burden of this nonsensical act." He added that the guilty persons should pay the highest penalty. More of the same kind of comment continued in the national press from time to time, before and after court proceedings, which took place later in the year.

Those accused who went to trial on the murder charges were acquitted. A United States district judge dismissed the Federal indictments; the Justice Department appealed directly to the United States Supreme Court. At the end of March, 1966, the Court ordered the indictments reinstated.

New trials ensued. In one, a jury declared that two of the men were guilty, but the court ordered the verdict sealed until the conclusion of the second trial, a week later. The other four defendants were found not guilty. The withholding of the first verdict is an interesting technique, and the care taken to follow that course may have been a consequence of today's intensified concern about potentially prejudicial news.

The convicted men have said that they will appeal.

9. Almost identical in terms of the prejudicial publication problems that it raises (although the arrests came hard on the heels of the crime) is the case of Viola Liuzzo, a civil rights worker from Detroit who was shot to death by nightriders on March 25, 1965, between Selma and

Montgomery, Alabama. The next afternoon, President Johnson appeared in a special nationwide television broadcast from the White House to announce that Hoover had advised him of the FBI's arrest of four Klansmen, charged with the murder. The President's speech included a vehement attack on the Klan and an avowal that no "hoodlums or bigots can defy the law and get away with it."

One of the four men, it soon appeared, was an informer for the FBI. One of the other three, Collie Leroy Wilkins, was brought to trial for murder in May; the process ended in a hung jury. He was tried again and acquitted in October by an all-white Alabama jury. A second defendant was acquitted in September, 1966. The three defendants were also tried in Montgomery on Federal charges of violating the civil rights law. They were convicted in December, 1965, and received ten-year prison terms. At this writing, appeals are pending. One defendant died a few months later (and was buried with full Klan honors), one is serving a one-year term for another offense, and the third has been sentenced to a two-year term, also on another offense.

As almost everyone remembers, the nationwide publicity about the case during the nine months it was active was enormous; comment was virulent. Details of the May trial were extensively reported and were doubtless well known to the jurors in the two trials that followed.

In these last two cases, as in most of the others, it is impossible to assess the real effect of the prejudicial publicity. It could conceivably be argued that with Southern juries, the antagonism from "outside" sources —from Federal officials and the "Yankee" press—helped rather than hurt the defendants. But the theoretical issue remains, and it is with this that we are concerned.

Could the press have suppressed or postponed the adverse remarks of FBI director Hoover, Governor Sanders, and President Johnson? Should it have withheld the identification of the defendants with the Klan? To put the question in its most impossible aspect, should the national television networks not have carried the President's statement, assuming they knew in advance—which of course they did not—what he was about to say? How could the press have avoided fully reporting the various trials, each, presumably, conditioning the minds of jurors chosen for subsequent trials in the same way as the earlier trials may have done—in theory—for the Seabee's killer, Talbot, and the musician Rees?

The question, we suggest, is not what the press should have done, but rather whether officials, from the President down, should have withheld all comment. Should the FBI have disclosed that the Penn murder suspects were arrested before, during, or after a Klan meeting, or that the identification of the Liuzzo murder defendants was made by an informer inside the Klan? Less easily answered is whether those disclosures helped or hurt the Klansmen at their trials.

And what should be the proper behavior of the press in anticipation of future court proceedings for the men who are appealing their convictions in the Penn and Liuzzo cases? The possibility cannot be dismissed that they will be granted retrials before new juries, and presumably the press should not prejudice those putative new adjudications. Therefore, until the cases are finally closed dare there be no reference that some have been acquitted by a state court and convicted by a Federal one? Would knowledge of those facts help or hurt in hearings before other Southern juries?

No concern on this score, apparently, inhibited the President of the United States. Even as he had done on the occasion of the arrest of the Liuzzo suspects, Mr. Johnson issued a statement after their Federal court conviction and after their attorney had announced that they would file appeals. The President said: "The whole nation can take heart from the fact that there are those in the South who believe in justice in racial matters and were determined not to stand for acts of violence."

However apt and moral those remarks may have been, they probably were, as a newspaper publisher observed, "a great national example of constructive contempt of court for comment on a case still in the process of adjudication."[7]

Potential Prejudice from the Facts of the Crime

The two preceding examples and the Speck case raised the question peripherally of the potentially prejudicial consequence of the description of the crime itself and the circumstances of arrest. The problem is worth examining further. Must some sort of prohibition against disclos-

[7] Raymond Spangler, "Open Court and Fair Press," *Nation*, April 11, 1966.

ing those details or otherwise preventing their publication be undertaken? Most of the currently proposed measures to solve the free press,
fair trial issue do not call for such limitations but accept the necessity of
describing the crime and telling what happened at arrest in rather full
detail (e.g., the Attorney General's instructions, the Philadelphia Bar
Association rules, the Reardon Committee's proposals, the various press
codes, discussed in Chapter 8).

10. "Trial by newspaper" could be said to have been accomplished
by the first news report in this case. It read as follows:

> MIAMI, Aug. 8 [1965]—A Coast Guard boarding party investigating
> what appeared to be a derelict coastal freighter today found three
> crewmen shot to death and four others missing.
>
> They also found one crewman alive, who told them he had been
> hiding in the chain locker since he saw the first mate and the captain
> shot.
>
> The boarding party discovered the bodies of the captain, the first
> mate and a crewman, all apparently slain yesterday. The survivor,
> Elvin Burywaise, told them he believed a fourth man had been heaved
> overboard.
>
> A 14-foot skiff was missing from the freighter, the Seven Seas. A
> search was immediately launched for the skiff, on the asumption that
> the missing men were aboard it.
>
> Burywaise said the Seven Seas was heading from Tampa to Miami
> with eight persons aboard yesterday when he saw a crewman shoot
> the first mate in his bunk.
>
> He rushed on deck to the bridge, Burywaise said, to tell the captain.
> But he found the captain shot to death. Burywaise then fled to the
> chain locker and hid. He apparently did not see the third man slain.
>
> He told the rescue party that when he hid in the locker, the skiff
> was still aboard, and when he came out, it was gone.

We suppose that even those most fastidious in their concern about
the possibility of an unfair trial would not say that this dispatch should
have been forbidden. The story is gripping, full of mystery and suspense,
with a Flying Dutchman overtone. If publication of such a story is taboo
until some statute of limitation on prejudicial publication has run, the
world, not to mention its press, will be lamentably duller. More practically, it is apparent that some such report was required to aid in
apprehension of the presumed murderer and to warn coastal sailors of
the probability that somewhere between Tampa and Miami a skiff was

afloat containing a dangerous character. Yet inherent in the story is the possibility that sooner or later a person or persons in the missing skiff will be found, against whom the suspicion of murder will rest.

The next day, when the abandoned ship was towed to port at Key West, investigators questioned the rescued seaman, Burywaise, in order to determine whether there had been mutiny on the high seas or whether it was simply a case of a sailor going berserk. But Burywaise went on to tell newsmen about one member of the crew, Roberto Ramirez, whom, Burywaise said, he saw in the dark crew quarters where the shooting occurred; he related how he had talked with Ramirez earlier in the day and heard from him how pleasant his life had been in Cuba, where he was born, had worked, and where his wife and child remained.

A day later, the skiff was found drifting off the Florida coast. In it was the Cuban sailor, Ramirez, and in his possession a revolver, knives, and silver-tipped bullets. He made a full confession of killing five men —or, more precisely, a source described as "a Federal official who declined use of his name" said he did. But had Ramirez said nary a word, and had there been no report of the weapons found with him, Ramirez would still have been, in theory, a victim of prejudicial publication, not because the jury might have read the only vaguely incriminating account of Burywaise on the second day but because it might have read the highly incriminating facts published the first day when the drifting ship was first discovered and before his name or his existence had even been mentioned.[8]

In fact, the charges of murder and piracy against Ramirez were dismissed; he waived extradition to Panama and at present writing awaits trial there.

11. In mid-July, 1965, two safes in Miami's Jordan Marsh department store were cracked open and $150,000 worth of jewelry was stolen. The

---

[8] As it happened, however—and this raises a whole new series of legal or philosophical questions—Ramirez' confession tended to be exculpatory. He asserted that the captain of the ship pulled a knife on him and threatened an attack. If we are concerned about a man facing a biased jury, what are the merits of prior publication of the defendant's side of the story, in order to offset the possible prejudice against him that arose from the description of the mere circumstances of the event? Looking toward the ultimate day of the trial, one may ask if the defendant's confession—an exculpatory statement—tends to injure him or to help him. If the latter, should its publication, pretrial, be forbidden or encouraged?

story was important in itself, and its news interest was enhanced by the fact that it followed by only three days a $100,000 jewel theft, also seemingly the work of professional safecrackers, from another Miami store.

Acting on a tip four days after the theft, police staked out the Miami Greyhound Bus Terminal, and arrested a man and a young woman after they opened a locker and withdrew an airplane flight bag. It was found to contain the bulk of the Jordan Marsh loot, some of the pieces with the department store's price tags still affixed.

The Miami *Herald* milked the story for all it was worth. It noted that the locker where the loot was stored was only six removed from the one in which had been stashed the Star of India, taken six months earlier in the tremendously sensational American Museum of Natural History theft, in New York. The paper recorded that the man who was arrested, Richard Duncan Pearson, was a friend and associate of the beach boys who committed the New York museum theft; that he was wanted for questioning by the Pennsylvania police in connection with the murder of a hoodlum friend; that he had had a long, involved, and unsavory association with known criminals in the Miami area. There were other similarly tendentious items. As for the young woman who was arrested, the newspaper disclosed that she had been a former Playboy Club bunny and that she took a swing at a photographer while she was being booked. She was described as "bosomy, in a pink pullover sweater and skin tight red toreador pants."

Reporting of that sort was hardly calculated to secure the two defendants the most objective and unopinionated jury possible in the Miami metropolitan area. But it is interesting to speculate on what kind of press treatment even under postponement rules *could* have been accorded to the event that would *not* have been almost as prejudicial to the two persons accused, in terms of its potential impact on future jurors. The key element in the story of the arrest was the fact that the flight bag Pearson and his girl pulled out of the bus terminal locker contained the Jordan Marsh loot; the two were arrested with the flight bag in their hands. Had no imputation been made of Pearson's past relationships with the beach boys who stole the gems from the American Museum of Natural History, had nothing been said about involvement in the Pennsylvania murder of a gangster, had there been no allegation of associations with Miami's crooks and jewel thieves, a future juror would still have known, before trial, the most damning possible piece of information: police said they saw Pearson withdraw the loot from the locker and had arrested him with the boodle in his hand.

Some of the reporting was gaudy embroidery, prejudicial from first to last. But if it is proper to publish the incriminatory circumstances of the arrest (as permitted by most of the current postponement proposals, including the policy proclaimed by the Attorney General of the United States), then the most matter-of-fact account would have engendered as damaging a preconception about Pearson's guilt as the report of the Big Springs killings did about Pope's (pp. 164–166).

Pearson was convicted of the Jordan Marsh theft on November 30, 1965, and sentenced to five years in prison; his companion was acquitted. At this writing, Pearson is appealing the conviction, as well as one handed down with a ten-year sentence for a part he played in connection with the ransom of the DeLong ruby, part of the American Museum of Natural History loot. (He did not raise the question of prejudicial publication at his trials.) He also faces charges for jewelry theft in Georgia. If he ever stands trial on them, the Georgia press may be confronted with a difficult problem: how to state who Pearson is in a way that is both realistic and not prejudicial.

The issue of possible creation of prejudice from the reports of the facts of the crime is further illustrated in the next three examples—in none of which, however, did its hypothetical presence seem to injure the defendant. It may be argued from them that if one of the many tributaries to the stream of justice is polluted, its effect may not be important, or that the procedures of justice ignored it. The case may never even reach a trial or a jury.

12. The issue of "prejudice from the facts" is underscored by this story which appeared in a Washington, D.C., newspaper on August 10, 1965:

> Wilbur J. Moore, 49, former star for the Washington Redskins, was shot to death yesterday afternoon in front of his home at 16425 Abbey Road, Mitchellville, Md. His 38-year-old wife, Clara, was charged with murder by Prince Georges Police.
>
> Mrs. Catherine Burke, who lives three doors away from the Moores, was working in the kitchen at the time of the shooting.
>
> "I heard a noise," she said. "Then I heard the Moores' 4-year-old son John cry. I ran outside and saw Wilbur Moore stagger onto the street and fall down.
>
> "He had blood on his neck and chest. John ran after him yelling,

'Daddy, daddy. Call a doctor. Call an ambulance.' Mrs. Moore followed John out into the street. When I ran up there I took John."

The Moores moved to a large modern home in Mitchellville last December. They were separated last April. . . .

Sgt. Packet said when he got to the Moores' house, above five minutes after the shooting, Mrs. Moore and John and Mrs. Burke were standing in the street.

He testified that Mrs. Moore told him, "That is my husband and I shot him and I'm not sorry."

He said she then led him into the house and pointed out a pistol on the kitchen counter.

Last week, Mrs. Moore called The Washington Daily News to report abuses which she said she suffered at the hands of the ex-Redskin halfback.

"I have papers from a doctor which prove that Wilbur hit me and broke my nose in three places," she said. "He also hit me and broke my ear drum. . . . Now he wants to divorce me.

"Our divorce trial was scheduled for July but was postponed. I asked him how he expected me to live and support a child for $35 a week and he said to get a job as a waitress."

Mr. Moore played with the Redskins from 1938 until 1947. He coached the backfield till 1949 and then went to George Washington University as an assistant coach. . . .

The passage about Mrs. Moore's telephone call to the newspaper a week before the slaying may have been laden with potential prejudice to her; on the other hand, it may have helped her plea—innocent by reason of insanity—in demonstrating her distraught state of mind. But quite aside from that element in the coverage, was the rest of the report damaging to her—or was it essential to the chronicling of the tragic event?

The question became academic. Mrs. Moore was acquitted on grounds of insanity and was given an indefinite commitment to a state hospital.

13. In the early morning of October 23, 1963, an Alexandria, Virginia, resident, Robert F. Powers, was found by his wife slumped in front of his television set, dead of a gunshot wound. There were no clues, no weapon, and no suspects. A week later, by a remarkable freak of weather and wind, a pistol was laid bare on the Potomac mud flats of the Alexandria waterfront; police linked it to the slaying. The weapon was traced promptly to a gun shop, where the record showed the purchaser to be a Mrs. McKelleget. But on the same day, when the owner of the shop and Mrs. McKelleget were brought together, the seller

made a definite and negative identification: Mrs. McKelleget was not the purchaser. As the police stated at the time, however, and as the press reported—and as neighbors well knew—she was a friend of Mrs. Powers.

From that moment on, the prejudice against Mrs. Powers was implicit. It could be argued that the police should never have disclosed the circumstances that gave rise to it. They made the matter worse, perhaps, when they announced, many months later, on May 5, 1964, that they knew but would not disclose the identity of the purchaser, who had presumably forged Mrs. McKelleget's name on the forms executed when the gun was bought.

But two weeks later, Mrs. Powers herself took action that reduced the degree of whatever prejudice already existed against her to a relatively small part of the whole: in her behalf, her lawyer filed suit for payment of a $13,000 insurance policy on her husband's life. It stated that the Travelers Insurance Company of Richmond had "ignored" Mrs. Powers' demand for payment. Unless the press was to ignore the suit— which, of course, it did not—the news of it was, itself, startlingly prejudicial; the implication was strong, if not precise.

After two more weeks, on July 6, Mrs. Powers was indicted for murder. Three days later, she attempted suicide and was found with a note at her side proclaiming her innocence and her fear that a jury would not believe her.

The problems of the press that this episode raises are worth thinking about. A murder, of considerable interest and concern to the people of a quiet residential neighborhood in Alexandria, has been committed; curiosity, already high, is further piqued by the discovery of the murder weapon and of its suspicious but unclarified history; the widow takes legal action that has the effect of revealing publicly that an insurance company, if no one else, entertains some suspicions about her. No indictment has issued, the police have identified no suspect, so all of this, one must suppose, is perfectly legitimate information for publication; none of the proposed protective strictures would forbid it. Then follows the indictment and thereupon the suicide attempt, both occurrences being news of a sort that the press would be remiss in failing to publish. The matter of the suicide note and its contents are more questionable: would it be admissible in Mrs. Powers' future trial, and if not, would its press publication tend to corrupt the objectivity of a future jury with the knowledge of an extra-record fact?

Or, to look at it from the opposite point of view, was the content of the note such as to create the presumption of innocence? If so, its publication might help the defendant's plea—and injure the government's case.

As it happened, the note was admitted in evidence at the trial, almost a full year later. By that time, July, 1965, the interest was intense, the courtroom was packed, and the emotional content of the case was enormous. Mrs. Powers was found not guilty.

For purposes of the present discussion, the verdict is immaterial. What the case shows is that, whatever the verdict, a copious amount of potentially prejudicial news was published, the most consequential part before the indictment and the rest just after it. Almost none of it would have been inhibited even under the strictest of the proposed prohibitions against publication currently advocated. It might be argued that after reporting the death of Powers, the press should have said nothing about anyone possibly connected with the case until an indictment was issued and should have kept silent thereafter until the trial. Yet if no one was ever charged, when would the statute of limitation on silence have run? This would have produced a Kafkaesque total secrecy, something intolerable in law enforcement. And once Mrs. Powers was indicted, should nothing she did until trial, even including the publicly discovered attempt on her own life, have been mentioned?[9]

---

[9] Although publication of nonjudicial information can injure a defendant, it is also true that withholding its publication can injure a defendant (as with Mrs. Powers' exculpatory suicide note) or a third party, equally deserving of consideration. A case involving disgusting slander of Senator Thomas H. Kuchel of California is illustrative. Its publication was of a sort that none of the proposed prohibitions would touch (although a clarification or change in California law might).

In the fall of 1964 and during a hot political campaign in California in which Kuchel's position was important (although he was not standing for re-election), Kuchel discovered that a vicious affidavit alleging he had committed homosexual acts was being covertly circulated in the state. A member of the liberal branch of the Republican Party, Kuchel was long a prime target of California's extreme right wing; as might be expected, the document was among the literature available—at least under the counter—in John Birch Society and other "pro-Blue" bookshops. The affidavit was executed on June 3, 1964, by a former Los Angeles police officer, who said he had arrested Kuchel in 1950 on seeing him commit a homosexual act, which was described explicitly.

Copies of the document and the gossip deriving from it began to spread furiously. Kuchel's problem was acute: if he ignored the slander it would proliferate; if he took legal action, the process might attract even more attention. He chose

14. On occasion, it is the legitimate reports published about the *victim* of a crime that may raise prejudice against the eventual defendant. Here are excerpts from a newspaper story of October 13, 1964, about one of Washington's most publicized recent murder cases:

> Mary Pinchot Meyer, a Georgetown artist with "a hundred thousand friends," was shot to death yesterday as she walked along the towpath of the C&O Canal. She had often walked the same path with Mrs. John F. Kennedy.
>
> Mrs. Meyer, 43, was a niece of Gifford Pinchot, twice Governor of Pennsylvania and chief of the Forest Service under President Theodore Roosevelt. Her father, Amos Pinchot, a leader in the Bull Moose Party, was the brother of Gifford Pinchot. . . .
>
> William Walton, chairman of the Fine Arts Commission, said Mrs. Meyer was "one of the most beautiful women I have ever known" and said her painting was "full of promise." He described her work as "feminine, glowing and lyrical."
>
> Mrs. Meyer was a close friend of the John F. Kennedys from the days when Mr. Kennedy, then a Senator from Massachusetts, lived near her N Street studio.
>
> Her other friends included writers, artists, Government officials and newspapermen. Bradlee [Benjamin Bradlee, Washington bureau chief

---

the latter course and demanded that Los Angeles County authorities investigate. They did, with the result that a grand jury eventually indicted a former policeman and three of his associates—another police officer, an editor of an ultra-rightwing publication, and a former public relations man for the Schick Razor Co.—for conspiring to commit criminal libel against Kuchel.

If trial followed close on indictment, perhaps no additional harm would have come to Kuchel from failure to disclose anything beyond the words of the indictment until the matter came to court. But the speculation is academic, because the full 816-page transcript of the grand jury hearings was promptly made public, as is customary in some areas of California. For Kuchel's needs, nothing less would have sufficed. For not the least perverse aspect of accusations of perversion is a public tendency to believe the worst, to circulate the charge despite denials, and to nourish its growth with sniggers and barnyard wit. Only the compelling detailed demonstration of the falsity of the charge and of its malicious invention that emerged from the grand jury testimony was powerful enough to put to rest the libel to Kuchel and the mental reservations of the doubters.

By all theoretical standards, the publication of the transcript potentially prejudiced the chances for the defendants to obtain an unbiased jury. Whether the potential would have become real we shall never know. The matter was ended four months later, in June, 1965, when the defendants finally pleaded nolo contendere to lesser charges.

of *Newsweek* magazine] described her as "a wonderful person—gay, sensitive." Her neighbors spoke of her as being beautiful and polite, a lady who moved and dressed in an elegant manner. She wore primarily blue or green clothes, they said, which seemed to alter the color of her light eyes to match them.

She also kept cats at her N Street home, where she had lived for eight years. Last night a sign remained on her door which said "Free Kittens—Ring Bell or Call." The kittens cried outside the darkened house.

The same story reported the arrest, within an hour after the crime, of one Raymond Crump, Jr., a twenty-five-year-old Negro laborer. He was charged with murder. News stories disclosed he had been recently released from a sixty-day prison term for petty larceny.

As it happened, Crump was acquitted. The jury determined that the government had not proved the charge against him beyond reasonable doubt. Reporters covering the trial and others tended to agree that the case had not been made.

Does the episode prove that a jury was able to set aside the prejudice against Crump that may have been inherent in the sympathetic report on the victim? Or that the newspaper description of Mrs. Meyer did not in fact generate prejudice against Crump?

In any event, to move from the specific to a matter of abstract principle, the case poses the question of whether the press could or should have refrained from what was, at least in its potential, a prejudicial report. There is no question that it could have. Yet in fairness to the dead woman, a tribute to her, recognizing the admiration in which she was held, was surely in order. It might have been placed elsewhere in the newspaper, presumably on the obituary page (a device not available to the electronic press media, however), but it is questionable even then how much it really would have been dissociated from the murder account in the minds of the readers—some of whom would become the jurors.

15. A final illustration is offered of a case where all of the potentially prejudicial publicity could have been avoided and presumably would have been under almost any of the current postponement formulas. What good the avoidance would have done remains, as in many of the previous examples, one of those questions that no one can answer. It is, however, about as clear a prototype as may be found of a large

number of frequently occurring news stories, involving crimes committed by a repeater, or by a person free on bond awaiting trial. Inevitably, these stories raise the issue of publication of prior criminal records.

Thomas Washington, twenty-two, a laborer, was arrested in the District of Columbia on August 9, 1965, on charges of rape and robbery. It was promptly noted by the press that he had been arrested for rape twice before in the last nine months. The charges in the first case, in November, 1964, were dismissed a week before trial when the complaining witness committed suicide. In the second case, in February, 1965, Washington was charged with the knife-point rape, along with five unidentified men, of a seventeen-year-old girl. U.S. District Court Judge George L. Hart, Jr., "reluctantly" dismissed that case on June 17 because of police failure to obtain a warrant before seizing the incriminating evidence—the girl's clothing—from an automobile Washington was driving.

The most recent arrest came about when police were notified that a woman was being dragged, screaming, into a garage. Arresting officers told how they found a trail of blood leading to the garage from the point where the woman was seized, and inside the garage, Washington himself in the process of committing the attack. The victim's hand had been cut by Washington's knife, police said.

Within a week, Washington had been charged with two more rapes, one on July 31 and one August 6. In both cases, the victims identified him on confrontation.

Washington was tried before a jury on the August 9 case in February, 1966. He admitted the act but pleaded insanity; his court-appointed counsel contended he was the victim of an irresistible impulse. Psychiatric evidence was apparently unconvincing, for the jury returned a guilty verdict. A month later in a different trial, Washington was found guilty of the rape of August 6; here, his defense was an alibi which the jury chose not to believe.

To what degree was Washington injured in his defense by the rather considerable news coverage in August? There were ten newspaper stories from the three Washington dailies, one of them containing an extensive interview with Judge Hart, in which he lamented having been obliged to free Washington the previous June and deplored what he termed "extreme technical rules" on search, seizure, and arrest that were violated by the officers in the earlier case. Hart said he had granted a defense motion to suppress the evidence against Washington seized by the police "most reluctantly and because I felt that I was compelled to because of the holding of our [U.S.] Court of Appeals."

Hart added: "Much has been said about protecting the rights of persons of deprived background who are accused of crime. It is time we consider protecting the rights of people such as Washington's latest victim, who was equally deprived." Each of Washington's alleged victims was, like him, a Negro from a slum area.

There was no further publication about Washington between mid-August and the first trial six months later, and none except a note of his conviction between then and the March trial.

The defendant's court-appointed counsel has related that he was deeply worried about the impact of the publicity the preceding summer, particularly the interview with Judge Hart, but he found no member of the panel from which the jury was selected who would admit on voir dire even to having heard of the defendant. He was nevertheless convinced, from courthouse corridor gossip and from the fact that the customary court observers and hangers-on turned out in such unusually large numbers as to pack the courtroom, that his client had earned something of a Jack-the-Ripper reputation and that the case was well-known and had been much discussed. He had considered asking a change of venue, but saw little tactical advantage to having his Negro client tried before a Virginia or even a Maryland jury (where the odds of racial prejudice might have been greater than in the District of Columbia), which would have been the only geographically feasible options.

If the defense counsel was right in his doubts of the jurors' sworn denial of preconception, this is a case where a man received one or perhaps two trials from jurors who had prior knowledge of nonadmissible information. Could it have been avoided? The answer presumably is yes. On its own initiative or under some postponement regulation, the press might have reported Washington's arrest on August 9 with no mention of the earlier indictments, and thereafter, when he was charged with committing two further rapes, have left them unreported or in reporting each at least made no mention of any other. And the press might have left Judge Hart's blast unpublished. Judge Hart might even have refrained from making it.[10]

Would such silence have caused any loss to the community? Assuredly, some. The public was entitled to know, one can agree, that the processes of the law—or, more exactly, the processes of the arresting officers—had failed in the past to remove from free circulation what looked like a dangerous citizen. Perhaps even the judge was entitled to comment publicly on what he felt were antisocial decisions by higher courts. And if the press should keep silent on inadmissible information until the trial is over, and then make whatever presentation to the community it felt was needed, the question would be: Which trial? The problem is reminiscent of that in the Rees case. When does the ban lift? Only after the last trial on the last charge outstanding is completed? With a man like Thomas Washington as defendant, that might take quite some time.[11]

---

[10] Another striking example of potential prejudice created by high officials charged with the administration of criminal justice emerges from a situation in Detroit in 1966.

Early in January, a police raid on a suspected gambling establishment in Detroit led to the seizure of what looked like payoff lists. Two men, identified with the Detroit "Mafia," were subsequently indicted on gambling charges. Their pretrial examination was held in June before a Michigan judge sitting as a one-man grand jury. The chief prosecution witness was a policeman who testified that he was paid off by the defendants and had seen his name recorded in one of the lists.

The state district attorney general asked to have all the seized lists admitted as evidence. The judge allowed only the one page on which the policeman's name appeared. A few minutes later and unknown to the judge, the prosecutor gave the lists to the press in the judge's outer chambers, permitting photo copies to be made. They contained about two hundred names, crudely coded and rather easily identifiable, of other policemen. Needless to say, the Detroit press made the most of the story.

The argument can easily be made that the press should have refused to publish the material, so clearly prejudicial to probable future defendants, that the prosecutor had handed out for the clear purpose of having published. The only thing wrong with the argument is its hollow sound.

[11] If an absolute rule existed against mention of prior charges or convictions—and it is hard to see how one that allows reasonable exceptions can be framed without vitiating the rule itself—some difficult or even ludicrous consequences could come about in the most unlikely places. To speculate in terms of situations current at this writing, how does one report a trial against James Hoffa on grounds of jury tampering without alluding to the trial where the jury was allegedly tampered with? How can one report a case of a major civil rights leader without referring to a dozen other pending charges against him—deliberately incurred to test racist laws to whose

In almost all of these cases, it is manifest that the suggested devices for postponing publication of potentially prejudicial material would not have acccomplished their purpose. In most, the method would have been ineffective; in others, its attempted application would have been unrealistic.

The cases where the proposed solutions would have been futile are principally those where the potentially prejudicial material came from publication that was unavoidable, that is:

—From previous trials, as with cases like the Seabee murder (#5), Melvin Rees (#6), former Congressman Johnson (#4), where some of the hypothetical prejudice for the future may actually lie in a dissenting opinion of the Supreme Court, and as with the alleged Penn and Liuzzo killers (#8 and #9), where, furthermore, it is by no means sure whether whatever prejudice was inherent was or will be unfavorable to the accused or just the opposite;

—From public investigations, as in the Patman hearings on the Crown Savings Bank defendants (#7), and again in the case of Johnson and the Maryland savings and loan defendants (#4);

—From potentially prejudicial comments of the highest officials—again the Crown Savings Bank (#7) and the Penn and Liuzzo cases (#8 and #9), with the same ironic question of whether what President Johnson, J. Edgar Hoover, and Governor Sanders said was potentially hurtful or helpful.

The proposed solutions would have been of no use in other cases because none of the suggestions undertakes to stop publication when the accused are fugitives, as in the Nebraska bank murders (#2), the Oregon-California abductions (#1), and the murder of the eight Chicago nurses (#3).

And as long as it is conceded that the press may report the circumstances of the crime and the arrest, the solution of postponement would have done little if anything to prevent potentially prejudicial publication in the cases of the sailor Ramirez (#10), the jewel thief Pearson (#11), the football coach's wife, Mrs. Moore (#12), and Crump (#14), the

---

overturn he has dedicated his life? If a student who has burned his draft card and has been convicted for that act goes on to commit what is charged to be another violation of the law requiring military service, and if he did it as a deliberate next step in his campaign against war, must the first crime remain unmentioned?

man accused but acquitted of killing the Washington artist. It can be argued that in all these cases, and surely also in the Rees and Seabee cases, much of the potentially prejudicial publication could have been postponed (although what could have been avoided was less prejudical than what could not have been). Yet some of the results suggested that in these, as in what must be a multitude of other similar instances, the potential prejudice was immaterial (Mrs. Moore pleaded insanity), or not influential, as with Crump and the case of Mrs. A——, discussed in Chapter 4, where the juries acquitted.

There remains the case of the Alexandria woman, Mrs. Powers (#13), where potential prejudice arose from an ancillary act of her counsel, a suit for payment of her husband's life insurance, and possibly from her suicide attempt (although it is by no means clear whether publication of her suicide note injured her or helped suggest her innocence), and where again the jury acquitted. Presumably one or another of the proposed solutions would have forbidden the Alexandria police to report the finding of the pistol,[12] but it seems certain that none would have forbidden the press from reporting the attempted suicide.

Finally, there is the case of the rapist, Washington (#15), where potentially prejudicial publication would clearly have been postponed under most of the proposed corrective measures. In this case—and in this respect it is typical of most of the troublesome situations—the information of largest potential prejudice came from the statements of law enforcement officials; indeed, the nonjudicial material seen by Washington's counsel as the most damaging item of all came from an indisputably judicial source, namely, a judge.

[12] Note, however, that the most prestigious and important of the proposals, that of the Reardon Committee, permits the authorities to make public all evidence at the time it is seized.

CHAPTER 11

WHAT PRICE

POSTPONEMENT?

The remedy of postponement of publication has been advocated in many combinations and permutations: postponement of publication of almost all information about a crime and the persons accused of it, or postponement of publication of only certain stated categories of information, such as the accused's prior criminal record, the existence of a confession, certain kinds of incriminating evidence or certain kinds of statements by witnesses, and views about probable guilt from counsel and law enforcement officers.

In many crime stories, even highly newsworthy ones, the press could—in theory—withhold some potentially prejudicial information, neglecting it forever or resurrecting it later. But should it? Dare it? And at what cost—cost to itself, in its ability to function as an essential instrument of a democracy; cost to the public, in terms of loss of needed information and needed surveillance of society's agents? There is even the cost of publishing a nonsensical product.

It is not enough to propose that the press withhold publication of information that could conceivably corrupt some future juror's detachment, to state in three or four embracive categories what the forbidden information is, and then to assume that the job is done. It is not enough to say that inasmuch as the Sixth Amendment promises an unbiased jury it is only necessary to proclaim that goal, to state one or another method that would supposedly achieve it, and then to remain indifferent to its costs and consequences.

Yet it seems to us that that is precisely what much of the advocacy of the postponement solutions amounts to. Astonishingly few discussions supporting a policy of restriction have included a consideration of its practical effects, the reduction it would bring to the flow of information and the loss in public scrutiny of the administration of justice. Instead, the easy assumption has been made that the information held back before and during trial can be published later, if there is need or desire for it. To be sure, almost all of the articles and speeches advocating postponement have included a bow to the First Amendment and an endorsement of its high purpose. But few have bothered asking to what degree that purpose would be undermined by the fundamental change in press procedure that would be the inescapable result.

Equally curious, the press organizations and spokesmen themselves have failed to point out or to analyze the effects of postponement on press and public; instead, owners and editors have tended to carry on the debate by proclaiming their devotion to the First Amendment and defending it in much the same terms that antebellum gentlemen used to defend Southern womanhood. The next step is to examine the cost of plausible theory, whether feasible in practice or not.

It was to put flesh on some of what we believed were distressingly naked bones in the anatomy of the free press, fair trial argument that we have presented so many examples to show that plausible theory is too seldom feasible practice.

Every restriction on crime news, no matter how necessary, effects some reduction of press scrutiny and public knowledge of the law enforcement process. Some of the proposed restrictions entail reductions that seem to us to be within reasonable limits; others do not. But a certain loss is inevitable in all of them.

Here also, much of the argument of those who focus solely on the goal of fair trial is based on an unspoken and generally unchallenged premise that the perfection of the process of law in theory produces perfection in its day-to-day operation, and that public monitoring is supererogatory. Were it so, society could forgo all inspection of the administration of justice, confident that once an arrest is made and a charge filed, the law will move inexorably in perfect course. Unfortunately for the ideal, due process of law is not executed by a computer in a space capsule, grinding out justice by its own internal dynamics. No matter how carefully the processes of justice are prescribed in the American democracy, and ordered to be shaped by law, they are, like all other operations of government, conducted by men. It follows, under the American system, that they must be watched over by other men.

The police and the courts are agencies of the society, and society knows no way of supervising its agents except by accompanying them as monitors on their daily tasks. It knows better than to believe that law enforcement officers, prosecutors, counsel, and judges are computers and that the law operates on its own energy; it properly refuses to send the courtroom into the untouchability—and invisibility—of outer space.

W. S. Gilbert put the matter tersely in the Lord Chancellor's song:

> The Law is the true embodiment
> Of everything that's excellent.
> It has no kind of fault or flaw,
> And I, my Lords, embody the Law.

Some of today's Lord Chancellors, like Iolanthe's, may be "highly susceptible" ones; they are also surrounded by even more highly susceptible functionaries.

In Chapter 2, we discussed the social utility to the public of the press's watchdog role in criminal affairs. We turn now to the effect of postponement proposals on the institution of the press itself. The device of delayed publication in crime coverage deeply affects the very essence of the operations of the press, and the larger the amount of postponement and the longer the period, the deeper the effect. Argument about essence is necessarily abstract, but nevertheless real; if the principles of the law are important, so also are the principles of the press.

At first glance, the solution of postponement appears entirely plausible and feasible. The only drawback that comes to mind at once, forfeiture by the press of its ability to serve up juicy details of a crime with the circulation-grabbing dew of freshness still on them, may be dismissed. Society is under no obligation to make the dissemination of information a profit-making enterprise.

Nevertheless, it is not a contradiction to insist that Liebling's Law is valid. The late press critic, A. J. Liebling, stated as a commandment that the first duty of a newspaper is to survive. It must survive not only financially but also in terms of its purpose, its basic function and *raison d'être*.

A newspaper or a news program has as its function the presentation of news. By definition, news is what is new or, to stretch the definition to its limits, what is newly discovered. A magazine, a lecture, a documentary program, an editorial column, a panel discussion, a brochure,

a book, or an encyclopedia can discuss to good purpose something that
took place a week or a year or a millennium ago. So, to be sure, can a
newspaper, as long as that kind of subject matter constitutes only a part
of its total output on any day. The main or central part must be reports
of events that just happened, or are just now known about. It is for those
reports that the public buys a newspaper or turns on the news program.
It is to meet this need, to satisfy this desire, to perform this function that
the news media exist. If there is no such need, then there is no reason
for the medium; but as long as there is need—and sixty million Americans testify to it by buying a newspaper every day—the news media
must perform it. The press must not be transformed into an institution
to do something else.

As is obviously inherent in another definition, a journalist[1] is a person
who deals with matters of the day. To him, it is a palpable incongruity
to say he should report on everything else that goes on as soon as it
happens, but to put aside, for use at some undetermined time in the
future, all crime news save the bare announcement that a crime or an
arrest occurred. It is asking the newsman, the journalist, to deny his
designation.

In a sense, it is like the Throne asking the Poet Laureate to compose
a lethargic and noncommital epithalamium on the marriage of the
Crown Prince because it is not quite certain how the marriage may turn
out—with a promise, of course, that he can crank out a real sizzler a year
or so hence if everything goes right. The enjoinder may have a worthy
social purpose, but it goes against the grain of the journeyman, bidding
him act contrary to the imperatives and goals of his craft.

To say this is not to imply that the editor or reporter rejects the cure
of postponed crime publication because it affronts his *amour propre*.
The point, rather, is that he recognizes the procedure as one that would
not merely change him, but also his medium, and thereby his service
and purpose, from something they are to something they are not.

Essentially, the postponement proposals presuppose an incongruity:
a newspaper or news program that does what a news medium is expected to do in all things but crime news. In this single category of
human events it is called upon to avoid presenting information on a

---

[1] In America, the newsman is inclined to resist the word, as being pompous or
precious, conjuring up the picture of someone entirely too couth, with cane and
yellow gloves.

current basis on the grounds that it would directly injure a specific man and disrupt the legal process. But to warrant a change as fundamental as that, the editor asks for a justification sufficiently convincing to set at rest his deep doubts.

To be sure, today's press no longer follows the formula of the Age of Enlightenment. The tidy logic of that era called for the publication of whatever anyone chose, right or wrong, good or bad, and with no hindrance. The faith in the Lockean self-righting process was that the truth would find its way against all odds, that falsity would be recognized as such, that only good would emerge from the welter of utterly free publication. This pure libertarianism has given way over the years to what is generally called the doctrine of social responsibility: the news medium is restrained in what it publishes not merely by the laws of libel, but by many other social considerations, not omitting decency and the editor's own views on what serves or injures the public welfare.[2]

There are easy problems and there are hard ones in carrying out that doctrine. It is easy to decide to withhold the name of a woman who has been raped, it is harder to know whether to mention the name of an accused rapist when there are some indications that the charge may have been made out of spite or as a means of evading parental wrath. The editor will ordinarily find no trouble in suppressing the news that a respectable citizen made a spectacle of himself at an overly liquid Chamber of Commerce dinner; he will be harder put to know how to handle the fact that the city fathers think a race riot is threatening and are moving to prevent it but that publishing the news could well fulfill the forecast.

But among the hard choices a news executive must make every week there are also a thousand pieces of noncrime news potentially harmful to one cause or another—and some causes with no less Constitutional endorsement than fair trial—the legitimate publication of which the editor, and everyone else, takes for granted. It would never occur to an editor that he should not report a professor's or a Senator's speech sharply critical of some foreign policy program of the Administration, on grounds that it conflicts with the President's Constitutional powers in foreign affairs and that his arm should not be joggled by public

---

[2] For an excellent discussion of the evolution of press principles, see Siebert, Peterson, and Schramm, *Four Theories of the Press* (Urbana: University of Illinois Press, 1956).

pressure in so serious a matter. Quite properly, the editor would think anyone insane who would urge that he wait until the President had decided the matter and then report the speech as interesting history. It would rarely occur to an editor not to publish such a speech, or some other story reflecting on conditions or opinions in this country, because some hostile foreign country could grasp the item and make political capital of it. It would be a rare—and wrong—editor who would refrain from recounting the essence of a serious local controversy on grounds that the issue would be better solved if it were handled in the absence of public agitation about it—and that he can escape the charge of shortchanging his readers if he tells them all about it after the fight is over. Vital to the operation of a democracy, as Lord Bryce noted, is the role of public opinion based on public scrutiny of government.

The question to publish or not to publish has been discussed here in some length only because it is against this tradition that the press weighs the proposal to delay publication of all possibly prejudicial news of crime until its admission at trial or after the end of legal action. Conditioned as he is by that tradition, the editor finds it hard to believe that his acts have injured or will injure defendants in general or any defendant in particular as gravely as he believes the community would be injured by his failure to print the news, including news of crime, while it is new. He suspects that his product serves the public because it provides fresh information, not because it suppresses or postpones its publication.

Postponing publication of crime news could, to be sure, abate sensationalism and breed calm in some circumstances, but there are other situations, such as an outbreak of crime that creates real or incipient panic, when the only antidote is immediate publication of all the news. That news may contain what is in theory or even in fact material prejudicial to some criminal defendant.

The example of examples is, of course, the November 22, 1963, tragedy at Dallas, and the castigation of the press for the superb work it performed in steadying a distraught nation—castigation from the President's Commission on the Assassination of President Kennedy, the American Civil Liberties Union, law professors, and bar associations—bewilders us. It appears as an amazing setting of the facts upon their heads, a dreamlike construction built for a nonexistent world. The situation is considered in some detail in Appendix C, but a few words are appropriate to the issue discussed in this chapter.

Not since Pearl Harbor day had the United States experienced such an emotional trauma as that caused by President Kennedy's murder. Half of the citizenry dropped whatever their business was on hearing the news. For four days, half of all Americans remained glued to their television sets for hours on end. There was no other focus of interest but the crime and its consequences. We can take as evidence of the force of the impact the certainty that almost every adult American will remember until he dies, as he remembers of Pearl Harbor day, where he was at the moment and the depth of his feeling.

But there was more to the matter than that. As a fine piece of research has shown,[3] there was instant fear that the act was conspiratorial, set in motion by agents of Communism, Castroites, or other left-wing segregationists or even political adventurers. Rumors of more than one assassin spread by word of mouth; wild speculation was immediate. The likelihood of dangerous action against various leftist or even rightist organizations and against Mrs. Lee Harvey Oswald and her friends cannot be lightly dismissed. Fear of an ongoing conspiracy was not irrational; the new President and his entourage entertained it in fullest measure.

Into this situation, the press poured the only reassurances possible: a clear statement of the facts, with only trifling discrepancies. It was immediate and, above all, it was thoroughly detailed. Ten months later, after voluminous investigation, the Warren Commission had nothing to add on major points to what the press reported (mostly from utterances of Dallas law enforcement officials) and nothing of significance to correct.

That the United States could tranquilly have dispensed with the detailed information the press published during the first hours and days after the assassination seems to us patently impossible. Never, for the sake of calm and reassurance, was immediate news, *and about who the assassin was and what the evidence was,* so urgently needed.

The daily press can perform its job only in the here and now, not as a retrospective commentator.

The reader expects timeliness—the element of the present, which is to say "news"—in his paper and his radio or television program, and rejects

---

[3] Bradley S. Greenberg and Edwin B. Parker, eds., *The Kennedy Assassination and the American Public* (Stanford: Stanford University Press, 1965).

disclosure in slow motion. So also, he expects completeness; he assumes that the story will tell him what there is to be told. This is not to say that he will be outraged if the report of yesterday's events in the Senate is anything less than a transcript of the *Congressional Record;* obviously, he expects selection, summarization, and economy in the chronicling. But he suspects and resents a report that seems to be failing to relate consequential and interesting facts any competent reporter would know. The old-fashioned catechism for the cub reporter, that he write the who, what, when, where, why, and how, is merely a reflection of the commandment that insofar as time and space permit, and within the limits of significance, interest, and what the reporter has been able to discover, the report must be complete; it cannot be partial or fragmentary. When the report is manifestly incomplete, and when there is no evident reason for the lapse, the reader may become irritated or cynical.[4] Human nature being what it is, he is likely to believe the worst of what he is uninformed about.

The newspaper that loses its readers' confidence in respect to crime news is likely to find their loss of faith spreading to other categories of news. A projection of that sad state of affairs may be viewed as suspect when it is conjured up by news executives whose principal concern is loss of readership. But there are more detached journalists as well who fear that eventuality, and deeply. They are entitled to the presumption of some confidence in their projections, for their ability to judge reader reaction is not only their specialty but also their means of survival. The judgment is reinforced by the fact of the lack of trust in the news media in tyrant states—those of the past in Hitler's Germany and Mussolini's Italy and those of the present behind the iron curtain and elsewhere. When news of national policy is withheld, reports of all else become suspect. That the consequence of withholding substantial news is a loss of trust in the press is not a far-fetched notion but an elementary one. And crime is substantial news.

The journalist who is not only honest in his purpose but honest in his appraisal of his product knows that even in the best of circumstances

---

[4] Even when there is a reason, as for example the unwillingness of those involved to discuss what happened, or their unavailability for comment, or the lack of time to dig into the event, the experienced reporter takes pains to note the reason, and does so precisely to forestall what would otherwise be annoyance of the reader at being served up with less than the full story.

the press does not have so abundant a treasury of reader credibility that some of it can be casually frittered away. He knows the dubiety of too large a proportion of his audience—the seemingly inevitable and perhaps quite healthy attitude of a large segment of society to mistrust what it reads and hears. He knows the prevalence of the comment: "You can't believe what you see in the newspapers." Above all, he recognizes the intrinsic elusiveness of the truth, and knows how hard it is to capture it in cold print or hot electric images, given all the talent and sensitivity and honesty in the world. The problem of maintaining credibility is hard enough, he figures; to eliminate from his daily account a set of facts of which a portion of his audience is already aware, and whose existence most of his audience has deduced, is to portray himself as running a news gathering organization that is emasculated.

The size of each "portion" may be small, but there will be several of those portions a day—multiplied by 365 every year. Each holdup, each investigation of a burglary, each alarm over an assault attracts a crowd of spectators. Exactly as a concertgoer or baseball fan reads the music review or the sports page more avidly next day if he has been to the event itself—a phenomenon every editor knows—so every neighbor who has been attracted to the scene of a crime or has heard of the affair from a bystander wishes to read about it in the paper or hear the news item over the air; if it is not forthcoming, he will wonder why.[5] People pay a dime or twist a dial for news, not for the omission of it.

The newspaper's and the news program's concern with timeliness is not a failing; it is an imperative, and the notion—implicit in the recommendations of those who espouse postponement of crime news until the legal proceedings are completed—that the press will return to report an old story is naïve.

What Sybille Bedford and Rebecca West have written about criminal trials is magnificent—as literature, history, or social comment. But their

[5] Whether it is a good reason or not, this is why most editors reject (callously, as it always seems to the grieving family) appeals to omit the news of a suicide: a certain number of people have been attracted to a spot where police and ambulance have gathered; a certain number of passersby have seen the throng and have sensed something other than a natural death; a certain number of friends and neighbors have heard the news or rumor by word of mouth; all will be curious and will want to know next day what it was all about. They will distrust the news medium if what they saw is not reported, and they will be inclined to consider it either incompetent or subject to persuasion to suppress news.

books and magazine articles are not news and were not written for immediate report. There are distinct needs for both contemporaneous and retrospective reporting, but they dare not be confused. For the news media, the powerful dynamic of today's event commands the track, pushing last week's happening aside. It is a rare story, about crime or anything else, that can be put on ice and heated up in the newspaper at some later date. Accordingly, the idea that the news medium that has refrained from telling pertinent details before a trial will tell all the "postponed" data later can be entertained only by someone who has never taken the trouble to inquire how news media work and what their basic drives and imperatives are or what readers want. And to concede that timeliness may be an essential, but declare that it is a foolish one, is to conclude that it is foolish for bears to hibernate. It may be, but it is in the nature of bears to do so.

A requirement to delay publication of certain important information in a criminal case will be in effect a rule that results, in most cases, in not publishing the information at all. First paragraphs such as the following, we suggest, are not going to see the light of day:

> John Doe, 25, who was found guilty yesterday of robbing the Elm St. Hardware Store of $38 last summer and received a suspended sentence, has twice before been charged with burglary and was out on bail on a third charge at the time of the holdup. . . .

> Joe Jones, whose conviction for violating the gaming laws was upheld yesterday by the State Supreme Court after two years of litigation, was the principal figure of the notorious 1959 "Joe Jones bribery scandal" involving Lt. Gov. Jim. . . .

> Richard Roe, convicted yesterday of selling narcotics, was arrested nine months ago for the offense only because an alert police officer got wind of his activities from an addict the officer was befriending. . . .

The reason why such stories will not be printed is that the press will have better things to do, fresher news to report, and an audience that would reject fallen soufflés. So what? one may ask; is anyone the poorer for not seeing the stories? The answer is that out of a multitude of such stories the community learns the anatomy of crime and of justice, the state of its law enforcement, and of society's carrying-on. It will not obtain that knowledge without those stories—and those stories will not be published except when they are fresh.

A final point: No news medium operating under a news-postponement system is going to publish a story such as this:

> William Williams, acquitted yesterday of last year's slaying of a Japanese farm worker, has twice before served prison terms for aggravated assault on Japanese farm laborers in the Eastern Valley truck farm area. He was organizer and president of the Americans Only Farm Employers Association which a state legislative committee branded as "despicable" after hearings in the Fall of 1962.
>
> In the most recent case, the pistol with which the victim was shot was not admitted into evidence because police who took it from Williams were acting upon an improperly issued warrant.
>
> During the trial, but not in the presence of the jury, the presiding judge ruled that evidence was inadmissible that Williams' 15-year-old daughter was pummeled in a school melee with Japanese-American students on the day before the murder.

The reason why no such story would ever appear is obvious. After a jury has declared a defendant innocent, no news executive in his right mind will publish an inference that he was really guilty, for he will be inviting a close to indefensible libel suit. We can assume that the judge ruled impeccably in the hypothetical example above. But should or should not the public, as distinct from the jury, ever learn the non-admissible facts?

To expect the news medium to carry out the watching brief on the administration of justice that the community assigns it, but to report what it finds out on some system radically different in time schedule from the one that serves as its holy writ on all other matters, is to expect the impossible. "Maintain your vigil at the gatehouse of justice, cock a piercing eye at the police, guard the right of each misfortune in the sheriff's hands, worry over the moves of the prosecutor, watch every step even in the court, the mansion of justice—and tell us about anything wrong or troublesome in a month or a year or two years, when the whole process is ended"—that is a mandate for failure.

Some sensible restraint and some reasonable postponement in publishing material harmful to a defendant in a current case is possible and sensible. But all-embracing commands, being both impossible and ridiculous, may destroy what chances there are for reasonable programs.

CHAPTER 12

THE PEN AND THE LENS

The Special Problems of Television

As a sword for public enlightenment, television is rusting in its scabbard, Edward R. Murrow once said. The average fare on television today does little to challenge that judgment. The medium has inclined toward frivolity in its fiction; the good presentations tend to fall by the wayside of commerce, stricken by a kind of special Gresham's Law of the airwaves. And in the area of crime and trial news reporting, television's failure is highlighted; all the complaints made against the press in general are aimed at television with particular vigor, and its youth and its vagaries have put it in a specially vulnerable public position. The men of the television medium have been charged with all the sins imputed to their brethren of the print press in pretrial coverage of crime news; but as for trial coverage, they alone have been sentenced to banishment from the courts.

There are two separate free press, fair trial problems raised by television: one is the general effect of its pretrial reporting of news of crime and judicial procedure; the other is its reporting of trials themselves.

In its general pretrial reporting, television is treated the same as and acts no differently, for the most part, from the rest of the press. In some circumstances its audience is larger[1] and its impact and pervasiveness may create greater and different problems. In its far-reaching coverage of crime and trial news, television's sins against taste have been frequent and—what is our present concern—the potential prejudice it can create

[1] While there are 60 million newspaper buyers in the United States (there are more readers), about 130 million people watch 72 million television sets every day. A recent survey showed that over half of the American public received most of its news from television.

against a defendant's later fair trial equals or exceeds that of the newspapers.

A distressing set of examples of offensive television coverage of crime news was reported in the *New York Law Journal* of January 27, 1964. In one case television cameras filmed a suspect just arrested for homicide in Brooklyn. When he dropped his head and tried to conceal his face, a police officer grabbed him by the hair and jerked his head back so that his features were exposed to the cameras. In another case, an elderly former New York official whose leg had recently been amputated was being moved out of a grand jury room on a stretcher after he had testified in a highly publicized and controversial matter. "In a rush by reporters, photographers and television men to interview Mr. Epstein, one of the news media representatives actually fell across Mr. Epstein on his stretcher," it was reported. In another incident, several high school boys being booked at a police station for the murder of an elderly woman were questioned oppressively by television reporters. Reporters chivvied the boys until they incriminated each other; the reporters dragged out of them, through leading questions, many assertions that would undoubtedly be disputed later at trial. The scene was hectic, obnoxious, and in potential seriously prejudicial. It is incidents like these that provide part of the substance of the indictment of television.

Another grisly example of television at its most repulsive, noted in Chapter 10, was provided in Baltimore after the Rees case. The night before Rees was to be sentenced for murder and kidnaping, WBAL-TV presented a taped show on which nine of his twelve jurors appeared as a panel at the studio and re-enacted their deliberations. The spectacle was described by Jack Gould, television critic of the *New York Times*, as "chilling in the extreme." The station oozed virtue by declaring that it was registering a first in public service, an "exciting and lasting tribute to the American jury system"; and one newspaper (owned, as was the television station, by the Hearst Corporation) said the program was "a reportorial breakthrough of the traditional silence of the jury room." It was not, to most observers, a best foot forward for television. As Gould commented:

> The champions of electronic journalism may regard it as terribly old-fashioned but the discussion of whether a man is to live or die may not strike everyone as just another Goodson and Todman package.

The legal rights of a defendant, let alone the dignity of court procedure, are not things to be broken through just to titillate the curiosity of the idle TV mob.

But the larger significance of the WBAL-TV episode is the comfort it will afford to those who would hobble the legitimate news aspirations of the TV medium. If a station is so insensitive to the need for coupling initiative with reasonable restraint, one can hardly blame those who contend TV may turn serious proceedings into a three-ring circus. At least it would seem desirable to draw the line at having jurors weighing death sentences double as TV artists.

The indictment of television does not end with the problem of tastelessness. Its pervasiveness also may create special difficulties in securing an impartial trial jury. On occasions, its ability to picture an event in progress can make the task close to impossible, as when the viewing audience is presented the drama of a crime being committed before its very eyes. For example, banks are now equipped with secret cameras which may be triggered to record a robbery. The resulting film can be turned over to law enforcement authorities and become evidence. But before it does, it may be available for the evening news broadcasts.

The entire nation was treated to such a perverse crime show when Jack Ruby shot Lee Harvey Oswald. Some forty-two million people were watching their television sets at the precise moment that cameras in the Dallas Police Station were televising the act that fateful Sunday morning after the assassination. Repeat broadcasts brought the incident to the eyes of 90 per cent of the adult population of the nation within a few hours. There is something otherworldly and eerie and, until our era, utterly unthinkable about sitting in one's living room and watching a man commit a crime. Its potential effect on the subsequent empaneling of an impartial jury is impossible to know; but it appears to be the extreme in potential pretrial prejudicial publication.

Despite these and other ghastly instances, most television coverage of crime is not outlandish.[2] As one spokesman said, the unfortunate thing for television newsmen is that their sins are committed more openly than those of anyone else—on the 6:30 news for everyone to see

[2] The National Association of Radio and Television Broadcasters has a television code enjoining misleading or alarming drama, exposition of sex crimes, appearances or dramatization of people in crime news except to aid law enforcement, and the avoidance of sensationalism, bad taste, and panic. The affirmative duty to inform about public events is also stated.

and cringe over.[3] What is needed may be better crime reporting, not necessarily less of it.

The problem with television crime coverage is not principally in this area. Its sins here are parallel to those of the print press. To the extent television coverage may prejudice a future trial, it does so (with some offbeat exceptions) in precisely the same way as newspapers are accused of doing. Whether television's pervasiveness and its increased vividness and greater impact convert a difference from one of degree to one of kind is an exercise in metaphysics; the point is that the problem before trial is the same with newspapers and television.

Where television's influence on fair trial seems to be different—where the difference is said to be one of kind and not just one of degree—is during the trial process, in the courtroom itself. For the most part, television is barred from the courtroom; this curb raises deep and difficult issues special to the medium in the free press, fair trial dispute.[4]

"Photographing or broadcasting of trials," Justice William O. Douglas has said, "imperils the fair trial of which we boast. It is not dangerous because it is new. It is dangerous because of the insidious influences which it puts to work in the administration of justice."[5] Whether the charge is true or not, and whether the problems are caused by newness or by something else, one fact is unmistakably clear: traditionally there *has* existed in the minds of most members of the bar and in practice in the courts a marked distinction between the pen and the lens. While

[3] William Monroe, speech to National Civil Liberties Clearing House, Washington, D.C., March 20, 1964.

[4] In one phase of the general complaint against television, its failure to report important events (like judicial proceedings), the television industry is not all to blame. It is unfair to damn television for what it does not do while telling it all the while that it may not do it at all in the area of trial reporting by the one method that is its unique specialty: filming and recording the event as it takes place. On the one hand, the Federal Communications Commission and the public insist, properly, that television broadcasters provide programs of information on current affairs. But, on the other hand, television has been denied permission to bring its equipment into committee rooms of the House of Representatives and into courtrooms. There is then an apparent contradiction among governmental bodies; what one demands (with the public) another makes impossible.

[5] "The Public Trial and the Free Press," 46 *American Bar Association Journal* 840 (1960).

no one has seriously questioned the right of newsmen to be in court, to write in court, to draw pictures in court—in fact, special places are provided to guarantee and facilitate this nonjudicial courtroom activity—the photographing or broadcasting of proceedings is taboo. Whatever the reason, and whether there really *is* a difference, and however debatable the logic, the distinction surely is made.

Media spokesmen argue that the distinction ignores the evolution of the electronic press in America and favors one medium of communication over another. "The old assumption that a newspaper reporter was in effect the representative of the unseen multitude no longer can be narrowly applied; the camera now enables the public to see for itself in full attainment of the democratic principle of an open court," Jack Gould has written in the *New York Times*.

The history of television and broadcasting in courts is clear and consistent.[6] Canon 35 was first adopted in 1937 by the House of Delegates of the American Bar Association. It called for dignity and decorum in the conduct of court proceedings; it prohibited photographs in courtrooms during sessions of the court or recesses between sessions and the broadcasting of court proceedings on grounds that they would detract from the dignity of the proceedings, degrade the court, and create misconceptions about the trial system. Canon 35 arose out of the work of a special committee of press and radio created in the wake of the crude coverage of the Hauptmann case (the news media withdrew and did not join in the recommendation). Radio broadcasting of court proceedings was disapproved by the American Bar Association's professional ethics and grievance committee in 1941. In 1952, another special committee on television broadcasting issued a report recommending that Canon 35 be amended to include a ban on televising court proceedings. In 1954, a special bar-media committee on free press, fair trial met with representatives of the communications media. The committee concluded, again to the dismay of the industry, that television would impose undue policing duties on the trial judge and have an injurious psychological impact on the participants, consequently affecting the trial adversely. Thereafter there were American Bar Association com-

---

[6] See 11 *University of Florida Law Review* 87 (1958) for an extensive résumé. An appendix to Supreme Court Justice John Marshall Harlan's decision in the Estes case (see below) also includes a history of the rules governing television in courts.

mittee investigations into television in 1955 and 1962; eventually, in 1963, Canon 35 was amended to include within its prohibitions televising of court proceedings.

The Canon now reads:

> The taking of photographs in the courtroom during sessions of the court or recess between sessions, and the broadcasting or televising of court proceedings are calculated to detract from the essential dignity of the proceedings, distract the witness in giving his testimony, degrade the court, and create misconceptions with respect thereto in the mind of the public and should not be permitted.

This conclusion is now adopted in Rule 53 of the Federal Rules of Criminal Procedure:

> The taking of photographs in the courtroom during the progress of judicial proceedings or radio broadcasting of judicial proceedings from the courtroom shall not be permitted by the Court.

This rule has been reaffirmed by the United States Judicial Conference and applies in all Federal courts in the United States. Moreover, all the states except Colorado and Texas have similar rules. According to one survey of state laws,[7] though most states have adopted Canon 35 by law or custom, some minor qualifications do exist. Some states allow photographing ceremonial proceedings such as naturalizations or where professional legal educational purposes or public service would be accomplished (law class viewing of certain trial proceedings and Law Day observances are permitted). Massachusetts, North Dakota, Oregon, Virginia, and Wisconsin give judges some discretion to allow television in courts. In Washington, press and bar committees are experimenting with taping certain court proceedings. But for the most part Canon 35 prevails.

In the many articles, speeches, and debates about television in the courts, certain standard objections have been raised by advocates of the status quo on public information about criminal trials.[8] It is said

---

[7] Harold R. Medina, *Radio, Television, and the Administration of Justice* (New York: Columbia University Press, 1966).

[8] For examples, see American Bar Association, Report by Special Committee on Proposed Revision of Canon 35 to the House of Delegates (adopted 1963); 40 ABAJ 838; 40 ABAJ 217; 42 ABAJ 341, 834, 838, 843; 46 ABAJ 1295; 47 ABAJ 761; 48 ABAJ 429, 615; 49 ABAJ 59; 50 ABAJ 1037.

that the mere presence of television equipment distracts participants and disrupts trials; that television in court spoils the judicial atmosphere at trials and would lead to commercialization and the vulgarization of the trial system in the public's mind; it is feared that only the odd and sensational cases would ever be telecast, that the privacy of jurors, witnesses, and defendants would be violated; it is speculated that television might impede justice by scaring off sources of the truth. The argument holds that juries should be free from public pressures and reactions that the medium would cause, and that although trials are not for public diversion, television wants to use them as ready-made pieces of entertainment.

In response, supporters of televised trials have pointed to the educational potential of television, the strong strictures of the First Amendment, and the strictly subjective nature of the opposing claims. Television, they assert, could be today's Forum. They ascribe a watchdog role for television in the administration of the courts: the answer to *in camera* proceedings is on camera proceedings. Furthermore, television advocates contend, publicity discourages false testimony and instead stimulates the production of evidence; it ensures good conduct from officials, eliminates public fear of the judicial process based on unfamiliarity, and advertises the impartiality of the judicial system. It is pointed out that photography and broadcasting are exact reproductive techniques and therefore less distortive than writing alone; that a hidden, quiet camera would be less distracting than a frantically scribbling newspaperman whose reactions openly punctuate the evidence as it develops; and that television is a modern branch of the press entitled to the Constitutional dignities of its brethren. It is pointed out that recent technology has so refined the medium that old arguments about obstruction are obsolete.[9] As a matter of fact, some observers feel that filming and taping trials would be a far better method of official recording than is being used now.

At the root of these strong, emotional, and contentious policy arguments

---

[9] *Life* magazine had the famous photographer, Eisenstadt, photograph an American Bar Association meeting and no one knew it was being done. NBC-TV televised a District of Columbia Bar Association meeting while the free press, fair trial issue was being debated and some were arguing that television coverage inevitably disrupts and degrades. No one present realized that the whole proceeding was televised. The experiment is often duplicated at press-bar gatherings.

lies—along with the competing, vital doctrines of Constitutional law about the institutions of the press and the courts—the historical guarantee of a *public* trial. The broad question of what constitutes a public trial must be considered first before television's role can be debated.

Historically, at common law the right to a public trial was developed to make sure that powerful officials would not be able to take advantage of individuals.[10] A public trial was thought to be a better way of getting at the truth than secret proceedings. The United States Constitution embodied this value judgment and ordered that in all criminal prosecutions the accused shall have a "public trial by an impartial jury."

But while everyone is against Star Chamber, the concept of a public trial raises some hard questions. How to ensure both a *public* and an *impartial* trial in circumstances where the reality of one may impinge upon the other? Whose right is it to insist on a public trial; how public need a public trial be?

Whether the Sixth Amendment's guarantee of a public trial creates a right for the defendant alone or whether it belongs to the public and the press as well still stirs lively debate. However, the consensus of historians is that the right to a public trial belongs to the defendant and that the rights of the press derive from the First Amendment and from its derivative rights to be present at a trial as part of the public.[11]

New media like television raise the question how public a public trial has to be and whether the defendant may waive the right to a public trial if he feels open proceedings will work to his disadvantage. May he choose a private trial and bind the press and public to his decision? The answers to these questions remain undecided. Indeed, modern changes in the nature of the American press have created a paradox. As Professor Harry Kalven has said, "The defendant is entitled to a public trial, but the rule would appear to be: not too public a trial, and that is a very delicate question to decide."

In any event, for present purposes, the following is clear: Trials must be public and the press will be allowed in the courtroom as part of the

---

[10] Max Radin, "The Right to a Public Trial," 6 *Temple Law Quarterly* 381 (1932); Sir Matthew Hale, *History of the Common Law of England,* Chapter 12 (Remington's edition, 1820), p. 343.

[11] See *Jelke v. New York,* 308 N.Y. 85 (1954); but see James Russell Wiggins, *Freedom or Secrecy* (New York: Oxford University Press, 1964), p. 38.

public. Reporters from all media will be accepted providing their tools are the same: notebook and pencil. The question, then, centers on the different tool, the camera. Should it be barred, and if so, why?

The distillate of almost two decades of argument on this precise question poured forth in 1965 in the opinions of the United States Supreme Court in the Estes case. It provides as complete a tour of this legal horizon as has been made to date.

The television issue was provoked by a nationally known defendant who had been convicted of a series of crimes resulting from a gigantic nationwide business fraud. The scene of the trial was Texas, one of the two states where televising trials is permitted. The American Bar Association and the American Civil Liberties Union filed amicus briefs with the Supreme Court urging the condemnation of televised trials; the television industry filed in its own defense.

On June 7, 1965, the Court handed down its decision in *Billie Sol Estes v. State of Texas,*[12] a decision which for the present poses a large barrier to television's access to courtrooms and which, in fact, came within one vote of barring all television from all courts on Constitutional grounds. The Court held that in this case notorious pretrial publicity, disruptive use of television at a pretrial court hearing, and partial televising of the trial itself, all over the defendant's persistent objections, combined to deprive Estes of his Constitutional right to a fair trial.

The case divided the Court curiously and variously. There were, in all, five opinions; and the associations of the Justices are interesting. The majority opinion was written by Justice Tom Clark, who was joined by Chief Justice Earl Warren and Justices William O. Douglas, John Harlan, and Arthur Goldberg. However, in an opinion of his own, Justice Harlan limited and separated his opinion from that of the other four in the majority. And the Chief Justice also wrote a separate concurring opinion in which he was joined by Justices Douglas and Goldberg, expanding upon the decision of the majority and reflecting the three men's strong antitelevision attitudes. The dissent was written by Justice Potter Stewart and was joined by Justices Hugo Black, Byron White, and William Brennan. Additionally, Justice Brennan wrote a brief opinion of his

[12] 381 U.S. 532.

own, stating simply what he thought the intricate separate opinions meant, and observing that the Court's actual majority holding was "not a blanket constitutional prohibition" against televised state trials.

Billie Sol Estes' financial maneuverings and the collapse of his business house of credit cards had captured the nation's attention and held it for many months. Eventually Estes was tried in Federal and state courts for a number of criminal violations arising out of his business deals. The particular case from which this decision emerged was a Texas trial in 1962 for swindling.

The massive pretrial national publicity—press clippings filled eleven volumes—had forced a change of venue from Reeves County to Smith County, five hundred miles to the west. Even so, all seats in the courtroom were filled. More than thirty people stood in the aisles.

The initial pretrial hearing, in which defense motions for a continuance and to prevent telecasting, broadcasting, and news photography were heard, was carried on in a small courthouse and was broadcast and televised live by both radio and television. Twelve cameramen were engaged in the courtroom. Cables and wires snaked across its floor. Microphones were on the judge's bench and others were beamed at the jury box and counsel table.

When the trial began, thirty days later, the coverage was very much less disruptive. A booth had been constructed at the back of the courtroom and was painted to blend in with the room. A small hole allowed the camera lens an unrestricted view of the courtroom, but all photographers were confined to the booth. Gone were the cables and special lighting. Live telecasting was in fact prohibited during the greater portion of the trial. The opening arguments, the closing arguments of the state, and the return of the jury's verdict and its receipt by the trial judge were all carried live with sound. Upon request, the judge prohibited all television coverage of the defense summation.

Video tape recordings of the trial were telecast extensively in the regular news programs in the area. Commentators discussed various parts of the testimony; otherwise the reports were unexceptional. One video tape of the earlier pretrial hearing was rebroadcast later.

The Constitutional consequences of that scene and the effect of those events upon the fairness of the trial were what the Supreme Court was called upon to consider.

Justice Clark's majority opinion began with a consideration of the concept of a "public trial." The purpose of this Constitutional requirement, he said, was "to guarantee that the accused would be fairly dealt with and not unjustly condemned." Turning to a discussion of the First Amendment, Clark held that its protections do not extend a right to the television medium to enter the courtroom. Nor, he asserted, can television say that it has been discriminated against. "The news reporter is not permitted to bring his typewriter or printing press."[13]

Confining his opinion to the particular facts of this case, Justice Clark noted that "we will have another case" should advances in the art of television bring changes ameliorating the hazards to a fair trial present in the Estes case. But the majority of the Court found those circumstances inherently suspect. It condemned television for compounding unknown but potentially prejudicial effects of trial publicity arising from coverage by any of the press media. The Court felt itself forced to draw lines between the media.

Clark listed the likely or potential impact of television on jurors, on witnesses, on the trial judge, and on the defendant himself: The jury's attentiveness at trial would be affected by the obstructions of television equipment, and the distraction resulting from knowing that televising was being done. The quality of testimony in criminal trials would become frightened, cocky, given to overstatement and forgetfulness, and in general would tend to lack the testimonial accuracy that should typify the search for truth. The trial judge's undivided attention would be diverted if he had to supervise the telecast; he also would have undesirable reactions to the psychological impact of the presence of television.

Turning from the general to the specific, Justice Clark pointed out that even in the Estes case, the trial judge was harassed by the presence of television, though he consistently voiced a strong commitment to the compatibility of television with trials and a firm belief in his ability to control it. Initially, Clark recounted, the judge had decided to permit the telecasting of the trial. Then he decided that a booth should be built to confine the operations. Then he decided to limit coverage to parts of

---

[13] At least half of this traditional analogy is inexact. Television's equivalent to a printing press is the transmitter and the panels of electronic gear plus a huge broadcasting tower. Courts would object to typewriters, which are noisy, but it is less certain whether they would forbid a newsman's use of a silent stenotype machine, which, of course, is the tool of many official court reporters and, along with pencil and pad, the equivalent of the hidden, silent television cameras.

the trial that could be televised live. Then he decided to film the witnesses without sound—for their protection. And finally he decided that the defense counsel's closing argument would not be televised over his objections. Said Clark: "Plagued by his original error—recurring each day of the trial—his day to day orders made the trial more confusing to the jurors, the participants and the viewers. Indeed it resulted in a public presentation of only the state's side of the case."

That there would be political as well as administrative distractions to trial judges if television were allowed in courtrooms was another point in the majority's general complaint.[14]

Not to be ignored, the Clark opinion pointed out, is the question whether television subjects the defendant to mental if not physical harassment of a third-degree nature. Without finding that this was the case in Estes, the majority opinion pointed out the ordeal of a defendant where every gesture, comment, and aspect was magnified onto a television screen.

The opinion discussed the fear raised constantly by critics of televised trials that the courtroom will be changed from the quiet, deliberate, confined crucible that it has traditionally been and converted into a kind of colossal cauldron in which typical propagandized, totalitarian trials come to a public boil. "A defendant on trial for a specific crime is entitled to his day in court, not in a stadium, or a city or nationwide arena. The heightened public clamor resulting from radio and television coverage will inevitably result in prejudice. Trial by television is, therefore, foreign to our system."

The essential feature of the trial process, the majority opinion went

[14] The Supreme Court's opinion that the trial judge should not have the discretion to allow television and thereby possibly to endanger fair trials echoes the arguments made elsewhere that judges must be spared the pressures the press would put them to if this discretion ever existed, and that only a uniform policy can save judges criticism, even political blackouts, from the medium. Where judges are elected, television's demands may become political weapons, which it is felt the legal profession can better withstand than could a single judge. Recall the Sheppard case where both the judge and the prosecutor were up for election and benefited from the notoriety of the case and the encouragement of the newspapers. The American Bar Association Report by its Special Committee on Proposed Revision of Canon 35, adopted by the House of Delegates February 5, 1963, tells (at p. 7) of other instances where judges who denied television access to a trial were blackballed by the medium and given no fair exposure in other community activities, to their detriment in subsequent elections.

on, is incompatible with television. Admitting that our empirical knowledge about the possible prejudicial impact of television in a courtroom is limited and that specific prejudice had not been shown to have resulted from television, the Clark opinion said that nonetheless the conditions caused by the presence of television created a more than hypothetical problem. "Truth . . . is the *sine qua non* of a fair trial," Clark said, and "the use of television . . . cannot be said to contribute materially to this objective."

An isolated case of actual prejudice to a particular defendant is not the sole criterion for determining the propriety of television, Justice Clark reasoned. Rather, the style of the proceeding itself may be so inherently or implicitly prejudicial as to warrant condemnation. In the majority's words: ". . . at times a procedure employed by the State involves such a probability that prejudice will result that it is deemed inherently lacking in due process."

The Court feared that television would present the public with only the more aberrational or notorious cases and thus discriminate against particular defendants. This general mistrust of television and its mysterious powers over courts and defendants was evident in Justice Clark's concluding remark: "The television camera is a powerful weapon. Intentionally or inadvertently it can destroy an accused and his case in the eyes of the public. While our telecasters are honorable men, they too are human."

Justice Harlan's concurring opinion, making a five-vote majority, confined its conclusion to the special facts of the Estes case and thus kept the Court's ban of television from reaching complete Constitutional proportions.

Justice Harlan shared the common fear about television's potential for disruption. But, taking a more conservative view of the Court's role, he contended that television must be judged as it is found and not as it could be imagined. Whatever might be television's mischievous potentialities, he declared, forbidding this innovation would violate the Constitutionally required separation of state and Federal governments—"one of the valued attributes of our federalism"—by not allowing individual states to pursue "a novel course of procedural experimentation."

Moving to the question of the rights of the press, Justice Harlan said that since the right to a public trial belongs to the accused, it is not a First Amendment right. The requirement of a public trial is satisfied if the court is open to those who wish to come. Actual presence of the public is not guaranteed, nor is there a concomitant press right to transmit the proceedings. The right to publicize what goes on belongs to the press as a part of the general public, but it does not include the right to bring in the mechanical facilities necessary for immediate publication. And though the press may of course be present to report what it has seen in the courthouse, as to its use of equipment, "the line is drawn at the courthouse door. . . . Within the courthouse the only relevant Constitutional consideration is that the accused be accorded a fair trial."

Harlan said that "the probable impact of courtroom television on the fairness of a trial may vary according to the particular kind of case involved"—that is, the question of the propriety may be answered differently in different cases. In the Estes case he agreed with the majority of the Court.

Although the legal establishment has long pronounced the verdict that television in the courtroom is bad per se, less than half of the Justices in the Estes case were willing to say the Constitution goes that far. Justice Harlan had restricted the majority opinion. But three of the Justices were ready to seize the opportunity offered by the Estes case and put the issue to rest finally as a matter of Constitutional law.

Chief Justice Warren's concurring opinion (of note in part because of the interesting combination of Justices Warren, Douglas, and Goldberg, joined by the American Civil Liberties Union and many other liberals, taking the strong American Bar Association–endorsed fair trial point of view) included a long account of the possible horrors of televised trials. Warren, long noted for his strong feelings about maintaining the traditional quiet and detachment of the courtroom, seized upon this case as, in his words, "the appropriate time to make a definitive appraisal of television in the courtroom." The record of the Estes case provided for him "a vivid illustration of the inherent prejudice of televised criminal trials," thus furnishing an appropriate opportunity to deal fully and finally with the problem.

The Chief Justice said that the purpose of the trial court is to assure calmness and solemnity according to legal procedures; certain practices can negate the fundamental concept of a trial even though the formalities of the trial process are followed.

The Chief Justice did not ignore the argument that the law must be adaptable and versatile enough to meet the changes of modern times.

Indeed, he insisted that "this court must be able to apply its principles to situations that may not have been foreseen at the time those principles were adopted." Nonetheless, he felt (and here his opinion moved beyond that of the majority decision), television in courts in and of itself violates the Sixth Amendment (if in Federal courts) and the Fourteenth Amendment (if in state courts). His conclusion rested on three grounds: (1) television diverts the trial process and has an inevitable impact on its participants; (2) it creates the wrong public impression about trials, detracting from the dignity of the court and lessening the reliability of the trial; and (3) certain defendants, whose trials are most newsworthy, will be singled out and subjected to special, prejudicial conditions.

As did Justice Clark, Chief Justice Warren dwelt on the physical problems likely to be caused by television in the courtroom—the noise, the distraction, and the temptations to dramatize. But the major thrust of his argument aimed at a different, less tangible concern: the effects upon the public or the community (as distinct from the immediate impact upon the trial participants) of the very presence of the medium.

Warren's opinion bespoke a concern over the commerciality of television, a nagging worry that it will tend to convert the trial process into a vehicle for entertainment. Warren noted that a rerun of the pretrial hearings in the Estes case was used by one station in place of the "Tonight Show" and by another as a substitute for the late movie. He pointed out that "commercials for soft drinks, soups, eye drops, and seat covers were inserted when there was a pause in the proceedings," and that "television commentators gave the viewing audience a homey, flattering sketch about the trial judge."

The Chief Justice was uncertain whether television was mature enough to be trusted with something so important as the description of the trial process. He referred to the quiz program scandals and the natural inclination (for commercial reasons or simply as a result of unprofessional irresponsibility) to heighten the dramatic appeal of a program. "Can we be sure that the public would not inherently distrust our system of justice because of its intimate association with a commercial enterprise?" he asked. "The sense of fairness, dignity and integrity that all associate with the courtroom would become lost with its commercialization," he swiftly answered. Televised trials, the Chief Justice argued, would not only affect those involved in the trial process but those who observe the trial process.

The purpose of a trial is not to entertain or even to educate the public, valuable as those goals might be, Chief Justice Warren declared. He implied that whatever its educational potential, a trial could easily be perverted into a propaganda vehicle, as has happened with publicized Soviet trials (where the concern is with giving the public object lessons more than with determination of the guilt of the individual on trial).[15]

The Chief Justice was also concerned that the television medium's selection of coverage could create a perverse image of the trial process in the public's mind. "The alleged perpetrator of the sensational murder, the fallen idol, or some other person who . . . has attracted the public interest would find his trial turned into a vehicle for television," he wrote. The opinion prophesied: "This court would no longer be able to point to the dignity and calmness of the courtroom as a protection from outside influences."

The Chief Justice conceded that as an institution the television industry is a great invention, with a proper role of defining and describing the activities of American society—but, he admonished, "that area does not extend into an American courtroom."

The principal dissent brought together an unusual combination of Justices Stewart, Black, White, and Brennan. Their opinion, written by Justice Stewart, was that television in the courtroom is at present so new an instrument that it would be extremely unwise to formulate a Constitutional doctrine about its general role at this time; nor were they able to find any prejudice in the Estes case. While recognizing that television invites many Constitutional risks, and detracts from the inherent dignity of a courtroom, Justice Stewart was "unable to escalate this personal view into a per se Constitutional rule." It is important to understand, he said, that "we deal here with matters subject to continuous and unforeseeable change—the techniques of public communication," in an area where, he noted, "all the variables may be modified tomorrow."

In answer to the fear of the majority that the public image of the trial process would be damaged by televising trials, Justice Stewart reminded

[15] The Chief Justice referred to a description of the Russian trial of Francis Gary Powers before two thousand spectators, the television cameras, and representatives of different countries, citing the conclusion of one scholar of Soviet law that the Russian legal system "uses the trial and indeed the very safeguards of justice themselves as instruments of the social and political objectives of the state."

the Court that "the Constitution does not make us arbiters of the image that a televised state criminal trial projects to the public." And to the argument that television is prejudicial per se, he responded: "If what occurred did not deprive petitioner of his constitutional right to a fair trial, then the fact that the public could view the proceedings on television has no constitutional significance."

The dissenters noted that there was no possibility in the Estes case for the jurors to hear from television evidence they did not receive at the trial, because they were sequestered in hotel rooms without television.

Nor did the dissenters feel there was need to fear any pervasive impact caused by continued television. Justice Stewart wrote: "We do not deal here with mob domination of a courtroom, with a kangaroo trial, with a prejudiced judge or a jury inflamed with bias." The only fear to be considered, he said, was whether television invited into the courtroom serious Constitutional hazards. No prejudice was proved, he insisted.

Turning to the First Amendment, Stewart said, "The idea of imposing upon any medium of communications the burden of justifying its presence is contrary to where I had always thought the presumption must lie in the area of First Amendment freedoms."

Joining in the dissent, Justice Brennan emphasized in his own one-page additional opinion that the majority opinion did *not* find television a Constitutional pariah; rather, that five judges merely decided that under the facts of this case (the grounds with which Justice Harlan agreed with the other four who made up the majority) there was an improper trial. In Justice Brennan's words, the decision in the Estes case "is not a blanket constitutional prohibition against televising of state criminal trials."

The antitelevision opinions in the Estes case, parading as they do current horrors and future fears, portray the Supreme Court in more of a professorial than a judicial role. The discussion was more of theory and potential—particularly in the Warren-Douglas-Goldberg concurring opinion—than of proven and inevitable faults. Justice Harlan as well as the dissenters confined themselves to determining specific problems in specific cases—agreeing in that principle but not about the particulars of the Estes case. In a sense, the close division in the Court was between those who saw possible dangers and those who focused on what were declared to be evident flaws. The dissenters dealt with the latter question, finding no particular prejudice in that case nor any duty to set an over-all antitelevision policy. As with many issues about which the last word remains to be said, the Estes case raises more questions than it answers. Among them:

Who should decide whether and under what conditions television should be admitted to the courtroom—judges or legislators?

If the advantages of televised trials are eclipsed by the disadvantages —if the hope for good is outweighed by the fear of the bad—then should not the prohibition come, if at all, from legislative or local administrative decisions?[16]

Does this difficult question of policy lend itself to determination on Constitutional grounds?

Was the Court really making a pragmatic decision concerning public information about trials, attempting to control the press generally in the only place where it might be possible to do so, in the courtroom?

Or was the Court merely acting out of its impatience with television? "Television," one of its spokesmen has admitted, "is a big, brash, nouveau riche medium that has irritated a lot of people who look on it as vulgar."[17]

Whatever the motive, the Court in the Estes case came perilously close to elevating an unknown into a Constitutional doctrine.

Much of the reasoning in the Clark and Warren opinions is puzzling. The contention that television's mechanical equipment will distract participants and encumber the courtroom is close to anachronistic. To provide for the unobtrusive presence of television cameras in the courtroom requires, it is clear from the Estes trial itself, nothing more than a booth or a partition at the back of the room. Once installed, the camera's potential for physically distracting judge, jurors, witnesses, and defendants could well be measurably less than that of the reporters in full

[16] Curiously, in the Estes case, the Warren group appeared to be reaching for the chance to decide the case on the broadest Constitutional ground, whereas the usual tendency of the Court is to avoid broad Constitutional rulings if there is a more limited basis for decision.

[17] William Monroe, Villanova Law School Symposium, April 16, 1966.

view at the press table, bustling or bored, impressed or scornful, and visibly reacting to the evidence as it develops.

To assert that television will discomfit the participants in some psychological way because of its newness and unfamiliarity is to argue in a circle. If television is forever banned it will be forever unfamiliar. When the print press first began to report trials, its presence also must have been unfamiliar and disconcerting. Acceptance and usage have removed whatever initial disruptive effect and nervous self-consciousness the new conditions brought about.

Most of the objections of the Court's majority to television seem based on fear of its power to injure either directly a single defendant in a specific trial or indirectly the institution of the court itself, degrading or transforming the whole process of the administration of justice. Yet all the objections dwell on the potential of the new medium without attempting to make any specific distinction between television's capability and what would appear to be the same kind of potential of the printed media. Each evil ability imputed to television is possessed by newspapers—and many, unfortunately, have been exercised by them. Why then, if the argument is in terms of potential, should the one instrument be admitted to the courtroom and the other barred?

There is only one sentence in the opinions specifically asserting a distinction. Justice Clark noted that the dangers of televising trials "are far more serious" than those of reports in print, but he offered no proof and made no argument.

The Clark and Warren opinions declared that televising a trial would inhibit testimony, since witnesses would be disconcerted, knowing that their remarks were being broadcast. But does not any person act under the same restraint when he knows his remarks are being taken down for any sort of publication?

There is, of course, an even more sweeping response to this line of the Court's argument. Bentham, Blackstone, Wigmore, and many others have pointed to the value of a public trial as a means of "clearing up the truth." Testifying openly, witnesses are discouraged from false testimony, and additional information may be stimulated from the public as it follows the developments. If the argument is valid, and there are many dramatic demonstrations of it, then the camera can serve the desired purposes as well as, or better than, the pen.

Television, the objections continue, will discriminate against that defendant whose trial is chosen for broadcasting. But if selection is tantamount to discrimination, then newspapers commit the same sin every day in the week, choosing to report the tribulations of one defendant, day after day, and printing no word about a hundred others.

The Court felt that television would tend to cover only the most sensational cases, and to broadcast only their most sensational episodes, thus distorting the case against the defendant and doing him an injustice. For "sensational" read "newsworthy"—the translation is reasonably exact—and the procedure is precisely that of the newspapers and magazines. They cover trials that are the most interesting, and select for reporting what they deem the most interesting testimony. They have no escape from this selectivity unless they are to report each trial and print its full transcript.

If the Court meant by this line of argument, however, that the television industry is less responsible and more wicked than the newspaper industry, then should not television reporters, as well as cameras, be barred from the courtroom? For the television commentator, reciting the news, also is free to distort a trial or to report it faithfully.

If this reasoning also means—and the conclusion is hard to avoid—that the Court is concerned about the quality of reporting, then logic should call for a discrimination to be made within a single medium, or even among the various reporters of one publication. Should no representatives from a scandal sheet be allowed to cover a case and only those of the *Christian Science Monitor* be given admittance? Are "good" reporters to be welcomed and "bad" ones to be forbidden?

The Court's worry over the possible "commercialization" of trials by television is also applicable to newspapers, which, after all, are enterprises as commercial as broadcasting companies. If "commercials" intersperse the telecasting of a trial, it is also true that advertisements for the same products flank the columns of the newspaper report of it. And, as in the preceding complaint, television's commercials are the same when an announcer reports the day's events on the screen as when they are shown on video tape. No doubt the difference, if there is one, is that in the one case the commercial is associated with the report of the event and in the other with the event itself.

Televising trials, the Supreme Court feared, will tempt a vain or exhibitionistic judge or lawyer to posture and strut, or a self-seeking counsel to play to the grandstand. But those same people can do the same things to win the same results by having their words and actions chronicled in the newspapers and news magazines or recounted by news commentators over the radio and television. As for its effect on the jurors considering the case, there should be no difference: the jurors saw the performance in the courtroom in any event.

The argument about ham acting, incidentally, is hoary with age, and arose, as might be expected, at the dawn of the Republic. The Senate voted against opening its doors to the press and public on February 25, 1791. Senator William Maclay of Pennsylvania entered his views in favor of open sessions in his diary:

> The objections against it, viz., that the members would make speeches for the gallery and for the public papers, would be the fault of the members. If they waged war in words and oral combats, if they pitted themselves like cocks, or played the gladiator, for the amusement of the idle and curious, the fault was theirs; that, let who would fill the chairs of the Senate, I hoped discretion would mark their deportment; that they would rise to impart knowledge and listen to obtain information; that, while this line of conduct marked their debates, it was totally immaterial whether thousands attended, or there was not a single spectator.[18]

The same considerations apply to the contention that televised trials will be put to narrow political uses by judges or prosecutors indulging in theatrics for the sake of promotion or re-election. The possibility has long since been converted to reality by the print press. One need only look at the Sheppard trial (Chapter 1) for an example of office seekers performing in such a way that the newspapers would serve their political ends. Here again, logic would require banning all of the press.

Televising trials will lead to propaganda trials, the majority Justices feared. Much was made in their opinions of how processes that should serve only the singleminded search for justice can be and have been perverted to become Roman holidays and propaganda spectacles. Chief Justice Warren referred to a situation in Nebraska where a trial was removed from a courtroom to a local Keith's theater to accommodate spectators clamoring to be admitted. The participants in the trial sat on

---

[18] As quoted by James Russell Wiggins in *Freedom or Secrecy* (New York: Oxford University Press, 1964), p. 21.

the stage and curious spectators sat in the pit. At one point of adjourn-
ment the bailiff was quoted as announcing from the stage: "The regular
show will be tomorrow, matinee in the afternoon and another performance at 8:30. The court is now adjourned until 7:30."[19]

But there were propaganda trials long before the instrument of television was invented; there still are in nations where it has never been
instituted, and there still can be in the United States even when television is rigorously excluded from trials. The printed page has both
the power and the pliability to be pressed into serving a government's
political objectives. South Africa's treason trial, the early Russian show
trials, even Eichmann's in Jerusalem (for effect on a nontelevision audience outside Israel) are examples.

The point need be labored no further. It may simply be noted that
one can take almost every specific complaint against television's effect,
either on a single trial or on the whole fabric of the judicial process, and
substitute the word "newspaper" for "television," "article" for "broadcast," etc. He will discover that whatever the validity of the accusation or the fear, it applies as a matter of logic as much to the one
medium as the other.

To yield to these fears is, in a sense, to admit an unbecoming doubt
about the integrity of the judicial process itself and about those who
administer justice. It is to suggest that temptation must be withheld
from judges and prosecutors and counsel lest they succumb. It is even
to declare that the processes may not be shown for what they are.

Should the presumption be that judges are such weaklings and so
tenuously committed to their responsibilities that with television present
they would change, Jekyll and Hyde fashion, into knaves and fools? Or
is the fear that television would make too clear who the knaves and

---

[19] Critics of television in court have pointed to such mockeries of justice as the
special prosecutions by the Castro regime before eighteen thousand people in the
Havana stadium. Justice Douglas (in 46 *American Bar Association Journal* 843) has
referred to another such situation in Baghdad in January, 1960. The Iraqi government turned a trial of seventy defendants into a mob circus by televising the performance. "The court was the people's court, the charge was a plot to assassinate
Premier Karin el Kassem. The accused were herded handcuffed into a pen ablaze
with kleig lights. A hand-picked studio audience jammed the room. The trial began
at 7:00 P.M. to accommodate the television audience. The judge and the prosecutor
vied for star billing while the studio audience, true to the cues, shouted and applauded."

fools are? Surely the dignity and integrity of trials depends on the participants, and not on television's portrayal of them. The performance of some attorneys at some trials is obnoxious, even without cameras; cameras would merely show it for what it is. On the other hand, during the Army-McCarthy hearings, Joseph Welch was dignified amid an unruly Congressional investigation; television showed that episode too for what it was. It is hardly an argument against the medium to assert that television may show a performance, good or bad, more vividly to more people.

If the foregoing argument is valid, must one conclude that the Clark and Warren opinions are illogical or inconsistent in seeking to bar one medium from the court but tolerating another possessed of the same kind of capability to wreak havoc? Does their argument collapse on the showing that they proved no differences between the kinds of danger that television and the print press threaten?

What the Justices must have seen was, if not a difference of kind, such profound differences in degree as to have become a difference in kind—in the likelihood of television's inflicting damage, in its greater power to do harm, and in its terrible proclivity for overwhelming and dominating the events it covers. The Justices in the Estes case who opposed televising trials seem to have been concerned about something hard to demonstrate but easy to sense: a widely felt feeling that written reporting already has a large potential to injure fair trial and that televising the proceedings would push the danger over the line.

The feeling surely comes in part from an attitude about television deriving from notorious episodes in its history, its scandals (more publicized than those of the newspapers, where a self-protective mechanism may be in operation), and the common image of its manners and its objectives.

Television came into being largely as an entertainment medium and has mostly remained so despite its significant news and educational accomplishments. As a result, there is a fear that it will transform whatever it touches into a theatrical diversion, that its objectives, regardless of the subject matter with which it may deal, will remain always to hawk more goods of the sponsors and advertisers, that it will sacrifice principle to money, and will abandon taste, fidelity, and integrity to win audience ratings.

Thus, although the Clark and Warren opinions never state it explicitly, there is an undercurrent of conviction that although the newspapers and news magazines are capable of it, television is more likely to sensationalize trials, to pick out for reporting the sordid and juicy ones, to load the account of them with offensive commercials, to disregard balance in the episodes it presents, to publicize them in frenzied voice, to be gauche, to misrepresent the trial's search for justice, and to warp it instead into the only mold it is supposed to know, the soap opera.

How fair is such a projection of television's behavior if it is permitted to broadcast trials?

The fear is real, and we share it. Yet we also feel that to let that fear become the decisive factor is to be oblivious to the potential for brilliant and honest reporting that television has demonstrated and to disregard the possibility of its progress toward maturity. It is also to reject a basic principle of criminal law—that an accused should be judged on the act for which he is charged, not on the basis of a previous record (much less on a subjective reading of his past behavior).

The conclusion of Justice Harlan, that television behaved badly in Estes' preliminary hearing and trial, seems a more reasonable one than that it is congenitally doomed to misbehave forever.

The second, and even more pronounced, undertone of the opinions hostile to television is that its potential for harm is vastly more powerful because of its greater impact on its audience, thanks to its ability to reproduce before one's eyes and ears the exact sight and sound of everything that transpires. It is a recognition of the truth of that most ancient cliché about a picture being worth ten thousand words. People believe that the act they see performed must be the truth; traditionally, they give less credence to someone else's report of it.

Television's prowess, particularly in its impact on the emotions, is undeniable, and trials have enormous emotional content. Trials are dramatic incidents; television is a medium for drama. The fear is that it will exploit the drama and diminish the deliberative atmosphere of a trial.

Finally, there is a concern—if not in the opinions themselves, then clearly behind the antitelevision arguments by members of the bar— that television is sovereign, that it swallows whatever it touches, transforming the purpose of whatever event it depicts to serve the different aims of television itself. That concern is not frivolously based, as anyone can testify who can compare the experience of being interviewed by a newspaper reporter with that of being the subject of a full-scale television interrogation. And anyone watching the telecast of a national political convention can be forgiven for wondering whether the purpose of the affair was to nominate a candidate or to produce a television spectacular.

Although there is no trace of it in the Estes opinions, there is still another objection which that portion of the bar that opposes television in the courts is charged with entertaining; it thus deserves to be discussed along with the other complaints. It is that the legal profession fears not only the blows television might strike against its dignity but also those against its mystery. Members of the bar and bench have twitted their colleagues with the accusation. Thus, Professor Fred Rodell of the Yale Law School has complained of how lawyers huddle within an abracadabra, hocus-pocus mysticism of exalted procedures and jargon of the past, less attached to modern needs and reasons than baffling and befuddling to the general public and assuring the myths and mazes that are necessary to the well-being of the lawyers alone. Much of this, he argues, is an empty, self-serving legal game that balks at innovation. The blackball of television conceivably may be a part of that same defensive motive.[20] The late Judge Jerome Frank also ridiculed as a superficial professional indulgence the ceremonial solemnity of the courtroom and the trial process—the architecture, the uniforms, even some of the procedures.[21]

That some of the antagonism to televising the courts arises from this self-protective attitude is attested to by the adamant refusal to permit the telecasting of even those proceedings where prejudice could not arise. For example, none of the stock complaints about the evil of televising trials can apply to televising appellate courts—except for the argument that some of the pomp and mystery of the courtroom might be lost.

Suppose, for example, that decisions of the Supreme Court were to be televised as an initial experiment. The Supreme Court has been referred to as a continuous Constitutional convention interpreting for

[20] "TV or No TV in Court," *New York Times Magazine,* April 12, 1964; and *Woe Unto You, Lawyers* (New York: Reynal & Hitchcock, 1939).

[21] *Courts on Trial* (Princeton: Princeton University Press, 1950).

each generation the most fundamental and vital principles of our nation. Would it not be, in the words of Judge J. Skelly Wright, a "matchless lesson in the meaning of our constitutional rights and principles for the people of the country to hear the decisions themselves?" The Supreme Court Justices announce their opinions periodically, some reading their opinions verbatim but most paraphrasing what they have written and generally explaining to the public that is present the issues of the case and their disposition. With a minimal change of existing procedures the public exposure to the Court could be greatly expanded. That this could be a tremendously edifying device is beyond question. As a matter of fact, it could do much to allay some of the criticisms of the Court that are based on misinterpretation of its actions. Not the least of its contributions would be to enable thousands of lawyers and the public to hear the opinions as they were rendered.

The law has always chosen to operate with its own rules and its own procedures, and television would, of course, familiarize the general public with what has been an awing situation—some of the awe coming from ignorance and not inhering in the specialty of the proceeding itself. As one writer has aptly said: "Familiarity may breed contempt, but lack of communication can breed suspicion, and one can be as destructive as the other to freedom and orderly government."[22]

How valid are the objections of the Clark and Warren opinions and the traditional ones of the bar? We suggest that preserving the mystery of the law—if that in fact is one of the objections—deserves little weight. We have also argued that determinations based only on likelihood or tendency are not built on solid or even fair foundations. And we have said that arguments about many of the specific dangers that are envisioned are full of logical incongruities.

Nevertheless, as we noted, there is an intuitive feeling, widely shared and not lightly to be dismissed, that television has a potential for mischief greater than that of the printed word because of the force of visual portrayal and the enveloping way it operates on an event.

Maintenance of the dignity and posture of the court is a legitimate concern. The court must be "a quiet place." Its singleminded purpose,

---

[22] Fred R. Travis, in speech to Vanderbilt Law School, "Free Press and Fair Trial: Viewpoint of News Media," April 16, 1965.

to find the truth and administer justice, dares not be diminished, much less changed. For the legal profession and for us all to worry about television on this score is to do no less than is proper.

But is this worry, this sense of possible danger, enough to warrant incursions on an institution protected by the First Amendment? Is it enough on which to base a far-reaching legal discrimination?

We confess to our own uncertainty about this central question.

But we believe that before it is finally answered more consideration should be given to the argument that television also has as great a potential to enhance the public view of the administration of justice as to degrade it. Television could report trials fairly and exactly and with solemnity, just as it has presented other events without any loss of decorum—the British coronation, royal weddings, the Kennedy and Churchill funerals, state visits, medical and scientific accomplishments, serious legislative debates, and the sessions of the United Nations.

Certain events are basically dignified, and all communications media can preserve their special quality. If a trial is dignified, there is no intrinsic reason why television cannot report it with dignity. If there is value to a public trial, there is no reason why as large a public as possible cannot see it, provided their numbers do not swamp the courtroom and convert the process into pandemonium. But a televised trial does not make that transformation; it is not comparable to a trial in the Roman Colosseum. The crowds may watch in a barroom, but they are not clamoring or shouting in the courtroom. Television brings the trial to the public, not the public to the trial. The organized bar has the right and duty to control proceedings in court, but once conduct there conforms to legal requirement, the bar's special interest ends. Where the news of trials is disseminated and discussed is a matter beyond the power of the courts and legal profession to control. Indeed, if they have faith in the legal process, they should wish that its performance be observed as widely as possible.

Because of the ban on television in courts, we have little evidence to argue what its effect either on trials or on the public's impression of the trial process will be. Without more courtroom experience, we can only speculate. But such little evidence as exists is by no means discouraging.

That a televised trial can be fair and decorous is demonstrated by the Graham case in Colorado (where Canon 35 is not followed). As a television executive reported:

Graham was tried in Colorado for placing a bomb on an airplane, killing 44 persons, to collect his mother's insurance. The proceedings were filmed from a booth in the back of the courtroom and excerpts on film and on audio tape were used in evening newscasts.

When the trial was over, the presiding judge, the jury foreman, the attorneys on both sides and the defendant's wife said that, to their knowledge, the broadcast coverage had not distracted anyone and had not interfered with the fairness of the trial. Veteran court reporters did not detect any awareness by witnesses of the broadcast operation. And the jury foreman's comment was, "Frankly, I had forgotten it was there."

Colorado Chief Justice Frank H. Hall, talking about the Graham trial, said the television coverage had provided a true picture of it.[23]

Another example of successful use of television in a criminal trial was reported by Abner McCall, a former law school dean. In 1955 in Waco, Texas, a murder trial was televised and a survey of witnesses and participants was made afterward. The results indicated that television caused no interference.[24]

These examples suggest that television need not be an all-engorging monster, and that it is not beyond the ability of a wise and firm judge to make it conform to the proper requirements of the courtroom.

We feel that states or local communities should be allowed to experiment with a new reporting technique like television. Without some experience we have little except personal preferences and hunches to guide our decisions about the effect of television in courts. During any experimental period, irreparable harm can be avoided by reversing decisions in cases where prejudice is shown. But without trying it—without experimenting—we will never know the existence, the extent, the inevitability, even the nature of television's prejudicial effect on fair trials or on the institution of the court itself. Those states and cities that choose to ought to be able to try televising trials—subject to being monitored by appellate courts alert to possible abuses—thus demonstrating either television's limitations or its promise.

A blanket bar at the present time would be premature. Television executives interested in opening new vistas of socially significant programing through televised trials ought to enjoy the cooperation of the

[23] William Monroe, Villanova Law School Symposium, April 16, 1966.
[24] "Courtroom Television," 19 *Texas Bar Journal*, 73, 106 (1965).

courts and the organized bar in developing techniques that are suited to trials and that avoid the pitfalls feared by the critics. Unfortunately, some of the few examples of televised trials in the past are poor advocates for television's cause. But the legal profession, too, owes an obligation to see whether traditional fears about the medium are well-founded. While the bar's distrust of television for what it might do to trial participants is real and must be considered, what the administration of justice will be shown to be or how it will be portrayed are not things to be feared in a free and open democratic society.

Television, it must be remembered, is part of the press. And we agree with Justice Stewart's remark in the Estes case that the First Amendment gives the presumption of access to the press. Any inroads upon freedom of the press should come, if at all, only after proof of clear and imminent specific dangers—to be demonstrated by those calling for press restrictions. This is a burden not to be switched in the negative to the press itself.

We conclude:

1. The physical intrusions of television in courts must be ended before access can be allowed. But that poses no problem.

2. The interferences with participants to the trial thought to be caused by television are exaggerated. They are those posed, in theory and in fact, by the print press. They would be likely to fade with experience, and they could be kept under control by the court.

3. That the image of the law inevitably would be vulgarized and commercialized we see as a super-conservative bugbear. If the basic nature of the judicial process were proved to be endangered by television, we would change our minds. But this has yet to be demonstrated, and it does not seem likely.

4. Public trials require access to the press. And the value of public information about trials, law, and life is too clear and important to be whittled away casually or peremptorily. If television is to be relegated to a Constitutional role different from the rest of the press, this decision should come only after sound reasons for such a second-class citizenship are demonstrated.

5. Those states that want to should be allowed to experiment for themselves and for the edification of all of us. Other states that now prohibit television in the courtroom should be encouraged to relax their total ban and begin experimentation.

CHAPTER 13

OUR CONCLUSIONS

In the law, as elsewhere, the easy problems are solved; only the hard ones remain. The free press, fair trial problem is one of the hardest. It has invited simplistic solutions, but it is not likely to be solved by them. Its special nature makes its resolution refractory; as Justice Hugo Black once wrote, "Free press and fair trial are two of the most cherished policies in our civilization, and it would be a trying task to choose between them." We do not want a press that is free, more or less, just as we should not tolerate trials that are almost fair. And, to complicate the issue, it is evident that a free press is one of society's principal guarantors of fair trials, while fair trials provide a major assurance of the press's freedom. The paradox is that neither value can be absolute, yet we cannot accept the diminution of either one.

The conflict is the more perplexing because it is between two civil liberties. Where the issue is a dispute between, let us say, property rights and civil rights, a freedom-conscious decision-maker sees more clearly where the preference lies and where the balance must fall. What confounds our problem is, in G. K. Chesterton's phrase, its competition not between right and wrong but between right and right.

Contrary to agreeable and buoyantly American folklore, there is no guarantee in either logic or metaphysics that merely because a problem exists there must also exist a perfect solution. There are only better or worse ones, or solutions by default.

Because the press and the law are different institutions—each serving society but in different ways and by different means, differently premised and with different natures, motivations, and functions—it may be that the free press, fair trial dilemma will remain without a complete solution for a long time, perhaps as long as the law and the press and human nature endure. Yet their goals are not so far apart as to prevent improvement in a situation that needs improving.

In the search for that improvement, however, the danger of the best becoming the enemy of the good must be avoided. A perfect solution—neat, automatic, invariably effective—is beyond attainment in a real and imperfect world. The drive toward perfection tempts the seeker into the perilous course of changing basic institutions, unaware that what he is doing is in fact undercutting principles and practices that lie at the heart of America's democratic system. It proposes growing the perfect rose by destroying the garden. The Reardon Committee found that the problem of prejudicial publicity "is of limited proportions." The techniques of solution must be limited as well.

Prejudice created by the press has a dangerous impact almost exclusively in the extraordinary crime, the *cause célèbre*, the sensational case. By all the evidence we can gather, that is also the rare case. It may appear otherwise, which is not surprising, for by its nature the sensational case is the remembered one, the notorious one, the one that is seen and talked of. It creates the impression that Garibaldi sought when he dressed such few troops as he had in red shirts to make them seem more numerous than they were.

Public impressions to the contrary, press-engendered prejudice is either not operative, or at worst is readily neutralized or neutralizable in most criminal cases. These include not only the great majority that escape almost all press mention, but even those that are given rather extensive coverage but not enough to convert them into either intense or long-lived sensations. The prejudice that is theoretically possible from press coverage does not seem to become real, as is demonstrated by the remarkable absence of any large number of appeals mounted on grounds of prejudice.

The sensational case remains as ninety-nine per cent of the free press, fair trial problem. Nevertheless—and we underscore what we have said before—however small in numbers, these cases may not be dismissed as insignificant. The problem raised here must be met. But we urge that it be done in the philosophy of accommodation rather than absolutism. In theory, prohibiting all potentially prejudicial news might be an airtight solution, just as in theory procedures advocated by Senator Joseph R. McCarthy might have guaranteed that the Federal service would be purged of any employee about whom there was the faintest taint of disloyalty. But in practice what looks like an airtight solution is less certain.

And its price is too high. Most of its cost, furthermore, would be levied against the administration of justice itself. As it now operates, with all its faults, the press serves the cause of justice far more than it subverts it. For it is the agent of public scrutiny.

To shackle the press is to curtail the public watch over the administration of criminal justice. To use Professor Kamisar's fine metaphor, the press serves at the gatehouse of justice. Additionally, it serves in the manorhouse itself and all along the complicated route to it from the police station and the streets to the purlieus of the prosecutor's office, to the courtroom corridors where the pressures mount and the deals are made.

There is an assumption, rarely subjected to examination, that if only the press would go away, fair trials would be automatic. The thought is that justice flies out the window when the reporter comes in the door. The truth, of course, is that there are many other serious and difficult obstacles to fair trial.

In saying this, we do not mean to try to exculpate the press by denouncing the law and the courts in fishwife recrimination. We mean only to say that for the sake of balance it is necessary to remember that if the press behaved precisely as its severest critics wished, the much worse roots of unfair trial would still remain: coerced confessions and other outrageous police procedure, absence of competent counsel, racial prejudice, clogged calendars, various economic discriminations, shabby conduct by attorneys in court, archaic attitudes about psychiatric testimony, political pressure, community prejudice, and plain and simple corruption.

This is not to argue that the problem of prejudicial publicity may be ignored. It is, rather, to underline the fact that in the very exercise of the function that provokes the fair trial problem, the press is at the same time serving as the community's most effective instrument for detecting and exposing those other, more serious enemies of fair trial.

Indeed, among the sins of the press, those of its omission—in not sufficiently covering the processes of justice—are more serious and melancholy than those of its commission. Judge J. Skelly Wright has properly complained of press failure to examine the underlying causes of crime and the results of the courts' judgments and sentences.[1]

"All too often," he declared, "the news media limit themselves to re-

---

[1] *American Bar Association Journal*, December, 1964.

porting the crime, the capture and the punishment. This is not enough; it misses the essentials. . . . The very workings of the system are distorted. . . .

"The mass media must remember that the trial and appeal are occasions for judicial supervision of a whole set of police practices and that this supervision is devoted to protecting the rights of all of us. The narrow-sighted newspaperman may see only the defendant, but the courts are obligated by their oaths to inspect also the conduct of the prosecutor, the police and the others involved, to the extent that their actions have influenced the trial itself."

But laws and regulations that would make news coverage perilous would gravely reduce the potential of the press to monitor the step-by-step march of each defendant along the road to justice. It is unrealistic to expect the press to be the vigilant watchdog while at the same time it is being threatened with punishment for publishing something which may seem to it central to an exposure of justice going awry but which may appear to the court as willful disclosure of some item on the list of taboos.

The point may be illustrated by a consideration of pretrial confessions, something at the top of almost every press critic's roster of items that should never be published before trial. Frequently the press publishes a report that a defendant has made a confession; it would be fatuous to assert that the press always does so to serve a lofty objective. But, whatever the intent, publication may nevertheless serve that objective. For the real social problem is not the publication but the coercion of confessions.

If a confession is truly voluntary, it will be admitted at trial, and the damage that the press may bring about by prior publication will be inflicted against principle but not practicality. If, however, the confession is coerced and is *not* admitted at trial, then pretrial news of the confession may hurt the defendant's chances of getting an impartial jury. But it also constitutes a highly necessary and perhaps the only notice to the public of police misfeasance. There has been harm to the defendant, perhaps avoidable. But which was the greater harm to him, the coercion of a confession, or the publication that a confession was made? Consider the matter in the negative: if the press consistently avoids mention of indications that the defendant has made a confession while in the hands of the police, what is to prevent police coercion from continuing forever? Or is the answer merely that police coercion of confessions does no damage provided no news of either the coercion or the resultant confession ever escapes to the public?

The press is damned, to take another major complaint, for mention of a defendant's prior criminal record. But here too is it not being condemned for an evil that lies at another's door? The real problem for the defendant here is a bad rule of evidence, about whose unreasonableness Dean Erwin N. Griswold has spoken in a remarkably candid way:

> The man with a prior criminal record in this country is far more at the mercy of the authorities—police and judicial—than seems to me to be warranted. And if he is arrested and put on trial, he has two almost hopeless alternatives in many states. He can take the stand and deny his participation in the crime now charged. If he does this, his prior conviction can often be shown to impeach his testimony, in which case he is very likely to be convicted. Or he can refuse to take the stand, resting on his constitutional privilege, in which case he is also very likely to be convicted. Ought we not, even with persons who have once offended against society, undertake to develop procedures which will seek as far as possible to bring out the truth about the crime now charged, not some prior crime?[2]

Yet when the press publishes the prior criminal record of a defendant in a sensational case—as it invariably does—it receives universal condemnation from its critics in the legal profession. Maybe it deserves it, but the criticism may be suspected of being disingenuous; sophisticated members of the bar know quite well that prior records do play a significant role in trials, injuring defendants in the very real sense that Dean Griswold described. To reverse the usual phrase, here is a situation where bad law makes hard cases. Certainly if the bar really succeeded in eliminating the impact of prior records once the trial begins, the press would be subject to criticism if it published them before trial; but without mutuality, the case for restraint is weak.

A third important criticism of the press is its reporting of comments of lawyers and public agents about pending criminal cases—the major source of crime news.

[2] From an address to the American Bar Association convention, August, 1964.

If the processes of justice are for the press to monitor, they are for the legal profession to administer. With respect to information about crime, it is unreasonable and perverse to command an institution whose function is to gather and report news to withhold, under threat of punishment, prejudicial material that officers of the law were so foolish or irresponsible as to have uttered. The renowned legal scholar Thomas Reed Powell has been quoted[3] as saying that if one can talk about a major premise that clearly relates to another premise without referring to it, one has a legal mind. It is that kind of legal mind that would order the press not to publish what the police chief freely disclosed to reporters in the headquarters press room.

The remedy for all but a small portion of the whole free press, fair trial problem is surely reasonable silence by the official sources of prejudicial news. We shall return to this point in a moment.

First, however, it is useful to examine an assumption upon which many of the proposed restrictive measures against the press are premised. It is most clearly implied in an oft-quoted remark of Justice Felix Frankfurter: "The Court has not yet decided that, while convictions must be reversed and miscarriages of justice result because the minds of jurors or potential jurors were poisoned, the poisoner is constitutionally protected in plying his trade."[4] That view harks back to English common law and reflects present British practice: the law may punish anyone who injects nonjudicial matter into the stream of justice, whether the act was done before the stream even began to flow, whether the "poisoner" was aware of the stream, or whether the polluted waters ever actually arrived at the spot where justice was administered. It also assumes the fact of the poisoner and the purity of the stream.[5]

It seems to us that the implications in that view endow the law with a reach that exceeds the grasp to which it is entitled. It appears to say that the law has a right to punish the engendering of any possible prejudice to every possible defendant wherever in time and place the potential prejudice was created. The question that is raised is whether the courts are entitled, in order to preserve the proper environment for possible future trials, to control an infinite number of events outside

[3] Sidney E. Zion, "What about Confessions?" *New York Times,* July 5, 1965.

[4] See Appendix B, p. 306.

[5] See Appendix B, p. 273.

their institutional bounds. Some of those events, however darkly the courts may view them, may have valuable social uses. Must the attitude of the court toward them, particularized to its needs, always prevail?

May the abbot forbid strolling lovers and sleek Cadillacs from the public walks and streets around the monastery, lest the sight of them tempt the monks to break their vows and imperil their souls?

The dedicated staffs of the big city centers for rehabilitation of juvenile delinquents no doubt wish there were no honky-tonks or juke joints in their neighborhoods. The motives are worthy; surely the removal of temptation would aid rehabilitation. But society has other values, some good, some bad, that cause it to leave the situation as it is, uncorrected.

Many useful things that society needs done have the potential of poisoning the stream of justice as that stream is conceived in the world of Justice Frankfurter. The very detection of crime by a civic investigating body, a legislative inquiry, a complaining private citizen, or a snooping reporter, coupled with the publication of their findings, may produce a "poisoning" of the stream of justice; they may create some measure of prejudice against some future defendant. As we have shown, the proceedings of one court can prejudice in a very real sense the processes of a future one. The necessary disclosure of information by police or the FBI to aid the capture of a fugitive prejudices his presumed future trial in some degree, and often in great degree. The mere identification of a defendant by his calling, his race, or his affiliations—strip teaser, Gypsy, civil rights leader, Communist Party official, or stockbroker—is replete with potential or actual prejudice, depending upon the times, the community, and the makeup of his future jury.

Publication of information necessary for the workings of a democracy or serving a legitimate need of its people dare not be made subject to suppression on the decision of any one man that it might conceivably inject something nonjudicial into the stream of justice.

Procedures for the Bar and the Law Enforcement Agencies

We have contended throughout this book that society has a need to be informed and the press an obligation to tell on a timely basis the essential news of crime and punishment. But it is not inconsistent with that contention to add that a rule of reason can be followed in the determination of what is necessary and useful to disclose. Prejudicial characterizations, tendentious and peripheral information, juicy tidbits and gratuitous judgments by the legal establishment and its agents do not fall into the category of data that must also be immediately made public.

If the administrators of justice are not entitled to veto every act outside their walls that they believe might affect their procedures, they nevertheless have the duty to control their own institution and servants. It is by doing just that, we conclude, that the major cure will be realized.

If institutional changes are necessary, they should come from the institution whose primary duty is the assurance of fair trials; not from the press, whose function is the dissemination of public information.

In the Sheppard case, the Supreme Court saw the problem most clearly and pointed precisely to the best and most nearly complete solution. The Court made no excuses for the press; indeed, its summary of the newspapers' behavior in Cleveland was devastating and its excoriation was fierce—and warranted. But after having made that denunciation, it turned for corrective measures not to the press but to the courts and officialdom. Justice Clark wrote:

> Of course, there is nothing that proscribes the press from reporting events that transpire in the courtroom. But where there is a reasonable likelihood that prejudicial news prior to trial will prevent a fair trial, the judge should continue the case until the threat abates, or transfer it to another county not so permeated with publicity. In addition, sequestration of the jury was something the judge should have raised *sua sponte* with counsel. If publicity during the proceedings threatens the fairness of the trial, a new trial should be ordered. But we must remember that reversals are but palliatives; the cure lies in those remedial measures that will prevent the prejudice at its inception. The courts must take such steps by rule and regulation that will protect their processes from prejudicial outside interferences. Neither prosecutors, counsel for defense, the accused, witnesses, court staff nor enforcement officers coming under the jurisdiction of the court should be permitted to frustrate its function. Collaboration between counsel and the press as to information affecting the fairness of a criminal trial is not only subject to regulation but is highly censurable and worthy of disciplinary measures.

Although the Court's language is clear, there were, apparently, some who gave it a curious reading. During the August, 1966, National Conference of State Trial Judges in Montreal, Professor Arthur E. Sutherland of the Harvard Law School told the gathering that the Sheppard decision was an invitation to judges to use their contempt powers against the press and prosecutors and pointed the way to restrictions on press immunity.[6]

The next day, Justice Clark appeared before the group and in an unusual departure from the Court's policy of silence, explained his opinion. He rejected emphatically Professor Sutherland's interpretation. He asserted, according to the Associated Press report of his remarks, that "the Court never held up contempt and maybe never will" because such action "may be too stringent." The Court's opinion "never mentioned any guidelines for the press," he said. "I'm not proposing that you jerk a newspaper reporter in the courtroom and hold him in contempt," Clark continued. "We do not have to jeopardize freedom of the press. The press has made sure our democracy works as it should." In a conclusion reinforcing the Court's post-1946 pattern of demanding retrials for defendants injured by publicity, but not suggesting contempt as a remedy, Justice Clark said, "If doubt comes to our Court that a defendant's rights have been jeopardized, I'm going to vote to reverse."

The thrust of the Reardon Committee proposals is much the same as that of the Sheppard decision. We have discussed them and stated our opinions in Chapter 8. In the same pattern, though less thoroughly and thoughtfully developed, are the ruling of Judge John J. Francis in the Van Duyne case, the Griswold proposal to amend the American Bar Association's canons, the proposal of the Philadelphia Bar Association, and procedures now being followed in several local prosecutors' offices, all of which we also discussed in Chapter 8 (pp. 126–131). The means to put these proposals into effect are simple and do not depend on elaborate negotiation or the passage of controversial legislation.

The courts have always had the power to control the conduct of attorneys in court. To give meaning to their professed concern for safeguarding fair trial, the courts should apply that power.

The bar associations also have ample authority to control the conduct of their members. For better or worse, those associations have what amounts to a life-and-death power over the professional activities of attorneys, and have exerted it—disciplining or disbarring lawyers—in other contexts. So far, the bar organizations have not matched that

[6] Associated Press, August 7, 1966.

power with action to achieve the ethical standards that they acknowledge are needed. They should.

District attorneys, who should be concerned with fair treatment of defendants, already have the power to enforce proper deportment by their subordinates. It is time for them to conform to proper standards.

The major problem, calling for the most extensive and drastic remedial action, is obviously in the police stations. The task of commanding silence from every patrolman and detective, humanly eager to see his or his organization's name attached to a piece of news indicating good work in arresting a suspect, is exceedingly difficult but not impossible. A major re-evaluation of news policy by the police is required in almost every jurisdiction in the United States. It can be encouraged by the courts, the prosecuting attorneys, the city and state governments, and, of course, by police officials themselves. The best way to obtain the correction that is needed is for the courts (in the face of inevitable criticism at the beginning from the press and some elements in the community) to condemn police practices that violate the standards for proper news release.

For reasons stated earlier, we believe that attempts to specify categories of information about which disclosure is absolutely forbidden breed rigidities that are so unrealistic as to be unenforceable. For example, Dean Griswold's call for "absolute prohibition against the release (pretrial and pending trial) . . . of any material relating to trial" is self-defeating since it would too often result in ridiculous anomalies. Guides commanding observance of general principles are much more practical, and therefore much more likely to be followed than detailed and precise *verboten* lists.

"Absolute rules do not offer useful solutions to conflicts in values," it has been observed.[7] The comment is applicable here where conflicts in values are at their sharpest.

For example, prohibitions on law enforcement personnel that forbid description of the circumstances of the crime and of the arrest would be improperly restrictive and, because they could not obtain the public acceptance needed to sustain them, unenforceable in practice. Some

---

[7] Oscar M. Ruebhausen and Orville G. Brim, Jr., "Privacy and Behavioral Research," *American Psychologist*, May, 1966.

sensible leeway must be allowed when comment is essential for the sake of community needs.[8]

To allow the leeway in publicity procedures that is a practical necessity is not to vitiate them. A sense of determination on the part of the courts and law enforcement agencies to protect defendants against the spread of potentially prejudicial news is more important than the exact words of any specific program.

If the will is present, the source will be quenched. With all credit to the energy and skill of reporters, the fact remains that almost all the news that plagues trials has originated in disclosures by policemen, prosecutors, wardens, bailiffs, coroners, or even judges. The exceptions are few.

In any community, the power of the court to enforce nonprejudicial behavior on its functionaries, and on the prosecutors and the police, is ample. So is the power of the legal profession over its members—under Canon 20, not to mention the proposed amendments—if only there were a determination to apply it. If those powers had been exercised in the past, it would have been difficult to find even a sensational case where the outrages would not have been prevented at their point of origin or at least defused of their danger.

The pattern of responsible silence that would appear if proposals were adopted in harmony with the Supreme Court's Sheppard opinion and the Reardon Committee's general philosophy contains one serious but not irremediable danger. It is that nondisclosure can be used as a curtain to cover deliberate injustice. As we have noted, a corrupt police officer, prosecutor, or judge would be happy to deny the public certain facts in order to railroad an innocent man or to conduct a collusive trial of a guilty one, or to prevent public knowledge of other abuses he is committing. That danger is particularly ominous in communities suffused with hostility about public issues, as for instance civil rights, and wherever persons accused have "connections" and where police and courts are corrupt. One shudders at the idea of putting another weapon, the right to reject inquiry and maintain silence about their acts, in the arsenals of those who use their power to abuse justice. We repeat our

---

[8] Wholesale exceptions to prohibitions suitable elsewhere were essential at Dallas. See pp. 200–201 and Appendix C.

hope that the Reardon Committee will take cognizance of this danger and amend its proposals accordingly.

But a vigilant and courageous press will not be powerless in the face of abuses of a basically sound principle. The press can live with a reasonable and realistic rule of silence, and should be able to combat its perversion.

The matter hinges on what is a "reasonable and realistic rule." It is easier to describe than to define. We have argued that it is reasonable for officers of the law to disclose the circumstances of a crime, the details of the pursuit of the suspect, and the events surrounding the arrest; it is unrealistic to withhold these facts. On the other hand, we hold that it is improper for officials to release conclusionary statements, opinions, or any other remarks designed to influence the course of the case, and that it is unreasonable for the press to demand such comment. We hope that the day will come when it will also be unrealistic for the press to demand it.

If such a rule were put into practice, it can be predicted that at first the press will be unreasonable about it. But that state of affairs is not likely to persist if the rule of restraint is basically sound and is exercised intelligently rather than rigidly and mechanically. On its side, the press is sensible and realistic enough that, sooner rather than later, it will meet fairness with fairness and reserve its protests for the occasions when protest is truly warranted—when the rule is used to conceal corrupt and ugly practice.

No journalist himself is ever in any doubt as to the real motives of his or another publication's complaint of news suppression—whether the cry is legitimate, for news that serves a proper public need, or self-serving, for news that is merely titillating and juicy. It is to be doubted that the discrimination of the public at large is much less sophisticated. Rather quickly, we forecast, the public would distinguish one case from another and bestow its support accordingly—to the press when its fight against secrecy is justified, and to the court when it is properly curbing prejudicial but nonessential news.

The Filtering Procedures

As we pointed out in Chapter 6, the law has devised a number of court procedures which, if used diligently and intelligently, can disarm much of the prejudice that may have been aroused in a community against a defendant. They may not be fully effective in sensational cases, where publicity has spread widely and sunk deeply. But in the majority of newsworthy cases, where some information has been released that could have a prejudicial effect but where the case has not become one of roaring notoriety, measures like continuance, change of venue, voir dire and challenges, instructions to juries and sequestration can go far to serve the cause of fair trial.

In the Sheppard case and elsewhere, the Supreme Court chided lower courts for failure to use these techniques. There are countless other cases, sensational and routine, where the same charge is deserved. Judges, we noted earlier, have been astonishingly forgetful of what one might have assumed would be an invariable injunction to the jury not to read about the case before it or listen to news of the case on radio and television. Local pride, surely the least valid rationale, seems to have inhibited judges from granting changes of venue in cases where it was obviously called for. Lawyers should look at voir dire with a view of putting it to the most effective use, and courts should allow challenges much more liberally when there is even a shadow of a question about a talesman's objectivity or any hesitancy on his part in declaring himself free of prejudgment.

Far too frequently, the fault is not the lack of filtering procedures, but the failure to apply them. As Justice Clark has made clear, they must be brought into play much more carefully and earnestly. Until they are, the Supreme Court has indicated it will not consider—nor should it—the more drastic measures against the press that some critical members of the legal profession demand.

Recommendations in this area by the Reardon Committee seem to us wise and admirable.

Television in the Courtroom

Our conclusions about admitting the television camera into the courtroom are spelled out in Chapter 12. Our recommendations, in summary, are against a blanket prohibition as being premature at this time. We favor much more experimentation with television than is now permitted, to determine its promise and its dangers.

Use of the Contempt Power

As we hope to have made clear, we oppose the use of the contempt power in the British manner or in its early nineteenth-century American form as an instrument to deal with the free press, fair trial problem. Its application against criticism of courts and judges, and its summary exercise without trial by jury and traditional judicial procedures, are unacceptable in America today. The Supreme Court has made this clear consistently, and we think quite properly.

For even broader reasons, exercise of the contempt power fails as a remedy. It is simply too dangerous. Its general use, or the threat of it, would imperil the free operations of the press in the crucial area of the administration of justice, where the press now performs essential functions. Moreover, the contempt power would presumably be used to enforce various proposed laws or regulations which, as we argued particularly in Chapter 8, endanger the proper flow of information and more often than not would be futile, incongruous, and ludicrous in practice.

But to oppose use of the general contempt power is not tantamount to saying that the press may forever willfully inflict injuries against a defendant's right to an impartial jury and remain forever unpunished. If every other element in the administration of justice is finally purified, if police and prosecutors and attorneys all behave with complete dedication to the rights of the accused, the press may not claim complete immunity from all sanctions if it deliberately injures those rights.

The press cannot and should not be prevented by law from publishing what it chooses. Its freedom from prior restraint may affront one's sense of fairness, but it should comport with one's sense of history and present political wisdom. It accords exactly with the policy and philosophy of the men who wrote the Constitution. They faced the question squarely. In accepting the First Amendment's prohibition of prior restraint, they saw no way of limiting the freedom it bestowed only to the good press or only to its good deeds. Freedom was also granted to those elements who would be irresponsible, reckless, and wrong. For they realized that once a distinction were attempted someone would have to be called upon to decide what publication was wrong, reckless, and evil. That umpire would have to be some instrumentality of the state, and this would have meant in its ultimate logic the subjection of the press to a state censor—a condition the Founding Fathers were determined to prevent.

They accepted the fact that freedom entails risk. The sense of those who adopted the Bill of Rights was that the value of freedom of the press overweighed the drawbacks of the inevitable misuse of freedom. Since 1941, that has been precisely the position of the Supreme Court in every case of press injury to defendants' rights it has dealt with.

But in one area of the free press, fair trial issue, the Supreme Court has not foreclosed itself from use of the contempt power, and the press must bear that potentiality in mind: No reversal of precedent would be required for the Court to sanction the punishment of an act that is deliberately intended to affect a jury verdict. Without being inconsistent with its earlier positions, the Court could find a publication contemptuous if it were demonstrated that it was calculated to disturb a trial, or if that would be its evident result.

We contended above that the courts cannot extend their arm to control a myriad of events that take place in the community outside the courtroom walls; by the same token, the press may not lay its hands on procedures that are permitted to take place only inside the courtroom.

What would constitute the intentional placing of the press's thumb on the scales of justice in a way that might be punishable? The most careful judgment and balancing of value is required for an answer. The endeavor may be undertaken only in an atmosphere dominated by one key concept: To curtail the press at all is to cut away at the known, demonstrable, and time-tested values of the First Amendment in favor of new procedures whose effectiveness is speculative and whose potential dangers are unplumbed. Thus any curtailment through the application of the contempt power must be for the clearest and most striking reasons and must be limited to the smallest compass possible. The criteria would have to be the nature of the information published, its timing, and above all its purpose.

First of all—however offensive the idea may strike the bar—editorial criticism of the courts, the law enforcement complex and its processes in general or with respect to a particular case dare not be made subject to punishment. To fulfill its function, the press must be assured of the right to speak its views, with no holds barred.

Second, to be punishable, the information it publishes concerning trial evidence must be, in the words of one judge,[9] "highly inflammatory, in volume great, and accessibility universal," reaching and entering "the consciousness of the overwhelming majority of available talesmen."

Third, to use a standard offered in a different context, the publicity must be without socially redeeming purpose. Watchdogging the processes of justice is essential and must be not merely protected but encouraged. But trifling by the news media when a man's life or freedom is at stake and exploiting the sensational elements of a case for circulation-grabbing purposes are matters of a different sort. The story of how a confession was illegally coerced by the police is not the same as a gratuitous report wheedled out of a policeman that the defendant has confessed.[10]

Fourth, in the period after the crime has been committed but before a suspect is named or before a named suspect is arrested, no inhibitions dare be placed against whatever the press chooses to publish (although there may well be some proper limitations to what law enforcement agents should disclose).

Fifth, the deliberateness of the press's action to stack the deck for the future trial must be demonstrated, and to the satisfaction of a jury and not merely, in summary proceedings, of a judge. The 1952 case of *Shepherd v. Florida* (Appendix B, pp. 299–300) would be an example of an attempt to force a finding had it gone to a jury instead of a judge. The 1954 Sheppard case in Cleveland (pp. 13–20) and the 1963 Gosser case in Toledo (pp. 24–29) are arguable examples. They can be distinguished from cases where the Supreme Court found that press misbehavior may have conditioned the minds of jurors, as in the Irvin and

---

[9] *U.S. ex rel. Bloeth v. Denno*, 204 F. Supp. 263 (S.D.N.Y. 1962), 313 F. 2d 364 (2d Cir. 1963).

[10] An elegant demonstration of the distinction is provided by the notorious case of George Whitmore, tried in 1964 for the slaying of two young women in their New York apartment. The details were lurid, the press treatment was sensational, and the pressure on the police to find the murderer had been intense. Whitmore's arrest and his subsequent confession, volunteered to the press by the police, received the most flamboyant publicity. Months later, diligent work by the press proved that the confession was not only coerced but false. At first, the press came perilously close to sending a man to execution; later, it was the agency that cleared him of a frame-up.

Rideau cases, but where deliberate loading of the dice was not asserted.

If in theory there is a case to be made for the limited application of the contempt power, the likelihood of the press suffering under it in practice is remote. If the agencies of the law once put their house in order and refrain from improper disclosures, the press will have little material with which to contaminate the courtroom; if, on the other hand, the source of the data that the press may have used to subvert a jury remains, as now, that which is wrongfully wholesaled by police and prosecutors, then the case for punishing the press for publication of material from official sources will be weak indeed.

The Supreme Court has yet to decide whether any attempt to punish the press by the contempt power is unconstitutional. Until it makes such a ruling, which is unlikely, the possibility of some contempt action remains.

When all else is done with complete respect for the defendant's right to a fair trial and the press nevertheless publishes information that is deliberately partisan, prejudicial in content, timing, and volume, and devoid of redeeming purpose, then the press should not expect to be exempt from contempt proceedings.

Remedies Within the Press

If, except in unlikely and utterly extraordinary cases, the press is to remain immune from legal punishment for such sins as it may commit against fair trial, will it stroll blithely on the course of irresponsibility? No such outcome is probable.

In the first place, if the agencies of the law end their dissemination of information that is truly and gratuitously prejudicial, the press will be substantially cut off from the raw material of the kind of news that is objectionable.

In the second place, if all other participants in the judicial process behave with maximum care for defendants' rights, the public pressure against press irresponsibility on that score will be immense. And, contrary to the usual impression, the public pressure can be effective. News executives—at least the successful ones—are inordinately sensitive to the attitudes of their audience, and for the simplest of reasons: the existence of their institution depends on its acceptance by its readers and audience. Accordingly, there is a role for the public also in protecting the rights of defendants. If the public is outraged at press sensationalism it has an easy way of making its sentiments known, and with considerable assurance that its complaints will have an impact.[11]

As it is, the argument of the press that it cannot be blamed for publishing what official sources freely disclose to it for publication is neither foolish nor hypocritical. But in a situation where other participants in the administration of justice have cleaned their houses, the challenge to the press's own sense of decency will come in much more impressive form than now.

Until that happy moment in history arrives, however, the question remains: What should the press do to improve the interim situation? The long-standing answer has been that it should voluntarily adopt codes of ethics and conduct.

For reasons implicit in the discussion in Chapter 8 of typical codes, we believe that they are without great promise. It is not merely that codes cannot be enforced, but that if they attempt to specify what may or may not be published they cannot be abided by. The real precepts for reporting crime and justice are like French grammar: there are more exceptions than rules. Flat prohibitions are unworkable. To subscribe to them and then be forced to breach them is worse than never to have stated them. As code drafters have discovered, they cannot proscribe the standard *index expurgatorius* as the bar would wish, and declare of the items on it, "The press shall not publish." At most, they can say, "The press should avoid publishing." And at that point, in codes like the Massachusetts *Guide* and the Toledo statement (pp. 123–125 above) that allow for exceptions, the adjurations become so fuzzy as to be meaningless in the notorious cases and supererogatory in the others.

As distinct from categorized codes, however, statements of decent resolve that avoid tabulating specific taboos have a use greater than cynics accord them. A resolution proclaiming such basic principles as

[11] The movie version, vintage 1930, of the "Front Page" editor and reporter, arrogant and hard-boiled, is romantically inaccurate. Most editors are thin-skinned to the point that a score of critical letters or a dozen angry phone calls create, in fact, a great deal more consternation and soul-searching—or at least tactics-searching—than their numbers warrant or than anyone outside the craft might suspect.

the presumption of innocence and the right to an unprejudiced jury can serve as both a reminder and a resolve-stiffener to reporters and news executives. A pledge to oneself is not entirely futile. For all its blandness, the statement adopted by the Oregon press and bar (p. 126) seems to have had a remarkably wholesome effect.

But certainly the most productive single course of action for the press is to indulge in some self-examination, with no more or less rigor and charity than it bestows when it examines other institutions. In the area of crime reporting, it will not, in most cases, find a pretty picture. It will see serious sins of omission—in failure really to cover crime with the constructive purpose of showing the community its origins and anatomy—as well as those of commission—in lurid, cheap sensationalism.

A defensive editor can take any bill of particulars against the press—the Reardon Committee Report makes particularly gruesome reading—and argue with some justice that in not more than one case out of a hundred did the publication injure the defendant at trial. But he must also concede that in many more cases what was published injured the cause of decency and good taste.

With distinguished exceptions, crime reporting in the American press compares lamentably in thoroughness, sensitivity, and responsibility with its increasingly expert coverage of other subjects. Quite apart from any considerations of prejudicing fair trial, its coverage of crime is coarse. If it debauches nothing else, it debauches the high standards the media proclaim and, in other fields, uphold.

A final useful piece of work for the press to uphold its role in improving the processes of criminal justice is to establish much closer and more frequent contacts with the bar to work on means for handling news of crime and trials in a responsible manner. There is good reason to believe that most of the press's real sins against fair trial are committed inadvertently—carelessly, perhaps, but without intent to do a defendant injury. The bar does the press a service in pointing out to it how and what kind of news is harmful and in calling attention to potentially dangerous material about which the press can remain silent with no loss to the public or itself.

On its part, the press will have no lack of useful comment for the bar, if only to give its members a better knowledge of the realities of news operations. Journalists can also show lawyers how they themselves often contribute to the very difficulty they complain about.

The recent history of press-bar contacts has been, unhappily, one of adversary proceedings and acrimonious debate. Often, the only result has been to make each group even more suspicious than theretofore of the motives and good faith of the other. This attitude of reciprocal bear-baiting is absurd and strangely out of keeping for two groups that in most other affairs of business and life are commonsensical and generous. There is no inherent reason why the mutual hostility should continue.

Press-bar discussions should be encouraged not for the purpose of drafting codes but to reach agreement on principles. If undertaken in good faith and good humor, they could lead in every community to a resolve not merely to work out procedures in general, but—what may be more important or at least more feasible—to ad hoc methods for responsible news handling in each potentially troublesome criminal case.

At a minimum, frequent meetings between representatives of the press and the bar at the local level would provide useful education to both sides. We suggest that both sides need it.

RESPONSES FROM PROSECUTORS

The authors sent letters in the spring and summer of 1965 to the attorneys general of the fifty states and the district attorneys of the fifty largest American cities. The following request was made:

Can you provide us with statistics showing how often prejudicial publicity is raised as a defense in criminal trials in your state and how often it has been dealt with on appeal?

Is it possible to gather any comparable figures for earlier years in order to determine whether the problem is increasing?

Can you provide us with any comments or thoughts or anecdotes about this general subject based upon your personal experience?

Summaries of replies that had information to offer follow.

State Attorneys General

The attorney general of *Alabama* reported that no statistics were available to show exactly how many times prejudicial publication was raised in his state as an objection to the conduct of a trial. He did report, based on his long personal observations, that objections on this score are frequently raised "when the crime has received wide publicity." In these cases, this is a common ground for objection. Without specific statistics he was able to report only that "we have heard more about the problem in recent years."

The attorney general of *Alaska* reported a unique situation: In Alaska, there are only five cities with daily newspapers and they are hundreds of miles apart. Only eight cities have television. Therefore, except for local news, newscasts are taped and shown after some days of delay. Adverse publicity before trial can be rectified, accordingly, by a change of venue to another city, although this process occasions some extra expense to the defendant and the government. In the past, publicity during trial has been a minimal problem. The attorney general knew of "several cases in which this has occurred. However, two or three cases have gone up on appeal on this question in the last few years but no conviction has been reversed on this ground." He did feel that the problem has increased in recent times.

The attorney general of *Arizona* reported that since 1904 seven cases have dealt with this issue and have gone as far as the state supreme court. In all of them the issue arose through a motion for a change of venue, occasioned by either high feelings in the community or a special or continuous treatment of the subject by the press. Three of the seven cases arose before 1940, but since 1961 there has been at least one case each year in which this question was raised.

The attorney general of *California* reported that his office becomes involved in criminal trials only after an appeal is taken. There are approximately 30,000 felony convictions annually in the state but only a small percentage are appealed. He had no records indicating the frequency with which the defense in question was raised in those appeals. He was able to report, however, that "a great percentage of criminal cases do not receive extensive press coverage with a consequent possibility of prejudice. It seems to be the consensus of opinion here that the problem is not increasing to any appreciable extent."

The attorney general of *Colorado* had no statistics with which to make an assessment. His office deals only with criminal cases on appeal. Only two cases then in his office involved the question of adverse publicity. However, he reported that members of the press and the bar in Colorado are concerned about the problem and are beginning a dialogue which, he expected, will lead to a mutual understanding of the problem.

The attorney general of *Delaware* reported that "an objection based on publicity is one of infrequent occurrence in the state of Delaware. From the best recollection of our staff there have been only two occasions in the past two years where the question has been raised. I would seriously doubt that we could say that the problem has been increasing in recent years." His assessment also, absent corroborative statistics, was based on personal experience.

The attorney general of *Florida* reported that his office handles only appeals and that there is no way of determining the frequency with which prejudicial publication is raised as a defense at trial. Moreover, this vagueness is compounded by the fact that when there is an acquittal or when no appeal is taken, the issue, even if raised at trial, is not preserved in any recordable court decision. He was able to report from his personal experiences that "through the years this objection has often been given as grounds for change of venue and in some cases venue has been changed because of this." He guessed that in recent years the complaints about trial publicity have been increasing simply because the range of media coverage has been increasing.

The attorney general of *Idaho* reported that "to my personal knowledge, the issue has not been a major one in Idaho at least in recent years." He stated that when objections are raised they are at trial and not on appeal. His opinion was that the problem is on the increase and will continue to be until "standards of conduct are laid down for the guidance of press media personnel." He preferred guide lines established within the media to the attempted imposition of restrictions from outside sources.

The attorney general of *Indiana* reported that since the Supreme Court's decision in *Irvin v. Dowd* "the question of undue publicity has not been properly raised in any criminal appeals in this state." He reported that the Federal courts in Indiana guard against the possibility of prejudicial publication "militantly" but that trial by newspapers is prevalent in the state courts because "defense lawyers enjoy basking in publicity as much as prosecutors."

The attorney general of *Iowa* reported that since January 1, 1965, when he took office, "this question has not been raised in an appeal." The policy in his office is that prosecutors will not make public statements which could prejudice trials.

The attorney general of *Kentucky* reported that after a diligent and exhaustive search of pertinent Kentucky cases, "we have found only a few cases in which the subject of publicity has played any part in the case or has been raised as an issue." Although exact statistics were not available as to how many times the question was raised on trial or on appeal, "from the digest of Kentucky cases it would appear to be negligible." He also concluded that the problem has neither increased nor decreased in recent years, and that any problem that does arise is taken care of by voir dire.

The attorney general of *Maine* reported that the only information he had was that in the past six months there were two murder cases in which changes of venue were requested on grounds of publication. Both requests were denied. The supreme court in his state has not passed on the subject.

The attorney general of *Maryland* reported that though statistics were not available, he was personally familiar with at least the important criminal cases in that state in the past four years and "it is my opinion that undue publicity has not been raised as a defense in more than 20 cases in that period." He was not aware that objections based on the ground of pretrial publication were increasing in any significant number in recent years.

The attorney general of *Michigan* reported that while statistics were unavailable, "it is our impression that the issue is very infrequently raised in this jurisdiction either at the trial or appellate level."

The attorney general of *Mississippi* reported that the problem is increasing in recent years. It is seldom raised on appeal if not raised at the trial. Based on his own experience he could state that there are about one hundred criminal appeals to the state supreme court each year but most of them are routine, run-of-the-mill criminal cases in which the publicity issue is seldom raised. The issue comes up only in extreme, sensational cases and he did not recall it being raised "in more than four or five cases in the past ten years." The issue usually arises on a motion for change of venue. No denials of these motions have ever been reversed by the state appellate courts. Often the trial judge will grant a change to a different county agreeable to the prosecution and defense. But in his long experience on both sides of criminal trials, "I have seen more guilty defendants acquitted because of favorable publicity than I could imagine not guilty defendants convicted. Publicity is, in fact, a two-edged sword."

The attorney general of *Missouri* said he has no jurisdiction over criminal trials and thus no way of determining the magnitude of the problem in his state. However, he does deal with criminal appeals and thus with the kinds of criminal cases "most likely to go the full route provided by the various aspects of due process of law . . . the type of crime which is most sensational, most newsworthy, and consequently, most apt to receive widespread publicity." About 150 criminal cases are processed by his office annually, the vast majority of which are routine or perfunctory. Even the cases which "make law" and have jurisprudential interest "are of a lackluster nature insofar as the press is concerned."

A few of these cases are publicized each year, while an equal amount of sensational cases involving important people or spectacular crimes receive extensive publicity. Out of all these cases, "perhaps no more than one annually will be such that it will deserve any more than cursory judicial scrutiny on the publicity issue." Reviewing the problem in his state historically, he judged that although it arises regularly the question of the effect of publicity on a fair trial does not "constitute a serious impediment to the administration of justice. I would say that serious widespread publicity has entered the picture in this state only on the order of every other year or so over the last century and the rate of occurrence does not seem to have accelerated with the advent of more expedient techniques of news distribution."

The attorney general of *Montana* reported that the trial judges in his state have coped with this issue so as to assure that publication does not affect defendants' rights. The incidence of objections on grounds of adverse publicity is low and there is no evidence that it is on the increase.

The attorney general of *Nebraska* stated that in his six-year experience the objection of undue publicity has been raised at trial on only two occasions. The issue arose in the context of motions for a new trial and a change of venue, neither of which was granted.

The attorney general of *Nevada* reported that "the issue of publicity in criminal trials is raised so seldom in Nevada that we have no statistics."

The attorney general of *New Jersey* reported that until the decision in *State v. Van Duyne* he considered the problem unimportant. Now, of course, this issue is the subject of much attention in New Jersey and is being actively considered by the various interested groups. He expressed no idea of the frequency of the issue.

The attorney general of *North Carolina* reported that this problem may be something to look to in the future, "but thus far has not caused us much trouble." The subject has come up in some isolated cases when mistrials were granted because jurors read news stories or saw television programs that tended to prejudice a defendant's right to a fair trial.

The attorney general of *North Dakota* stated that he keeps no statistics. However, he felt that from his experience he could draw three conclusions: "1. Although in proportion to the total number of cases tried, publicity is not often raised as an objection in the conduct of a trial it is raised often enough to warrant the attention it has been receiving. 2. It is probably raised more often at trial than on appeal. 3. The problem has been increasing in recent years."

The attorney general of *Oregon* reported that though statistics were unavailable, he believed that the problem has increased in recent years. He pointed out that the Oregon newspaper publishers association and the Oregon state bar have arrived at a joint agreement on pretrial and during-trial publicity in the form of a code which has received much national attention. He felt that he would prefer something akin to the British system adopted in this country even though he believed such a step would require a Federal Constitutional amendment.

The attorney general of *Rhode Island* reported that no statistics were available, but on the basis of personal experience he stated: ". . . the problem has arisen only very rarely in this state. On one or two occasions in the last ten years or so the Superior Court has granted a change of venue from one county in the state to another county when it appeared that because of local sentiment and/or pre-trial publicity there might be a question as to whether a defendant could receive a fair trial in the county in which the particular crime was committed. To the best of my knowledge this subject has never come up on appeal to our Supreme Court."

The attorney general of *South Carolina* had no statistics but guessed that there would be an increase in the frequency of the assertion of this defense because "the literacy of the people is on an ever increasing upswing" and because of "the tremendous impact television has had on the populace in the last decade."

The attorney general of *South Dakota* reported that prejudicial publication has been raised as an objection at trial very seldom, that it has never been raised on appeal, and that the problem has not been increasing recently.

The attorney general of *Utah* replied that "publicity is very seldom raised as an objection to going forward with a criminal trial or as a claim for prejudice after trial." He knew of only two cases in the past five years where the issue was raised, and in one the issue was abandoned on appeal. The attention given to this issue by the courts and counsel in criminal cases has increased in recent years but not remarkably. He pointed out that the problem is not one of critical importance in this state because "the newspaper policies of the major daily publications in the state of Utah are relatively conservative, and crime news is seldom treated in a leading fashion."

The attorney general of *Vermont* reported that though statistics were unavailable, "generally I can say that the question of prejudicial publicity has been raised during trials only on a few occasions and infrequently on appeal. I do not believe that there has been any noticeable increase in the number of cases where this issue is raised."

The attorney general of *Virginia* pointed out that his criminal jurisdiction applies only to appeals. He stated that in his opinion, "the question of publicity prior to the trial has only come up in a very few cases. This question has been raised primarily in habeas corpus cases." He said he believed that the recent attention given to this problem by the Federal courts will cause an increase in the assertion of this defense.

The attorney general of *Wyoming* concluded that, on the basis of "an examination of the Wyoming digest and personal recollection, in no cases has publicity been raised for the reason stated." Thus, if the problem did arise in any trials it must have been inconsequential or it would have been reported.

City District Attorneys

The district attorney in *Portland, Oregon,* stated that objections based on alleged prejudicial publicity are not often raised. He estimated that this objection comes up "in less than five per cent of all criminal cases prosecuted in this jurisdiction." He added that without doubt this objection has been increasing during recent years. However, in his judgment the rise was probably due less to an intensification of the problem than to the tremendous increase in the amount of literature emanating from the bench and bar about it. He added that the problem arises primarily in two cases: the publishing of reported confessions and prior records. He initiated a staff policy against commenting on pending criminal cases, making public only such information as name, address, age, and formal charge. However, he has no direct control over law enforcement officers. He said he felt that adverse publicity is not a serious problem in his metropolitan area but "our press is a highly responsible and ethical press and almost without exception exercises very good judgment in reporting crime news."

The district attorney of *Denver, Colorado,* replied that though statistics were not available, after a discussion with his associates he could estimate that "in approximately 1 per cent of the trials publicity is raised as an objection. On appeal it is raised in approximately one-tenth of one per cent of the cases. It appears that the problem will be increasing particularly since the recent decision in the case of Billie Sol Estes."

The county prosecutor in *Newark, New Jersey,* reported that "unfair publicity as a defense is not raised very often." In the few cases where it does come up, it arises in the course of a motion for a change of venue. "Such motions have always been denied and that decision has always been affirmed on appeal." He reported that the local prosecutors and the state attorney general are now considering the Van Duyne decision as well as the United States Attorney General's guide lines with the idea in mind of establishing rules to cover this situation in the future.

The commonwealth attorney in *Louisville, Kentucky,* reported that "the question of publicity and its effect on a trial in a criminal case is a problem but certainly not a perplexing one." In the day-to-day coverage of trials there is no problem and the reporters are fair and cooperative. "It is the exceptional case which creates unusual public interest prior to trial where we have some damaging effect." However, the newspapers do in sensational cases assign special reporters to cover developments and to conduct private investigation. Reporting such as this "obviously transcends that which you would normally expect from the press." Based on his experience, the issue is "seldom raised at trial and just as seldom on appeal. The problem has not been increasing in recent years. The number of those complaining about it, however, has increased greatly."

The state's attorney for *Baltimore, Maryland,* reported that his office handles the prosecution of about five thousand cases a year. "To the very best of my recollection the problem of undue publicity has arisen no more than six or seven times over the course of that six and a half years. It has come up . . . about once a year and almost always has been raised on a motion for a change of venue. Since the cases involved have all been rather notorious and with one exception have been capital cases, the change of venue was granted as a matter of right. The question has not been raised on appeal during this time in any of the cases coming out of Baltimore City."

The district attorney for *Norfolk, Virginia,* stated that publicity is seldom if ever raised as an objection to the conduct of a trial or on appeal. This problem may be increasing a little in recent years—"but very little."

The district attorney for *Philadelphia, Pennsylvania,* replied that defense counsel traditionally object to pretrial publication as one objection among many that are traditionally filed in advance of trial. However, "it has never been successful." In capital cases and in cases of high public interest, juries are usually locked up, shielding them from any exposure to publication during trial. The problem of pretrial publicity is at present a matter of controversy between the press and the bar, he noted. The bar association is attempting to develop rules to govern its members and early drafts are of a restrictive nature. The issue is usually raised in court through the application for a change of venue. However, he saw a noticeable decrease in requests of this nature in recent times, a circumstance he attributed to the wide dissemination of the information published and consequent realization of the difficulty of escaping from its impact by changing the locus of the trial. He was not certain whether the problem has been increasing in recent years but guessed that it is becoming more acute "due to the fact that it is presently given a very widespread discussion." He concluded that "to the best of my knowledge no appellate court in Pennsylvania has reversed a conviction because of publicity either before or during trial."

The district attorney for *New York City* stated that there is no statistical record of the frequency of the problem. However, a discussion with the attorneys assigned to the trial and appellate courts led him to the conclusion that "the objection is raised in practically every case that has received an unusual amount of publicity. It has been estimated that this occurs on an average of approximately once a month in New York County . . . only a handful out of the thousands of cases now disposed of each year." Nevertheless, he felt that this is too many and that the effect of this publicity "is to destroy the presumption of innocence and deprive those defendants of a fair trial."

The district attorney of *Houston, Texas,* reported that in his area the objection on grounds of adverse publicity is extremely rare. He said that out of thousands if not tens of thousands of cases with which he was familiar, "I can recall of less than a dozen instances wherein a serious objection has been raised regarding the publicity surrounding the offense of the trial." Until recently, he said, defendants seldom objected to trial publicity. The juries in felony cases are sequestered and isolated from exposure to publication. He felt, however, that recent Federal cases have opened up this issue as a new avenue of appeal and that as a result objections on this score have increased in the last few years. The problem has not increased but it is a new defense tactic, he noted. Local courts will not permit photographs or movies in the courtroom over a defendant's objection. Moreover, changes of venue are effective to avoid the influence of adverse publicity. Thus "it is in the appeal of convictions that the objection to publicity is most often and most seriously presented." He added that news coverage is intensifying and may lead to augmentation of the problem. He guessed that of the 27,787 serious crimes in this area reported in 1964 by the FBI Uniform Crime Report only about five hundred received any publicity at all.

The district attorney for *San Antonio, Texas,* stated that though there were no available statistics, he was of the opinion that the issue comes up in cases involving prominent people or crimes of extraordinary violence. The issue will be raised through a motion for a change of venue or in the qualification of prospective jurors. He estimated that "publicity is involved in about 7 to 10 per cent of the cases we handle. Most of this consists of small news reports of a more or less routine nature. In about 2 per cent of our total cases or less there would be more or less widespread coverage." He guessed that the problem is on the increase. He also estimated that approximately a third of all the daily news items in local papers involve crime and criminal conduct.

The district attorney of *Los Angeles, California,* reported that though statistics were unavailable, "the defense has not been common here." It has been raised in some highly publicized cases. No cases in that county were reversed because of any act of the press. He is attempting now to establish voluntary ground rules for his office to eliminate whatever problem may exist.

The district attorney for *Dallas, Texas,* reported that statistics were not available. However, he said he discussed the question with the district judges in the county and, on the basis of their joint memories, concluded that "during the last ten years pretrial publicity has been raised on motion for a change of venue fewer than five times per year. An average of one case per year has been transferred . . . on this ground."

The district attorney for *Santa Fe, New Mexico,* stated that his office has issued a set of guide lines to law enforcement officers and prosecutors which follows those recently promulgated by the United States

Attorney General. He felt that the problem is minimal and that whatever difficulties do exist can be worked out together with the press.

The district attorney of *Phoenix, Arizona,* stated that in his long experience as a prosecutor and before that as a defense counsel, "I can recall very few cases wherein publicity either prior to or at the trial was used to indicate that the defendant would not or was not having a fair trial. I know of no cases that have been reversed by our appellate court because of adverse publicity prior to or during trial." He concluded that there simply is no problem in his jurisdiction.

The district attorney for *New Orleans, Louisiana,* said that even though he knew of no statistics, a cursory examination of the cases in his state "does not reveal that the issue has ever been raised."

PRESS REGULATION BY LAW

The trail of the law leading to a vital Constitutional doctrine often begins at distant and unlikely points, makes unpredictable turns, stops and starts at places for sometimes practical and often imponderable reasons, until it evolves fully and clearly for all to see in a settled and steady direction. This is the pattern of the legal course of the regulation of the American press in its coverage of trial and pretrial news.

In American legal history, the free press, fair trial cases have seldom hinged on the question of prior restraint of the press. That particular form of censorship had been furiously resisted in Britain before the Revolution and was not about to be admitted into the new republic. The colonies had also battled over attempts by the Crown to control the press, and the framers of the Constitution encased this one bounty of their victory in the strong, clear words of the First Amendment: "Congress shall make no law . . . abridging freedom of the press."

The Supreme Court has consistently refused to weaken this prohibition. In the classic case, *Near v. Minnesota*,[1] in 1931, Chief Justice Charles Evans Hughes enunciated the rule holding the principal conception of freedom of the press to be immunity from previous restraints or censorship:

> In determining the extent of the constitutional protection, it has been generally, if not universally, considered that it is the chief purpose of the guarantee to prevent previous restraints upon publication. The struggle in England, directed against the legislative power of the licenser, resulted in renunciation of the censorship by the press. The liberty deemed to be established was thus described by Blackstone: "The liberty of the press is indeed essential to the nature of a free state; but this consists in laying no *previous* restraints upon publications, not in freedom from censure for criminal matter when published."

The law in this matter having been quite clear even before the Near decision, there has been little litigation in American legal history over

[1] 283 U.S. 697.

prior restraint of press coverage of trials. From time to time, however, attempts have been made to reanimate the very dead horse. Recent examples follow this standard pattern: A trial court judge orders the local press, under threat of a contempt citation for disobedience, not to report trial or pretrial developments that might be prejudicial if brought to the jury's attention. Almost automatically the press defies the court, publishing both the material ordered to be censored and the court's censorship order. Usually these direct conflicts have quickly dissipated, with the judge retreating (or ordered to retreat by a higher court), rueing his impotence, calling for reform, and admonishing the press that it is heading for trouble. No dramatic, national legal precedent on this point has been set, but the presumption is that any attempt at prior judicial restraint on the press would be ruled as violative of the First Amendment and would result in an embarrassing and enfeebling precedent for the courts.

Such was the case in Arizona when the state supreme court in January, 1966, prohibited a trial court judge from holding two newspapers in contempt for violating his order not to publish a certain pretrial hearing. Immediately prior to the empaneling of a jury for a murder trial in Phoenix, the defense lawyer had asked for a habeas corpus hearing aimed at dismissing the case without trial for lack of evidence. He had demanded that the press be excluded lest its coverage prevent a fair trial before a local jury later that day should his motion to dismiss be unsuccessful. The judge acquiesced in his proposal. During the hearing on the motion of the defense, certain incriminating evidence was brought out. The *Arizona Republic* and the *Phoenix Gazette* reported the open court hearing. The judge ordered them to show cause why they should not be held in contempt. The newspapers appealed and were upheld. The trial court's good faith attempt to assure a fair trial was held to violate both the state constitution's and the United States Constitution's guarantee of freedom of the press.[2]

Whatever the legal history, there remain the most formidable practical problems for any judge who would attempt prior restraint to protect the integrity of the court. He would face the difficult requirement of proving, first, that the press coverage would in fact be prejudicial and, second, that the ensuing prejudice would inevitably seep into the

[2] The Freedom of Information Center's January, 1966, Situation Paper No. 12 reports several similar cases between 1963 and 1965.

courtroom because the court could not protect itself against it. The first issue is imponderable and unprovable; the second implies an unnecessarily defeatist attitude of the court and its surrender to the environment outside its door.

The law governing press coverage of crime and trials has been developed for the most part through judicial construction of the contempt power of courts. Though there have been legal variations, this has been the main theme. And interestingly enough, although attempted regulation of the American press in its coverage of trials has emanated from the contempt doctrine, not all of the contempt cases developing the law have concerned the press. A review of the key contempt cases, along with some mention of the other attempts to cope with the problem of prejudicial publications, provides a rather complete picture of the course of the law of free press, fair trial.

The Source of the Law

The United States Constitution introduces the antagonists. The First Amendment declares in part that "Congress shall make no law . . . abridging the freedom of the press." Clearly, any law or decision inhibiting press coverage of crimes or trials would tend to abridge the freedom of the press. Yet, the views of some commentators notwithstanding, the press's freedom cannot and does not amount to absolute unfettered or destructive license. We draw lines. But in the case of the press the judgment is close to unanimous that any lines that are drawn must as a matter of policy allow the press the fullest area of freedom. The rule has developed that although the press may not be censored by restraints before publication, it may be punished for abusive publications against the public interest (e.g., for treason, incitation to riot, libel, or contempt). Even the Near case acknowledged that the First Amendment's protection of press publications was not absolute. Under exceptional circumstances limitations will be recognized.

Thus rests one Constitutional value judgment. On the other hand, although the exact words "fair trial" are not mentioned in the Constitution or in the Bill of Rights, the concept is clearly inferred from those rights explicitly guaranteed in both the Fifth and Sixth Amendments.

The Fifth Amendment states in part that no person may "be deprived of life, liberty or property without due process of law." Certain cases have led to the interpretation of this requirement of *due process* as one guaranteeing conformance with what are at least minimum civilized standards for the conduct of trials. This notion has been applied to cases where extreme publicity created such a general community environment or atmosphere at trial that the defendant was effectively denied due process of law.

The Sixth Amendment states in part: "In all criminal prosecutions, the accused shall enjoy the right to a speedy and public trial by an impartial jury of the state and district wherein the crime shall have been committed. . . ." It is, of course, this requirement of an impartial jury that is at the heart of the complaint that on occasion press publication deprives the defendant of his Constitutional right to a fair trial.

Most debates about the free press, fair trial issue have centered on the conflict between the First and Sixth Amendments. Actually, the "fair trial" guarantee is predicated upon rights emanating jointly from both the Fifth and Sixth Amendments. It should be noted that while these are Federal rights, all states have similar guarantees.

Not all aspects of the Sixth Amendment's admonition are always consistent. The right to a *public* trial may not be consistent with the right to an impartial jury (suppose the community is enraged about a case and that this sentiment is communicated to the jury by a hostile public at the trial, or if the jurors, drawn from the locale where the crime was committed, have been so suffused with news of the act as to have become prejudiced).

The first cases dealing with the publicity problem concerned the construction of the Sixth Amendment's guarantee of an "impartial" jury. Early cases placed the burden of proving partiality upon the defendant and, as if this were not difficult enough, the task was made almost impossible by the added requirement that actual prejudice be specifically shown. Apparently, preconceived notions about a case would not necessarily disqualify a juror. This issue, once raised, was left in flux for a long time, and only recently has it been revived for re-examination.

For the first half of the twentieth century, the doctrine of contempt by publication was the dominant law governing press coverage of trials. A brief examination of the course of this rule, its birth and development in England and its adoption and reformulation in America, is a necessary background for understanding the modern legal situation.

The History of the Contempt by Publication Rule

"There cannot be anything of greater consequence than to keep the streams of justice clear and pure, that parties may proceed with safety both to themselves and their characters." That remark by Lord Hardwicke in 1742 in an English case entitled *Roach v. Garvan*[3] is the basis for constructive contempt convictions against the press for its out-of-court publications about criminal cases.

That rationale and its application became clearer in a 1905 decision in *King v. Davies*[4] which followed the line of reasoning in the Roach case. It dealt with a newspaper article about a woman who had been arrested for abandoning a child, but had not yet been committed for trial. The *Southwest Daily Post* printed an article about traffic in babies, reflecting upon the character of the woman. Some short time later the woman was charged with attempted murder as a consequence to her abandonment of the child. Because of the article, the editor of the *Post* was convicted of contempt. Referring to Lord Hardwicke's "streams of justice" phrase, the court wrote:

> We adhere to the view we expressed in that case that the publication of such articles is a contempt of the Court which ultimately tries the case after committal, although at the time when they are published it cannot be known whether there will be a committal or not. *Their tendency is to poison the stream of justice in that Court, though at the time of their publication the stream had not reached it;* and as such articles are calculated to interfere with the power of the Court . . . that tries the case to do effective justice, it is a contempt of any Court which very well may try the case, but in fact does not do so, as well as of the Court which actually tries it. [Emphasis added.]

The editor, Davies, was made to pay a hundred pounds for his journalistic mischief because it was considered likely to pollute justice and thereby contaminate the public welfare through depriving the judiciary of its power to administer justice duly and impartially.

Through the years, English courts continued to apply and extend the polluted-stream theory with a Draconian doctrine of constructive contempt.

[3] 2 Atk. 469, 26 Eng. Rep. 683.
[4] 1 K.B. 32 (1906).

One extension of it occurred in 1956.[5] The Sunday edition of *People* published an article about vice and prostitution containing an attack on one Micallef. Unknown to the editors, publishers, or printers, Micallef had recently been charged with keeping a brothel. Shortly after the publication of the story, Micallef was committed for trial. The Attorney General moved for an attachment and the court agreed that a contempt had been committed. Lord Goddard, who wrote the opinion, said that criminal intent was not essential to constitute the crime of contempt. In holding that knowledge is no prerequisite for a contempt conviction, he called the newspaper publishing business "a perilous adventure," to be undertaken with the assumption of the risk of possibly publishing matters about subjects that the law will later forbid should they come up at trial.

This decision created a print-at-your-own-risk situation, since by its application the stream of justice could be poisoned even if it was not known to exist. The unknown stream of justice later took some further strange turns when the contempt power was extended to streams that had not begun to flow and streams whose flow had ended, and where the stream itself was not contaminated but the navigator of the stream of justice was exposed to the evil influences of the poisonous flow.

Two cases extended the constructive contempt doctrine to comments about judges as opposed to comments about defendants or about cases and the administration of justice. The first, in 1928, dealt with remarks in the *New Statesman* about a Catholic judge's verdict in a birth control case.[6] Dr. Marie Stopes, the famous birth control advocate, had been sued for libel by the *Morning Post*. She had suggested that the *Morning Post* refused to publish her advertisements because of Roman Catholic influences. The libel action against her was successful. Thereupon, the *New Statesman* commented: "The serious point in this case, however, is that an individual owning to such views as those of Dr. Stopes cannot apparently hope for a fair hearing in a court presided over by Mr. Justice Avory—and there are so many Avorys."

Supposedly recognizing the past legal authority that the judges as individuals *are* subject to criticism, the court nevertheless held this statement contemptuous as scandalizing "the court itself" as opposed

[5] *Regina v. Odham's Press*, 3 W.L.R. 796 (1956), 1 Q.B. 73 (1957).
[6] *Rex v. Editor of the New Statesman*, 44 T.L.R. 301.

to the judge as an individual. It was held that this was more than criticism of a judge personally but was an imputation of his partiality and therefore something that would lower public confidence in the administration of justice. Defendants may be held in contempt "not for the sake of the Judges as private individuals, but because they are channels by which the King's justice is conveyed to the people."

In a case three years later, *Rex v. Colsey*,[7] the editor of *Truth* was held in contempt and fined for his discussion of Lord Justice Slesser's judgment in a case involving the Minister of Labor. The editor had said: "Lord Justice Slesser, who can hardly be altogether unbiased about legislation of this type, maintained that really it was a very nice provisional order or as good a one as can be expected in this vale of tears." Lord Justice Slesser had been Attorney General in a former Labor government which supported the legislation referred to. This rather mild comment was held to have been contemptuous.

The constructive contempt doctrine was extended in another direction in the notorious Dr. Adams case.[8] In 1957, Dr. John Bodkin Adams was tried and ultimately acquitted for the murder of an old woman who was his patient and under whose will he was a beneficiary. The case created worldwide interest. The European edition of *Newsweek* magazine contained some comments that could have been said to be prejudicial to Dr. Adams. The article was written in the United States, printed in Amsterdam, and distributed in Britain. The London distributor obviously was ignorant of the prejudicial matter. Nevertheless, the court held him guilty of contempt.

The apparent reason for scooping so deep into the barrel of responsibility was that in the eyes of the court someone had to be responsible. Since only the distributor was available, he was held liable on the theory that he was in charge of circulation within the country and was therefore the only one whom the court could punish in a case of this kind. Were no one held to be punishable, foreign publishers could take advantage of their immunity and conduct themselves irresponsibly where local publishers, susceptible to the court's contempt powers, could not. This decision put the news vendor in a particularly hazardous position. Obviously, vendors do not know the total content of all the

---

[7] 47 L.Q. Rev. 315.

[8] *Regina v. Griffiths,* 2 Q.B. 192 (1957). A further discussion of the Adams case is found above, pp. 148–149.

magazines that they distribute. Yet, not knowing of the existence of the stream of justice, they are liable for its having been poisoned.

The Administration of Justice Act of 1960[9] made some relieving procedural changes in English contempt law. For example, lack of knowledge of the existence of prejudicial comments after reasonable care had been taken may now be a defense to contempt charges. Thus some of the more aggravated extensions of the contempt doctrine just mentioned would be alleviated. Nevertheless, Lord Devlin was recently quoted summing up the English rule as one that prohibited any comment about a matter before a court that might tend to influence a jury in any way, whether done with good or bad intent, with or without knowledge.

It is this tradition of a constructive contempt doctrine that the American colonies originally adopted from the English. It will be seen that the nature of the American press, the nature of America's courts, and the nature of her popular values and philosophical preferences led to an application of the contempt doctrine in the United States that has varied widely from the English pattern.

The American Rule

The most influential, however adventitious, source of the contempt by publication doctrine has been a strange old English case entitled *Rex v. Almon*[10] involving an unusual set of events. The case gave rise to certain legal language which has been adopted, extended, and is persistently proffered as the source of contempt by publication both in England and in the United States.

Recent scholarship has shown that until the 1700's in England, contempts were treated in the same way as ordinary offenses. Defined crimes were tried by juries. But in 1764, a bookseller named Almon was tried for publishing an alleged libel about Lord Mansfield. Justice Wilmot, the judge in the Almon case, stood in very close relationship to Lord Mansfield, having been elevated to his position by a cabinet under Mansfield's influence. Wilmot considered criticism of his patron sacrilegious. Owing to a procedural mix-up, the Almon case was improperly titled by the court, and because of this technicality the decision

---

[9] 8 & 9 Eliz. 2, ch. 65.

[10] See Sir John Fox, *Contempt of Court* (Oxford: Clarendon Press, 1927).

was never rendered. The action was abandoned and the opinion of Justice Wilmot in the case was never delivered. In 1802, however, Wilmot's son published the notes of his father.[11] These included the stillborn, undelivered opinion in the Almon case. It contained the language, allowing summary punishment for contempt out of the presence of the court, that has been so controversially referred to ever since.

> The power which the courts . . . have of vindicating their own authority is coeval with their first foundation and institution; it is a necessary incident to every court of justice, . . . to fine and imprison for a contempt to the court, acted in the face of it . . . and the issuing attachments . . . for contempts out of court stands upon the same immemorial usage as supports the whole fabric of the common law; it is as much the *lex terrae* and within the exception of Magna Charta as the issuing [sic] any other legal process whatsoever. I have examined very carefully to see if I could find out any vestiges or traces of its introduction but can find none. It is as ancient as any other part of the common law; there is no priority or posteriority to be discovered about it and therefore [it] cannot be said to invade the common law, but to act in an alliance and friendly conjunction with every other provision which the wisdom of our ancestors has established for the general good of society. And though I do not mean to compare and contrast attachments with trial by jury, yet truth compels me to say that the mode of proceeding by attachment stands upon the very same foundation and basis as trial by juries do—immemorial usage and practice.

The historical underpinning for Wilmot's pronouncement has been proved wrong but the doctrine has survived. One reason for its acceptance into American law is the fact that Justice Wilmot was a friend of the Tory, Blackstone. When Blackstone wrote his famous and authoritative legal treatise he consulted Wilmot about the law of contempt and thus propagated Wilmot's view of the law. Blackstone's statement on the subject was tremendously influential in the American colonies, where his treatises were religiously followed. Thus, the Almon case was accepted as the common law of contempt by the American colonies and the early American courts.

The first American legislation dealing with the power of contempt of court was the Judiciary Act of 1789. It gave Federal courts "the power . . . to punish by fine or imprisonment, at the discretion of said courts,

[11] Wilmot's Notes 255.

all contempts of authority in any cause or hearing before the same."[12] The words "all contempts" implicitly included whatever the contempt power was at the common law. That was the Almon rule; and the earliest American decisions in interpreting the 1789 law referred to Wilmot's opinion as the enunciation of the common law.

This interpretation of the common law rule of contempt was followed in the United States until the famous case involving Judge Peck. It was his proposed impeachment for exercising this power that occasioned the first important change in American contempt law.

The story of the Peck episode is told deftly and fascinatingly by Nelles and King in two articles published in 1928.[13] Briefly, Judge Peck and an attorney named Luke Lawless became engaged in a wrangle involving Lawless's prosecution of a series of suits involving land grants under the old Spanish law. Judge Peck had ruled in a way fatal to a whole mass of these cases, including several brought by Lawless. Judge Peck's opinion was published in the newspapers in 1826. Later, Lawless published in a rival paper a statement critical of Peck's decision. Peck found Lawless guilty of contempt and sentenced him to a day's imprisonment and temporary suspension from the practice of law.

Lawless, who was not without considerable political influence, sought Judge Peck's impeachment by Congress and eventually, in 1830, the Senate Judiciary Committee took up the matter. The issue was whether summary punishment for publications out of court constituted willful oppression for which a Federal judge could be impeached, or whether the judge could have legitimately believed that he possessed this lawful contempt power. After almost a year of debate on that point, the vote was 22 to 21 for acquittal. Soon after the vote, however, the Judiciary Committee, led by James Buchanan, drew up a new law, which was enacted in 1831. It defined contempt of court as "any misbehavior in the presence of the court or so near thereto as to obstruct the administration of justice."

The new Federal statute was clearly adapted from early Pennsylvania and New York laws (1809 and 1829 respectively). Neither gave the courts power to punish summarily any kind of contempt except that in their actual physical presence. Nelles and King concluded that "what the Federal draftsman meant by misbehavior so near the presence of

---

[12] 1 Stat. 83.

[13] 28 *Columbia Law Review* 401, 525.

the court as to obstruct the administration of justice was substantially any breach of the peace, noise, or other disturbance directly tending to interrupt proceedings." It was aimed against that misbehavior which, though not in the court, was so near to it as to have the same effect as if committed in the actual presence of the court, for example, pounding a drum in the hallway and interrupting the progress of a trial. Although it would not appear to have taken place precisely in the presence of the court, it would in actuality have upset the conduct of the trial.

A second section of the Federal statute of 1831 specifically provided penalties for certain obstructions of justice that were not likely to be attempted in the very presence of the court. The addition confirms the construction that the prior section was to confine the use of summary power only to acts in the physical proximity of the court and not to more remote obstructions which were provided for elsewhere in the statute.

Between 1831, the time of the statute, and 1903, there were no indications that the Federal judiciary considered using the "so near" clause to punish publications out of court. As Justice Baldwin said in *U.S. v. Holmes*[14] in 1842, if any doubt of its meaning could arise from the language, "the occasion and circumstances of its enactment must effectually remove them." He held that the only acts punishable as misbehavior in the presence of the court or so near it as to obstruct justice are those creating noise or disorder that actually disturbs the court while it is sitting and impedes it in exercising its functions. Most states followed and implemented the 1831 Federal statute. And it is the progeny of this statute that has been interpreted by the United States Supreme Court in the last half century as the law of contempt by publication.[15]

The American Cases

The first major American decision concerning the modern doctrine of contempt by publication arose in a case entitled *Toledo Newspaper Company v. United States*.[16] The opinion was written by Chief Justice

[14] The authoritative judicial interpretation is attributed to Supreme Court Justice Baldwin, as circuit judge in Pennsylvania in *ex parte* Poulson, Fed. Cas. No. 11,350 (1835) and *U.S. v. Holmes,* Fed. Cas. No. 15,383 (1842).

[15] Ronald L. Goldfarb, *The Contempt Power* (New York: Columbia University Press, 1963).

[16] 247 U.S. 402 (1918).

Edward D. White and dealt with a case involving an alleged contempt by the *Toledo News Bee.*

The Toledo Railways and Light Company controlled and operated the street railways in Toledo under a franchise that was soon to expire. Creditors of the company sued the City of Toledo and the company to enjoin the enforcement of a recently passed ordinance which would have set fares at three cents. The ground for their suit was that the ordinance would confiscate their property in the company and destroy their franchises, which they alleged should be in effect for a longer time.

There was tremendous public agitation and discussion about the issue. The newspaper backed the city in a continued and vociferous series of daily articles. It also published a cartoon criticizing the presiding judge. The managing editor was found in contempt for comments about certain actions of the court.

His appeal provided the Supreme Court with its first opportunity to interpret the words of the 1831 Federal statute defining contempt as misbehavior in the presence of the court "or so near thereto as to obstruct the administration of justice."

The Court held that the test in interpreting these words is the character of the act done and not its direct tendency actually to prevent and obstruct justice. The opinion stated that it is enough if there is a reasonable tendency that the acts would influence or bring about a baleful result. Thus, a causal connotation was given to the words "or so near thereto as to obstruct the administration of justice."

Justice Oliver Wendell Holmes wrote a dissent. The thrust of it was that the use of summary contempt power by a judge must be limited to situations where it is necessary to assure order and decorum in his presence and to prevent the court from actual interference. The words of the statute, he said, meant in the physical presence of the court or near enough to cause an actual interference with the court as an accomplished fact.

The effect of the Supreme Court's majority holding was, in the meantime, to interpret Federal contempt law in a way consistent with the English common law rule, and in a way that gave courts the power to punish publication of crime or trial news.

Lower Federal courts thereupon acquired the sweeping doctrine of the Toledo case. Eventually, of the forty-eight states there were only six in which summary punishment for out-of-court publication was not sanctioned by the precedent of decision or by at least a judicial tendency in that direction. This has been called a twentieth-century subversion of an American Constitutional rule that had been settled in the nineteenth century.

The law of the Toledo case prevailed until 1941, when the Supreme Court reversed itself in a case that had nothing to do with press publication or trial publicity, but nevertheless had a far-reaching effect on the freedom of the press. The case was *Nye v. United States.*[17]

Nye had persuaded an enfeebled, illiterate old man who was suing in the Federal district court in Durham, North Carolina, for the wrongful death of his son to drop the case against Nye's son-in-law and another man. Nye had the old man brought from South Carolina to Lumberton, North Carolina, a hundred miles from the court. He inveigled him into sending a letter to the judge in Greensboro, North Carolina, requesting that the lawsuit be terminated.

The court-appointed attorney for the old man became angry when he learned what had happened, and asked the court to find Nye guilty of criminal contempt. This the court did, even though only persuasion and no payments or promises had taken place. Nye's conduct, the court held, prevented the prosecution of a civil action in a Federal court and was done with the intent to prevent and obstruct a case being tried on its merits—all causing delay and expense and obstructing the administration of justice. The court summarily treated the case as a contempt committed in the presence of the court or so near thereto as to obstruct the administration of justice. Nye was fined. He appealed his case all the way to the Supreme Court.

Justice William O. Douglas wrote the Court's opinion, reversing Nye's summary conviction and, in the process, re-examining the law of contempt by publication. He began by dismissing the holding in the Toledo case, declaring: "The inaccuracy of that historic observation [the Court's interpretation in the Toledo case of the Federal contempt statute] has been plainly demonstrated."

The issue, Justice Douglas said, was whether the statute's words "so near thereto" have a geographical or a causal connotation. The Court's holding: geographical.

"It is not sufficient that the misbehavior charged has some direct

[17] 313 U.S. 33 (1941).

relation to the work of the court. 'Near' in this context, juxtaposed to 'presence,' suggests physical proximity not relevancy," the Court ruled. The fact that the judge received the letter that obstructed justice did not make the case one involving misconduct in the vicinity of the court. Summary contempt actions may only be had for noise or disorder that actually interrupt the court in the conduct of its business. The legislative history of the contempt statute, the interpretations of the Federal courts until the Toledo case, and the character and nature of the proceedings all lead to this substantial distinction, Justice Douglas held.

Furthermore, Justice Douglas's opinion pointed out, Congress's intention in this statute was to distinguish between two kinds of wrongs: those in the actual physical presence of the court, with which the court could deal summarily, and those involving the court but not in its presence, which should be tried as crimes in the ordinary way. Congressional intent would be nullified by any other construction of the words in issue and the distinction between which crimes could be tried without a jury and which need not would be obliterated. That reprehensible conduct is not reached via the summary contempt power does not mean the conduct can proceed with impunity, the Court reminded.

Justice Harlan F. Stone dissented, arguing that spatial tests are wrong where the evil effect of the conduct in question does not depend upon physical nearness to the court. "Near," he said, "is of significance only in its causal relationship to the obstructions of justice." But this was now an echo of discredited past thinking, and an approach that was laid to rest in cases that were to follow.

The Clear and Present Danger Test

The Nye case settled the construction of the contempt statute. Later cases engaged in another debate, this one about the meaning and application of the court-fashioned clear and present danger test to press publication cases. The issue came up in 1941 in the Bridges and *Times-Mirror* cases.

In *Bridges v. California* and *Times-Mirror Company v. Supreme Court of California*,[18] the Supreme Court dealt with the issue of contemptuous publication that involved neither criticism of judges or courts

[18] 314 U.S. 252.

nor published material alleged to be prejudicial to a defendant facing trial by jury. In these cases, the editorials in question dealt with matters that were under judicial consideration. One case involved a newspaper editorial attacking two union members accused of assault and urging the judge to deal strictly with them. The trial was over. The defendants had been found guilty. Only the issue of sentence remained. The other two editorials commented on accused persons who also had already been found guilty before Los Angeles courts and were awaiting sentence.

The first editorial was in the December 21, 1937, *Los Angeles Times-Mirror*. It concerned a recent conviction of twenty-two strikers and its implications for unionism on the West Coast and particularly in Los Angeles. The editorial spoke of union terrorism and continued:

> It is an important verdict. For the first time since the present cycle of labor disturbances began union lawlessness has been treated as exactly what it is. An offense against the public peace punishable like any other crime. . . .
>
> Government may have broken down in other localities; whole states may have yielded to anarchy. But Los Angeles County stands firm; it has officers who can do their duty and courts and juries which can function.

On May 5, 1938, the same paper printed the second questioned editorial, calling for tough sentences in a completed case. It was entitled "Probation for Gorillas," and read:

> Two members of Dave Beck's wrecking crew, entertainment committee, goon squad or gorillas having been convicted in Superior Court of assaulting nonunion truck drivers have asked for probation. Presumably they will say they are first offenders or plead that they were merely indulging a playful exuberance when, with slingshots, they fired steel missiles at men whose only offense was wishing to work for a living without paying tribute to the erstwhile boss of Seattle.
>
> Sluggers for pay, like murderers for profit, are in a slightly different category from ordinary criminals. Men who commit mayhem for wages are not merely violators of the peace and dignity of the state; they are also conspirators against it. The man who burgles because his children are hungry may have some claim on public sympathy. He whose crime is one of impulse may be entitled to lenity. But he who hires out his muscles for the creation of disorder and in aid of a racket is a deliberate foe of organized society and should be penalized accordingly.
>
> It will teach no lesson to other thugs to put these men on good be-

havior for a limited time. Their duty would simply be taken over by others like them. If Beck's thugs, however, are made to realize that they face San Quentin when they are caught it will tend to make their disreputable occupation unpopular. Judge A. A. Scott will make a serious mistake if he grants probation to Matthew Shannon and Kennan Holmes. This community needs the example of their assignment to the jute mill.

The third editorial (also printed after a jury had found the subject of the editorial guilty) appeared on April 14, 1938. It dealt with a local woman who had been a long-time political boss but who was recently committed for bribery. The editorial mused about her past, her political demise, and the irony of her case:

> . . . It is only fair to say that to her the power was much more important than the perquisites. When the inevitable turning of the political wheel brought new figures to the front and new bosses to the back she found her grip slipping and it was hard to take. The several cases which in recent years have brought her before the courts to defend her activities seem all examples of an energetic effort to retain and reassert her onetime influence in high places. That it should ultimately have landed her behind the bars as a convicted bribe seeker is not illogical. But if there is logic in it, the money meant less to Mrs. Warner than the name of still being a political power.

The companion (Bridges) case involved a telegram from labor leader Harry Bridges to the United States Secretary of Labor. The pertinent portions, published in newspapers in San Francisco and Los Angeles on January 24 and 25, 1938, read:

> This decision is outrageous. . . . Attempted enforcement of Schmidt decision will tie up port of Los Angeles and involve entire Pacific coast. International Longshoremen Warehousemen Union representing over 11,000 of the 12,000 Longshoremen on the Pacific Coast does not intend to allow state courts to override the majority vote of members in choosing its officers and representatives and to override the National Labor Relations Board.

Bridges was found in contempt of court and appealed to the Supreme Court. His case and the case involving the three editorials of the Los Angeles *Times-Mirror* were joined in one opinion of the Supreme Court. In all these situations, there was no prejudiceable jury to consider.

The trials were over and proceedings could be said to be pending only to the extent that sentence was yet to be adjudged. The Bridges telegram was made public while a motion for a new trial was pending. (It is interesting that only Bridges was fined for contempt and the Los Angeles and San Francisco newspapers that published it were not.) In the *Times-Mirror* case, the two labor unionists and the woman of politics had been convicted and were requesting probation. The editorials were printed some time before the date set by the trial judge for passing on the application and pronouncing sentence.

Justice Hugo Black wrote the majority decision overruling both contempt convictions handed down by the California courts. The Supreme Court held that the First Amendment guarantee of free speech and press invalidated English practices restricting that freedom and that, as a matter of fact, one of the very objects of the American Revolution had been to rid the new country of freedom of the press, English style. Recognizing the perplexity of choice-making in the press-trial conflict, the majority's choice was free press and speech. The opinion reflected the post-New Deal Supreme Court's preference for a strong if not absolute interpretation of First Amendment liberties which must predominate in almost all cases of conflict.

Justice Black's theory was that historically the intent of the Constitution's authors was to give the press a liberty of the broadest scope consistent with orderly society. Dismissing the issue of the state-Federal conflict, which the majority resolved by holding that the First Amendment is incorporated into the Fourteenth and therefore binds the states, the Court applied the clear and present danger test to the contempt by publication dilemma.

Enunciated in a different context by Justice Holmes in *Schenck v. U.S.*,[19] the clear and present danger test in effect gave protection to the Constitutionally guaranteed freedom of speech unless the words in question were "used in such circumstances and are of such a nature as to create a clear and present danger that they will bring about the substantive evils." Applying what it called the working principle of the clear and present danger test, the Court found that the publications were not likely to bring about substantive evils serious or imminent enough to be punishable. Disrespect of the judiciary and interference

[19] 249 U.S. 47 (1918).

with the administration of justice, it was held, was negligible, certainly not warranting censorship of utterances of public interest.

Justice Felix Frankfurter wrote a minority dissent, arguing that the majority's interpretation of freedom of speech tore at the historical powers of state courts to protect the state's administration of justice. In his view, free speech was "not so absolute or irrational a conception as to imply paralysis of the means for effective protection of all the freedoms secured by the Bill of Rights," such as fair trial. Drawing a distinction between comment and the free flow of doctrine and intimidation that subverts a pending judicial proceeding, Justice Frankfurter saw intimidation in the cases before the Court. His rationale for the use of the contempt power was that courts are not organs of popular will as are the executive branch and the legislature, and therefore stand in more serious need of this power to facilitate their function. The dissenters felt that the contempt power as a control of out-of-court publications was becoming useless with the Court veering more clearly and more strongly away from permitting its application.

Justice Black's majority opinion in the Bridges case (joined in by Justices Reed, Douglas, Murphy, and Jackson) held that the serious substantive evils to be averted were disrespect for the judiciary and disorderly or unfair administration of justice. It excluded the first as a substantive evil because to consider it so would be "to impute to judges a lack of firmness, wisdom or honor—which we cannot accept. . . . The assumption that respect for the judiciary can be won by shielding judges from published criticism wrongly appraises the character of American public opinion." The second evil, disorderly and unfair administration of justice, is then the substantive evil to be prevented under this application of the clear and present danger rule. The intimation was that it should be restricted to pending litigation. Courts must examine the specific utterance and the circumstances of its publication to determine the likelihood and the extent of the evil causing unfair administration of justice.

Justice Frankfurter, joined by Chief Justice Stone and Justices Roberts and Byrnes, drew the lines differently. The dissenters felt that criticism of courts and judges in general and the discussion of past or future cases should be permitted. However, publications that interfere with the impartial and calm disposition of matters under judicial consideration should be punished. Judges, in Justice Frankfurter's words, "however stalwart are human" and "the delicate task of administering justice ought not to be made unduly difficult by irresponsible print."

The Bridges case adopted the clear and present danger test as a guide for determining which out-of-court publications did in fact obstruct justice. That the clear and present danger test permitted press comments about courts and judges soon was made quite clear. In 1946, the United States Supreme Court issued two decisions dealing with contempts arising out of newspaper criticism of judges.

The first of these was *Pennekamp v. Florida*.[20] Because of two editorials, the publisher and associate editor of the *Miami Herald* were found guilty of contempt by the local circuit court.

The editorials, in October and November, 1944, criticized local judges for going out of their way to favor criminal defendants by allowing technicalities to delay swift convictions.

The first editorial described the local judicial complexion, and after some rather innocuous moralizing, stated:

> The seeming ease and past facility with which the criminally charged have been given technical safeguards have set people to wondering whether their courts are being subverted into refuges for law breakers.

And, after detailing some specific complaints about recent rulings, and pointing out the power of the people to elect judges, another editorial stated:

> This may be good law, exact judicial evaluation of the statutes. It is, however, the character of legal interpretations which causes people to raise questioning eyebrows and shake confused heads in futile wonderment.
>
> If technicalities are to be the order and a way for the criminally charged either to avoid justice altogether or serve to delay prosecution . . . then it behooves our courts and the legal profession to cut away the dead wood and the entanglements.

The second editorial was entitled "Why People Wonder." It discussed two cases, one in which it was suggested that the court acted too hastily, another where it acted too slowly, both to the disadvantage of the prosecution. The editorial commented:

[20] 328 U.S. 331 (1946).

Here is an example of why people wonder about the law's delays and obstructing technicalities operating to the disadvantage of the state —which is the people—in prosecutions.

After describing the two instances complained of, it concluded:

. . . There you have the legal paradox working two ways but to the same purpose against prosecution. Speed when needed, month after month of delay when that serves them better.

The editorials that constituted the alleged contempts were accompanied by a cartoon which caricatured the court tossing off charges and dismissing a case in favor of a powerful figure portrayed as a criminal, while at one side an individual labeled "Little Public Interest" vainly protested.

The newspaper's defense in its contempt case (one which came but three years after the Bridges case) was that there was no clear and present danger that the editorials or the cartoon would affect the administration of justice in cases pending before the court. Therefore, it was argued, the First Amendment protected the contemnors. The Supreme Court accepted this argument in an opinion by Justice Stanley F. Reed, holding that no present danger to the administration of justice in Florida was posed by the editorials or cartoon. The opinion noted that there was no jury in this case. Inasmuch as the criticism was aimed at judicial action that had already been completed, it was incapable of affecting the court's decision. The opinion said: ". . . the danger under this record to thwart judicial administration has not the clearness and immediacy necessary to close the door of permissible public conduct. When that door is closed, it closes all doors behind it."

The Court went on further to particularize the meaning of the clear and present danger test and its application to cases involving judges alone: ". . . too many fine-drawn assumptions against the independence of judicial action must be made to call such a possibility a clear and present danger to justice. For this to follow, there must be a judge of less than ordinary fortitude without friends or supporters, a powerful and vindictive newspaper bent upon a rule or ruin policy, and a public unconcerned with or uninterested in the truth or the protection of their judicial institutions."

As to the timing of the editorials and the status of the trial to which they pertained, the Court said: "Discussion that follows the termination of a case may be inadequate to emphasize the danger to public welfare of supposedly wrongful judicial conduct. It does not follow that public comment of every character upon pending trials or legal proceedings may be as free as a similar comment after complete disposal of the litigation. . . . Courts must have power to protect the interests of prisoners and litigants before them from unseemly efforts to pervert judicial action."

There were three concurring opinions: by Justice Frank Murphy, Justice Wiley B. Rutledge, and Justice Felix Frankfurter. Doubtless the most important was Justice Frankfurter's. His was an essay about the free press, fair trial conflict and an articulation of the view of a minority of the Court through the years which favored a contempt by publication rule more like the English. Justice Frankfurter argued that freedom of the press is not an end in itself but only a means to an end. While freedom gives power, power in our democratic society implies responsibility. The press has such a responsibility. Judges themselves are not free from criticism, but the functions which judges exercise need to be protected. Further, Justice Frankfurter argued for recognition of the principle that in state cases the administration of criminal justice (ordinarily considered to be a local matter) is owed a greater degree of deference by the Supreme Court.

Soon after the Pennekamp decision, the Supreme Court was again called upon to deal with the same subject. This case—*Craig v. Harney*[21] —involved a drawn-out donnybrook between the Corpus Christi, Texas, news media and a local judge.

The fight arose out of an unlikely and unglamorous forcible detainer case in the Corpus Christi County court. One man sought to regain possession of a business building in Corpus Christi from a serviceman who claimed to have a lease. He argued that the soldier had lost his interest because of nonpayment of rent.

At the close of the testimony on May 26, 1945, the judge instructed the jury to return a verdict for the plaintiff. Instead, the jury ruled for the defendant soldier. The judge refused to accept the verdict and again instructed the jury to reconsider and return a verdict as he ordered. The jury returned a second time with a contrary verdict. Again the judge refused to accept it. That evening the judge repeated his prior

[21] 331 U.S. 367.

instruction and when the jury did not comply he recessed the court until the following morning.

The local newspaper reported some innocuous facts about the case on May 26.

On May 27, a news item factually reported the court's original rulings and ended with the line: "The effect of this ruling was that Browning [the judge] took the matter from the jury."

Then, on May 28, the newspaper printed this statement of the defense attorney to the jury:

> . . . I now advise you that under the law Judge Browning has the right to compel you even against the dictates of your conscience to sign the verdict he has ordered.
>
> As a matter of fact it is probable that he has the power to put you in jail until such time as you do sign it and I rather imagine from what has heretofore taken place in this trial that unless you do sign the verdict he will cause you to be put in jail.
>
> As I and my clients feel that you have done all in your power to register your protest and revulsion of feeling at the effect of this decision reached by Judge Browning; as you are helpless to do anything further; and as making you suffer by remaining locked up will not do us a bit of good I suggest that you sign the verdict and return to your homes with a clear conscience in having done all that you could do to protect the rights of a man who I feel and evidently you feel has been done a great injustice.
>
> While we have no appeal from the court's decision in this case we do have the right again to appeal to his conscience by presenting a motion for a new trial in this action—and which motion we will file and argue strenuously with the hope that in the meantime he will see the error committed and will rectify the same.
>
> There cannot be any doubt that the action of you men in registering your protest against this decision as you have done will affect him. At least I can only hope that it will. I sincerely thank you.

The jury finally complied with Judge Browning's command, stating that its judgment was made under coercion of the court and against its conscience.

On May 29, the defendant moved for a new trial, and on the 30th an editorial criticized the judge and the practice of allowing nonlawyers on the bench:

> Browning's behavior and attitude has brought down the wrath of public opinion on his head, properly so. Emotions have been aggra-

vated. American people simply don't like the idea of such goings on. Especially when a man in the service of his country seems to be getting a raw deal. . . .

That was the travesty on justice. The judge's refusal to hear both sides. That's where a legal background would have served him in good stead. It is difficult to believe that any lawyer, even a hack, would have followed such high handed procedure in instructing a jury. It's no wonder that the jury balked and public opinion is outraged.

The fact that a serviceman is involved lends drama to the event. But it could have happened to anyone and it can happen to anyone with a layman sitting as a judge in a case where fine points of law are involved. True, the idea that only lawyers are qualified to occupy most public offices has been run into the ground and in most instances a competent layman would be better qualified but the county judge's office is an exception. He should be a competent attorney as well as a competent business man.

It's the tragedy in a case of this sort that the court where the controversial decision was handed down was the court of last resort. It's too bad that appeal can't be made to a district court and heard by a judge who is familiar with proper procedure and able to interpret and weigh motions and arguments by opposing counsel and to make his decisions accordingly. . . . There is no way of knowing whether justice was done because the first rule of justice, giving both sides an opportunity to be heard, was repudiated.

Also on the 30th, the newspaper reported a resolution issued by the Soldiers and Sailors Advisory Council of Corpus Christi concerning the judge's conduct.

Finally, on May 31, 1945, the last news story to appear pointed out that several local groups were seeking a new trial and asking the judge to disqualify himself from further action in this matter.

On June 4, an officer of the county court filed a complaint charging the defendants, a publisher, an editorial writer, and a news reporter on the local newspaper, with contempt of court based on the foregoing articles. And on June 6, Judge Browning denied the motion for a new trial of the civil case.

The newsmen were found guilty of contempt and the appellate courts upheld the conviction. The case was appealed to the United States Supreme Court. It threw out the contempt convictions, declaring:

A trial is a public event. What transpires in the courtroom is public property. If a transcript of the court proceedings had been published, we suppose none would claim the judge could punish the publisher for contempt. And we can see no difference though the conduct of the attorneys, of the jury, or even of the judge himself, may have reflected on the court. Those who see and hear what transpired can report it with impunity. There is no special perquisite of the judiciary which enables it, as distinguished from other institutions of democratic government to suppress, edit or censor events which transpire in proceedings before it.

The Pennekamp and Craig cases reflected a development in the philosophy of the clear and present danger test. In Pennekamp, the Court characterized the problem as one of striking "a balance between the desirability of free discussion and the necessity for fair adjudication, free from interruption of its processes." In the Craig case, the Court said that freedom of the press could not be impaired "unless there is no doubt that the utterances . . . are a serious and imminent threat to the administration of justice." "The vehemence of the language used is not alone the measure of the power to punish for contempt. The fire which kindles must constitute an imminent, not merely a likely, threat to the administration of justice. The danger must not be remote or even probable; it must immediately imperil."

The clear and present danger test has been reformulated elsewhere in noncontempt cases. Some of them carry the indication that the danger does not have to be imminent, and to the extent that that interpretation may prevail in the future, the courts would of course have more leverage in curbing publication.

In the famous Smith Act case, *Dennis v. United States*,[22] the Supreme Court placed emphasis on the magnitude rather than the imminence of the evil: "In each case [courts] must ask whether the gravity of the evil, discounted by its improbability, justifies such invasion of free speech as is necessary to avoid the danger."

The Supreme Court's opinions have left room for the inference that the clear and present danger test might lead to different results if jury decisions were threatened. This judge-jury distinction which recognizes that jurors may be more susceptible to influence than judges, and therefore may cause clearer and more present dangers, was advanced for the first time in *State v. Baltimore Radio Show*.[23]

The case arose out of three contempt citations issued by the Criminal

[22] 341 U.S. 494 (1951).
[23] 333 U.S. 912 (1950).

Court of Baltimore City imposing fines for broadcasting over the local radio stations news dispatches at a time when a defendant charged with murder was in custody of the police.

In the early afternoon of July 6, 1948, Marsha Brill, an eleven-year-old girl, was dragged from her bicycle and stabbed to death by an unidentified man in the northwestern section of Baltimore while she was playing with two other children. Similar crimes had recently occurred in this area; the residents were aroused and concerned about the safety of their children. That evening, Eugene H. James was arrested and held for investigation. On July 8, he was taken to the scene of the crime. He had admitted his guilt and directed the police to the spot where he had buried the murder weapon—a knife. That night he was formally charged with murder. A few hours later he signed a written confession.

Later that evening the police commissioner verified certain information put to him by the night editor of the United Press and disclosed other information about the case. Still later that evening, he was interviewed by the press outside police headquarters and responded to questions, although his answers were not in the form of a formal press release. Throughout the night of July 8, Station WITH continued to broadcast long and detailed analyses of the crime. The same information that the United Press gathered was teletyped to WCBM and WFBR, subscribers to the UP, and they also made broadcasts about the case. The local newspapers did *not* publish this detailed information.

On July 8, at 8:45 P.M., one broadcaster began a report over WITH with the words, "Stand by for a sensation." He went on to recount the crime and its solution. His story, only one of the several reports broadcast that night, follows:

> After three days of unrelenting hard work on the part of every man in the department the Baltimore police have just broken the Brill murder case—broken it wide open. Police Commissioner Hamilton R. Atkinson announced only a few moments ago that a man has been arrested and formally charged with the crime—the brutal and apparently pointless stabbing of eleven year old Marsha Brill in the Pimlico neighborhood Tuesday afternoon. The funeral of the little girl victim was held today and hundreds of persons attended. The man now charged with the Brill girl's murder is Eugene James, a thirty-one year old Negro and convicted former offender whose home is at 3311 Peyton Avenue not far from the scene of the crime.

The police said James not only admitted the brutal murder and another recent assault in the same area, but that he went over the scene of the crime with them late this afternoon and showed them where the murder weapon was buried. It turned out to be an old kitchen carving knife. Immediately after the finding of the knife, the prisoner was taken downtown to police headquarters for a formal statement. The story of how James came to be charged with the Brill murder is an account of police work at its best. James was taken into custody yesterday mainly because of his record. Police remembered that he had been charged or suspected in past years with a series of assaults and that about ten years ago he was sentenced to the Maryland penitentiary for an attack on a ten year old child. The police took into account also the fact that James's home was close to the scene of the Brill crime.

James was questioned along with other suspects but no information of much importance was obtained from him until today. The police did not use any force, of course, but questioned him persistently. Then this morning, according to the officers, James admitted an attack on a white woman recently in the same woods near where the Brill child was slain. In that case, too, James used a knife only to threaten his victim into submission. She wasn't otherwise injured. With more information supplied by James, police recovered the woman's pocket book which had been taken from her. Police said James was familiar with every foot of the ground on which the offenses, the assault on the woman and the slaying of the girl, occurred. James is not an obvious mental case. Throughout all his questioning, said the police, he seemed, as they put it, quite cute. In other words wary. When James freely admitted the assault on a woman the police were encouraged and renewed their interrogation with renewed vigor. They felt that James had admitted the lesser assault only to throw the police off the main track and the police felt they were close to a confession in the Brill case. They were in fact.

A few hours later, the prisoner broke again, and this time it was the break that broke the Brill case. James admitted that crime also and consented to accompany the police to the scene. On the ground, said the police, he made a more detailed admission. Among those who accompanied him to the scene of the crime were the highest ranking officers of the department. They were led by Commissioner Atkinson. With him were Chief Inspector M. Joseph Wallace, Inspector Joseph Itzel, who had directed the examination of James and other suspects, and Captain Oscar Lusby, the comparatively new commander of the Northern Police District.

The appearance of the high ranking police officials with an obvious suspect on the scene of the crime soon drew hundreds of idle spectators and for that reason the police did not linger on the ground any longer than necessary. Instead, they took James and the evidence they had accumulated downtown to police headquarters for a formal statement. From headquarters the prisoner was taken to the Northern Station. He probably will be arraigned in the Northern Police Court tomorrow.

The first hint that the police were close to an important break in the Brill case came with word from an officer of rank at headquarters that while no arrest had been made and no charges had yet been placed, the police felt they had a very good suspect. James was the suspect, of course. At that time he had not confessed the Brill crime, although he had admitted the earlier offense against the woman in the same neighborhood. Since the break in the case came so late in the day, the police at first were inclined to postpone making the actual charge against James until tomorrow. In view of the intense interest in the case, however, and in view of the alarm and agitation among parents and children in the area in which the crime occurred, Commissioner Atkinson decided to make the charge and the announcement immediately in order to relieve any anxiety among the families in the Pimlico area.

The police are deserving of the utmost commendation for the comparatively quick break in the case and the commendation is merited by every man who worked on the assignment from the highest to the lowest in the department. From the first, Commissioner Atkinson personally took charge of the investigation. The hunt for the slayer promised to be a long, hard, routine search. The killer had escaped from the scene despite a wide dragnet thrown around it soon after the alarm. Usually when arrest is not immediately made on or near the scene, such cases develop into long exhausting investigations that end usually only when police get some favorable break. In this case the officers made their own break by remembering James's record and taking him in hand promptly. Had the police not been so alert and so prompt, James might have fled the city. With the prisoner in hand, all the rest was accomplished by patient and skilled interrogation. Dozens of suspects were examined and released until the police felt reasonably sure that the lone man remaining in custody was the one they wanted.

The police ought to be congratulated and it is tragic that all the community can do otherwise is commiserate with the bereaved family. Fifteen hundred dollars in the award money has been offered for the arrest and conviction of the girl's slayer and the distribution of that money among those who have earned it remains to be decided. But, if I am not mistaken, the police do not consider themselves eligible for rewards.

Later broadcasts repeated similar incriminating stories, and dealt with the relation between court leniency and crime in the community. At one point the comment was made: "When James, the defendant in the Brill case, was up before for assaulting a ten year old girl, his sentence was 23 years. His release recently means, therefore, that he served only about ten years of the original sentence."

On July 9, James was indicted for the Brill murder and for the assault and rape of a woman some weeks before. About a week later, he plead not guilty and not guilty by reason of insanity. On September 20, 1948, he was tried in Baltimore without a jury, found guilty of murder in the first degree, and sentenced to death. His conviction was affirmed on appeal.

On July 20, citations for contempt were issued against the Baltimore Radio Show, Inc., the Baltimore Broadcasting Corporation, and James P. Connelly, a broadcaster for WITH. The difficulty in finding a resolution of the conflicting Constitutional issues raised by the case—even the problem of distinguishing the bad guys from the good guys—was evidenced by the fact that among the amicus curiae briefs supporting the contemnors was one of the American Civil Liberties Union, while the organization's affiliate, the Maryland Civil Liberties Committee, supported the court in an amicus brief urging that the greater need to protect defendants justified the contempt citation.

At issue was a rule, dating from 1939, of the Supreme Bench of Baltimore making it a contempt to issue statements relative to the conduct of the accused, or admissions, or matters bearing upon the issues to be tried, forecasts about the future course of the action by prosecutive or defense authorities, or "the publication of any matter which may prevent a fair trial, improperly influence the court or the jury or tend in any manner to interfere with the administration of justice."

At the contempt proceedings, the defense counsel for James testified that one of his reasons for waiving a jury was that he "felt that inasmuch as it was common knowledge throughout the city that James had allegedly made a confession, and that he had been previously convicted for crimes somewhat similar to his then present indictment, I did not feel that I could have picked a jury that had not been infected, so to speak, by the knowledge of this man's confession and his criminal background." During the trial, the written and oral confessions were admitted and in the course of medical testimony James's previous convictions and incarceration were brought to the court's attention.

The principal defense in the contempt proceedings was that the contempt power was limited by the First and Fourteenth Amendments which under the facts in this case barred a conviction. It was also argued that there was no deliberate attempt to influence the outcome of the case since the statements were not argumentative but factual. In the words of the Bridges case, "If there was electricity in the atmosphere, it was generated by the facts" more than by the "explicit statement of them." Moreover, it was argued, the broadcasts were mitigated by the circumstance that the statements were verified by public authorities.

A Baltimore trial court found the three Maryland broadcasting companies guilty of contempt and imposed fines. The lower court held that the broadcasts constituted "not merely a clear and present danger to the administration of justice, but an actual obstruction to the administration of justice in that they deprived the defendant of his constitutional right to have an impartial jury trial."

The Maryland appellate court said that these broadcasts did not in and of themselves make a fair trial impossible. The accused had his rights to examine on voir dire and move for continuances and to use all other techniques for attempting to sift out such prejudices as may have existed. As there was no direct evidence of prejudice because of the broadcast information, there was no clear and present danger to satisfy the appropriate constitutional test. The contempt convictions were reversed.

A dissent pointed out the interesting paradox that customarily in these cases arguments are made that (1) prejudice in a jury can always be prevented *so why worry,* and (2) there is a prejudice in a jury that can never be prevented *so why try.*

The dissent went on to point out that there were then almost 1,700 daily newspapers and more than 2,500 licensed radio stations disseminating information to the general public. There were also more than 83 million radios and more than one and one-half million television sets in the United States. It was estimated conservatively that every day more than 135 million people used services rendered by radio broadcasts, and these numbers were rising swiftly. Changes of venue, thus, will not prevent obstructions of justice. Procedures of this kind are only attempts to flee from the influence of the media, and flight from the media is futile. Moreover, citizens should not be forced to relinquish their right to a jury trial and submit to court trials in order to escape an intolerable situation that they did not cause.

The Supreme Court denied certiorari, thus letting stand the appellate court's reversal of the contempt citations. Justice Frankfurter filed an opinion nonetheless, pointing out the facts as the trial court had stated them, noting the compelling and widespread public interest in the matter, and describing what he obviously felt was the prejudicial broadcast of Connelly. He urged that the broadcasts in question must have had an indelible effect on the public mind. As to the usefulness of the techniques of voir dire, he quoted the trial court's statement: "It hardly seems necessary for the Court to say to men who are experienced in the trial of jury cases, that every time Defense Counsel asked a prospective juror whether he had heard a radio broadcast to the effect that his client has confessed to this crime or that he has been guilty of similar crimes, he would by that act be driving just one more nail into James's coffin. We think, therefore, that remedy was useless."

Justice Frankfurter also pointed out that the Supreme Court's refusal to grant certiorari meant only that fewer than four members of the Court wanted to review this state court decision and should not be construed as a condoning of the state court's decision. He described the rationales for denying certiorari and pointed out that denial indicates nothing about the merits of the case or about the law—that the Court's action "does not remotely imply approval or disapproval of what was said by the Court of Appeals in Maryland." He concluded by adding an appendix of recent English decisions dealing with the situation in the twentieth century (up to 1945) in ways contrary to the treatment by American courts and obviously more akin to his views.

A New Route

At mid-century, thus rested the Supreme Court's treatment of contempt by publication about trial and pretrial events. It seemed quite settled that the law had evolved in such a way as to provide the press with what amounted to near immunity from punishment by contempt for publication. Contempt was limited to misconduct in the presence of the court—the last place where the press was likely to indulge in prejudicial misbehavior.

But within a year or two, it developed that the Supreme Court, while not departing from its insulation of the press through a protective preference of First Amendment rights, would nonetheless seek a way to strike down convictions based upon jury trials held in an inflammatory and prejudiced atmosphere. Without punishing the press, the Court indicated in a series of cases that it would solve the problem by reversing on due process grounds convictions effected by prejudicial publication. This difference in perspective was first stated by Justice Tom Clark in *Stroble v. California*,[24] a case where the Supreme Court affirmed a state murder conviction in a highly publicized case. Justice Clark drew the distinction in these words: ". . . we are not faced with any question as to the permissible scope of newspaper comment regarding pending litigations . . . but with the question whether newspaper accounts aroused such prejudice in the community that petitioner's trial was fatally infected with an absence of that fundamental fairness essential to the very concept of justice."

The first case that found such a deprivation of due process was *Shepherd v. Florida*.[25]

On July 16, 1949, a seventeen-year-old white girl in Lake County, Florida, claimed to have been raped at pistol point by four Negroes. Community feeling at the time was extremely high and, in the words of the Supreme Court, was "exploited to the limit of the press." The defendants were taken to the county jail. Soon a mob gathered outside, demanding the prisoners. To protect them, the court transferred them to the state prison. But during the interim before trial the mobs burned Negro homes including that of the parents of one of the defendants. Negroes in the community moved their homes and fled in fear of being lynched. The National Guard was called in on three occasions and the 116th Field Artillery ultimately had to be summoned from Tampa to protect the peace.

The press played the story to the hilt. At the time the grand jury investigated the case, a cartoon appeared in a local paper picturing four electric chairs with the caption: "No Compromise—Supreme Penalty." Later, the newspapers published the sheriff's report that the defendants had confessed; and it was determined that witnesses and jurors had heard or read the account. Defense motions for a continuance and a change of venue were denied. The trial judge enforced strict decorum in the courtroom during the course of the trial and excluded the confession that had been reported in the press. Yet community climate was

---

[24] 343 U.S. 181 (1952).
[25] 341 U.S. 50 (1952).

such, the Supreme Court determined, that no juror would acquit the defendants.

In a concurring opinion to a decision reversing the conviction, Justice Jackson said: "It is hard to imagine a more prejudicial influence than a press release by the officer of the court charged with defendants' custody stating that they had confessed, and here just such a statement, unsworn to, unseen, uncross-examined and uncontradicted, was conveyed by the press to the jury." Dealing with the perplexities of the problem of assessing pretrial publicity, Justice Jackson added:

> But prejudicial influences outside the courtroom, becoming all too typical of a highly publicized trial, were brought to bear on this jury with such force that the conclusion is inescapable that these defendants were prejudged as guilty and the trial was but a legal gesture to register a verdict already dictated by the press and the public opinion which it generated.

Noting that the Supreme Court had "gone a long way to disable a trial judge from dealing with press interference with the trial process" in the Craig, Pennekamp, Nye, and Bridges cases, he said:

> . . . if freedoms of the press are so abused as to make fair trial in the locality impossible, the judicial process must be protected by removing the trial to a forum beyond its probable influence. *Newspapers, in the enjoyment of their constitutional rights, may not deprive accused persons of their right to fair trial. These convictions . . . do not meet any civilized conception of due process of law. That alone is sufficient . . . to warrant reversal. . . .* The case presents one of the best examples of one of the worst menaces to American justice. [Emphasis added.]

The conviction was reversed.

A question about prejudice of grand jury (as opposed to petit or trial jury) arose in 1962 in *Beck v. Washington.*[26] In this case, the notorious union leader David Beck argued that his conviction for grand larceny in the Washington Superior Court was invalid because adverse publicity, highly circulated by the news media in the vicinity of Seattle where he was indicted and tried, violated his right to due process and equal protection of the law under the Fourteenth Amendment.

[26] 369 U.S. 541 (1962).

Some of the questioned publicity emanated from the United States Senate Subcommittee on Improper Activities in Labor or Management. At its hearings on the connections between West Coast Teamsters and criminal interests, Beck was accused of controlling law enforcement in Oregon and being an irresponsible head of a union that had tie-ins with organized vice. The newspapers also reported that Beck used $250,000 taken from Teamster funds for his personal benefit. Beck invoked the Fifth Amendment before the committee. Seattle television stations broadcast live programs of the sessions, one of which ran for almost nine hours. Major national publications such as *U.S. News and World Report* published articles about the hearings. Finally, a special state grand jury was empaneled in Seattle and a former mayor was appointed as chief prosecutor. A Federal grand jury in Tacoma also ran an investigation into Beck's activities. Five days after Beck's Federal indictment, he was again called before the Senate Subcommittee. Again he declined some sixty times, on Fifth Amendment grounds, to reply to questions. All this received great publicity. He was then indicted a second time by a Federal grand jury for income tax evasion, and also by the state for grand larceny.

The local newspapers covered extensively his state trial for larceny. During the trial, Beck sought to quash the indictment. Three times he tried unsuccessfully for continuances of from one month to an indefinite period, and he also asked vainly for a change of venue to another county. He was convicted of grand larceny and appealed all the way to the Supreme Court, on the ground that voluminous and continuous adverse publicity deprived him of his Constitutional rights.

In an opinion by Justice Clark, the Supreme Court held that the trial judge had taken proper precautions in assembling the grand jury. Where evidence of prejudice appeared, the prospective jurors had been eliminated. Beck made no claim that any particular juror was biased. He merely said that publicity generally prevented the selection of a fair grand jury and also precluded the ultimate selection of a fair petit jury. He argued that since there had been such strong adverse publicity, presumably *any* jury in Seattle at the time must have been biased and therefore his motions should have been granted. The Court held that the news impact of the original press disclosures was diminished since Beck was not tried until nine and one-half months after he was first called before the Senate committee. All jurors who admitted possibilities of bias had been excused. All the rest had sworn that they were not biased and had not formed any opinions.

Justices Frankfurter and White took no part in the decision. Justices Black and Warren dissented, holding that the judge had not taken any steps to ensure an unbiased grand jury for Beck, and he had thus been denied equal protection of the law. "A fair trial under fair procedure is a basic element in our Government," they wrote. Justice Douglas also dissented on this ground and because the Washington law allowing one in custody to challenge grand jurors who were alleged to be prejudiced, but not allowing one who is not in custody at the time to have the same privilege, also was an unequal protection of the law.

It was never said, but it can be speculated, that the underlying reason for the majority's denying the claim of grand jury prejudice was that this body, unlike the trial jury, may and should hear all facts, opinions, even rumors about a case. It has been the traditional nature of grand jury proceedings to hear everything before the jury makes up its mind. Press comments are deemed an allowable part of the hodgepodge grand juries consider, although they are utterly forbidden to come to the attention of the trial jury.

The argument about generally versus specifically prejudicial publication was soon before the Court again. This was the landmark case of *Rideau v. Louisiana.*[27] In the opinion issued by the Louisiana Supreme Court, Justice Sanders described the factual background:

At 6:55 P.M., February, 1961, Wilbert Rideau entered the Southgate Branch of the Gulf National Bank in Lake Charles, Louisiana. He compelled three employees to fill a suitcase with money and, at pistol point, forced them into one of their cars and directed them to an uninhabited area northeast of town. He ordered them out of the car, lined them up abreast, and fired six shots at them. They scattered and fled. When one of them tried to rise to her knees, Rideau stabbed her with a hunting knife.

A few hours later the police apprehended Rideau and took him to the Calcasieu Parish jail. In the police car on the way to the jail, Rideau admitted his kidnaping, robbery, and murder. Handcuffed, he was not

[27] 373 U.S. 723 (1963).

advised of his right to make no statements or to have a lawyer. A large crowd was milling around the jail when the group arrived. Rideau was interviewed again in jail that night by the sheriff and confessed, still without advice of his rights and without counsel. Five days later he was interviewed by FBI agents in a 7′ x 10′ room and confessed again under similar circumstances.

The following morning Rideau was interviewed in his cell surrounded by the sheriff and two policemen; the episode was recorded on television. The twenty-minute television film was shown three times to viewing audiences estimated at 24,000, 29,000 and 53,000 in a parish of 150,000 people. Rideau was later charged, tried, convicted of murder, and sentenced to death.

Rideau's lawyers appealed the decision, arguing, among other things, that the defense motion for a change of venue was improperly denied, that specific jurors were wrongly allowed to be seated, and that the television broadcasts made a fair trial impossible in that place and with those jurors. Three jurors had seen the television show at least once; two were inactive deputy sheriffs. Some jurors said they had a fixed opinion in the case but, the judge having refused to sustain challenge for cause, Rideau was forced to use his peremptory challenges. Ultimately, he exhausted those allowed him and thus could not challenge the jurors who saw the television show. All the jurors testified that they could lay aside their opinions and judge the case on the evidence alone.

On appeal, the Supreme Court of Louisiana upheld the conviction on the theory that Rideau failed to prove such prejudice as would defeat the fairness of his trial. A number of witnesses had testified on the motion for a change of venue that in their opinions Rideau could not get a fair trial in Lake Charles; a large number of witnesses testified that he could. On the basis of this testimony the Louisiana courts held that the denial of the motion was proper.

The United States Supreme Court thought otherwise; at least, seven of the nine on the Court did. Justice Potter Stewart delivered the opinion of the Court that reversed Rideau's conviction. "We hold," the Court's majority opinion stated, "that it was a denial of due process of law to refuse the request for a change of venue, after the people of Calcasieu Parish had been exposed repeatedly and in depth to the spectacle of Rideau personally confessing in detail to the crimes with which he was later to be charged. For anyone who has ever watched television the conclusion cannot be avoided that this spectacle, to the tens of thousands of people who saw and heard it, in a very real sense *was* Rideau's trial. . . . Any subsequent court proceedings in a community so pervasively exposed to such a spectacle could be but a hollow formality."

Justice Clark, with Justice Harlan concurring, dissented on the grounds that state criminal procedures are not subject to the Supreme Court's general supervisory powers (as are the procedures of Federal courts) and therefore are not reversible unless they reach Constitutional proportions, which Justice Clark felt were not reached in this case. And since the objectionable television films were not used at the trial, the defendant, he felt, had not proved that they had otherwise "fatally infected the trial." The burden of showing this essential unfairness he placed on the defendant. The dissenters chose to accept the decision of the trial judge on this issue. "The determination of impartiality . . . is particularly within the province of the trial judge. And when the jurors testify that they can discount the influence of external factors and meet the standard imposed by the Fourteenth Amendment, that assurance is not lightly to be discarded."

The case was retried and Rideau was again convicted—this time under less prejudicial conditions.

Irvin v. Dowd,[28] decided in 1961, was a follow-up on the Shepherd and the Stroble cases. It arose out of a habeas corpus proceeding testing the validity of Irvin's conviction for murder and his death sentence in Indiana. Irvin argued that he had not received a fair trial and that his conviction violated the Fourteenth Amendment.

Six murders were committed in the vicinity of Evansville, Indiana, two on December 4, 1954, and four in March, 1955. The local news media naturally gave the events extensive coverage. There was tremendous excitement and indignation in the county and in the adjoining county, both rural. In April, 1955, Irvin was arrested. Soon thereafter, the prosecutor and police officials issued press releases stating that he had confessed to the six murders. They were published widely. When Irvin was indicted for one of the murders he successfully sought a change of venue from Vanderburgh County, but the court sent the

[28] 366 U.S. 717.

case to adjoining Gibson County. The defense counsel sought another change of venue but it was denied on the ground that Indiana statutes allow only one change of venue.

Voir dire lasted four weeks. Two more motions for changes of venue and eight motions for continuances were denied.

Justice Clark, who wrote the Supreme Court's opinion, pointed out that the right to a jury trial is the right to a fair trial by impartial, indifferent jurors, and failure to accord it violates the minimum standards of due process. He reiterated the established rule that jurors need not be totally ignorant of the facts involved since that would be impossible in this day of swift, wide-reaching and diverse methods of communication, and that those best qualified to serve as jurors are likely to have some impression or opinion about cases. Furthermore, Justice Clark conceded that the mere existence of a preconceived notion is not enough to rebut the presumption of a prospective juror's impartiality. "It is sufficient if the juror can lay aside his impression or opinion and render a verdict based on the evidence presented in court." It is always a question whether or not the juror's opinion, under the particular facts of the case, warrants the presumption of partiality. The task of proving it falls on him who makes the challenge.

Nevertheless, the facts of this case, Justice Clark found, made clear a showing of prejudice. The patterns of the daily popular news media were, in his words, "singularly revealing." It was the *cause célèbre* of the community. Curbstone opinions of guilt and punishment were solicited and recorded on the streets by roving reporters and were later broadcast. A barrage of newspaper headlines, articles, and cartoons was set off. Local newspapers were delivered to approximately 95 per cent of the dwellings in Gibson County. The radio and television stations carrying extensive newscasts of the case similarly blanketed the county. The press proclaimed details of the defendant's background, and referred to crimes he had committed as a juvenile, to his convictions for arson twenty years before and for burglary and A.W.O.L. by a court martial. The press accused him of being a parole violater and announced in headlines that he had been identified as the killer in a police line-up. When faced with a lie detector test, it was reported that he confessed and offered to plead guilty if he could receive a ninety-nine-year sentence instead of the death penalty. He was characterized by the press as being remorseless and without conscience but as having been found sane by a panel of doctors. On the second day of the jury selection the newspapers reported that there were strong feelings apparent in the courtroom, and frequent bitter and angry rumblings close to the surface. Twenty-seven of the first thirty-five prospective jurors were excused for holding biased opinions, and in the words of one newspaper, "a pattern of deep and bitter prejudice against the former pipe fitter" was evident. The newspapers quoted spectators as saying their minds were made up that Irvin was guilty and that he should be hanged.

Of the panel of 430 persons the court excused 268 as having fixed opinions about Irvin's guilt.

The voir dire record was almost three thousand pages. It showed that 90 per cent of those examined entertained an opinion as to guilt ranging in intensity from mere suspicion to absolute certainty. Eight of the twelve who were ultimately picked said that they thought Irvin was guilty and that they were familiar with the facts and circumstances of the case. Some said that Irvin would have to offer evidence to overcome their belief and one said that he could not even give the defendant the benefit of the doubt that he was innocent. One juror said, "You can't forget what you hear and see."

Vacating and remanding the case, Justice Clark said: "With his life at stake, it is not requiring too much that petitioner be tried in an atmosphere undisturbed by so huge a wave of public passion and by a jury other than one in which two-thirds of the members admit, before hearing any testimony, to possessing a belief in his guilt."

Justice Frankfurter concurred and went on to deplore the miscarriages of justice caused, he felt, all too typically by anticipatory trial by newspapers. He then made his oft-quoted remark about the recent increase in the free press, fair trial problem, concluding with the harsh admonition: "This Court has not yet decided that the fair administration of criminal justice must be subordinated to another safeguard of our constitutional system—freedom of the press, properly conceived. The Court has not yet decided that, while convictions must be reversed and miscarriages of justice result because the minds of jurors or potential jurors were poisoned, the poisoner is constitutionally protected in plying his trade."

Notwithstanding the minority interest in resort to the English contempt rule, it was not long before the Supreme Court reconfirmed its judgment about the inaptness of that doctrine. In *Wood v. Georgia*,[29] a 1962 case, Chief Justice Earl Warren delivered an opinion in which the Supreme Court again reversed a state court conviction for contempt.

In June, 1960, a judge of the superior court of Bib County, Georgia, empaneled a grand jury and instructed it to investigate a suspicious political situation in the county giving the appearance of a pattern of Negro block voting. The judge pointed out that there had been rumors and accusations that candidates for public office had paid large sums of money in an effort to get the Negro vote. All this took place in the midst of a local political campaign, and in order to publicize the investigation the judge had reporters from all the local news media present in the courtroom when he charged the grand jury.

The next day, while the grand jury was sitting, Wood, the sheriff of Bib County, issued a statement to the press, calling the investigation "one of the most deplorable examples of race agitation to come out of middle Georgia in recent years . . . this action appears either as a crude attempt at judicial intimidation of Negro voters and leaders or at best as agitation for a Negro vote issue in local politics." He added that singling out the Negro people in this manner was intimidation reminiscent of the conduct of the Ku Klux Klan. He hoped "that the present grand jury will not let its high office be a party to any political attempt to intimidate the Negro people of this community."

He concluded:

> If anyone in the community [should] be free of racial prejudice, it should be our judges. It is shocking to find a judge charging a grand jury in the style and language of a race-baiting candidate for political office.
>
> However politically popular the judges' action may be at this time, they are employing a practice far more dangerous to free elections than anything they want investigated.

The next day Wood delivered an open letter to the grand jury which implied that the court's charge was false. It asserted that in his opinion the Bib County Democratic Executive Committee was the organization responsible for corruption and the purchasing of votes and that the grand jury ought to investigate it.

[29] 370 U.S. 375.

A month later he was cited on two counts of contempt based on the two statements. It was asserted that they ridiculed the investigation and interfered with the grand jury, and thus constituted a clear and present danger to the administration of justice. The trial court, without making any findings or giving any reasons, judged Wood guilty on all counts and gave him concurrent sentences of twenty days in jail and a $200 fine. The conviction for the open letter to the grand jury was subsequently reversed. Wood appealed the contempt conviction on the remaining count.

The Supreme Court found that there was no evidence of any obstruction of the court, or in fact of anything more than the expression of views on matters of great public importance being considered by a grand jury. This could be no clear and present danger to the administration of justice, the Court said, and moreover there was no judicial proceeding pending; no one was on trial. It is important that grand juries, especially with investigations of this kind, have freedom of communication. Grand juries cannot operate in a vacuum, the Court held, in words reminiscent of its putative rationale in the Beck case.

The opinion stated: "The administration of the law is not the problem of the judge or prosecuting attorney alone, but necessitates the active cooperation of an enlightened public. . . . The petitioner's attack on the charge to the grand jury would have been likely to have an impeding influence on the outcome of the investigation only if the charge was so manifestly unjust that it could not stand inspection. In this sense discussion serves as a corrective force to political, economic and other influences which are inevitably present in matters of grave importance." The contempt conviction was reversed.

Two recent cases, *Billie Sol Estes v. Texas* in 1965 and *Sheppard v. Maxwell* in 1966, solidified this trend toward reversal. In both cases— probably two of the most notorious cases in the country in the last decade—highly celebrated criminal convictions were reversed. In one case television at trial and during pretrial proceedings was held to have deprived the defendant of a fair judicial proceeding. In the other, heavy coverage, bedlam at trial, and prejudicial comments by public officials were held to have combined to deny the defendant a fair trial. The former case almost resulted in a final ban on television in courts.[30]

---

[30] A full discussion of the Estes case appears in Chapter 12, pp. 215–223.

The latter set out a prospective rule that courts assume the responsibility of controlling trial news by controlling the sources of news. The Sheppard case, accordingly, is a particularly apt one in the present discussion.

The Supreme Court handed down its decision on June 6, 1966. In an opinion delivered by Justice Clark, the Court held that the trial judge in the Sheppard case had failed to protect the defendant from "massive, pervasive and prejudicial publicity that attended his prosecution" and that therefore Sheppard "did not receive a fair trial consistent with the Due Process Clause of the Fourteenth Amendment."

The Clark opinion spent eleven pages describing the details of pretrial publicity that attended the 1964 trial and five pages describing all of the publicity and commotion surrounding the trial itself. The opinion pointed out that all aspects of the problem of prejudicial publicity were present: participation by public officials, physical intrusions on the participants to the trial (including the defense counsel, the defendant, and the jury), and intensive national coverage. All combined, along with "virulent publicity," to create an environment which the Court described as "the carnival atmosphere," and "bedlam" reigning in the courthouse.

The Court then discussed the legal doctrine appropriate to this situation. "A responsible press has always been regarded as the handmaiden of effective judicial administration, especially in the criminal field," Justice Clark said. He went on to point out, "The press does not simply publish information about trials but guards against the miscarriage of justice by subjecting the police, prosecutors, and judicial processes to extensive public scrutiny and criticism." He noted the unwillingness of the Court to limit directly the traditional freedom of the news media to report about the process of justice.

But he added the qualification that legal trials cannot be carried out like elections, through the use of meeting halls, radios, and newspapers. Justice Clark pointed out that the Supreme Court has consistently insisted that the trial in criminal cases must be in a public tribunal, "free of prejudice, passion, excitement, and tyrannical power." The Court's description of the details in the Sheppard case showed that the requisite calmness and solemnity of the courtroom were absent and that there were good reasons to believe that the jury's verdict might not have been based solely on evidence received in open court.

The Court added that it is not necessary to show specific prejudice in deciding this question. Justice Clark repeated the statement made in an earlier case that "our system of law has always endeavored to prevent even the probability of unfairness." He held that in the Sheppard case the facts showed that "the totality of circumstances" demonstrated a lack of the requisite trial fairness.

The Court also pointed out that the available, ordinary legal techniques for filtering prejudice at trial were not used by the trial judge in the Sheppard case. The motion for a change of venue was denied; the jury was not sequestered; moreover, there were not even adequate instructions to the jury not to read or listen to published news of the case.

Compounding the bedlam of the case, the Court pointed out, was the fact that the trial judge did not make appropriate arrangements with the news media; thus Sheppard was deprived of the proper judicial serenity and calm to which he was entitled.

The Court placed the responsibility for balancing the competing demands of the press and the law with the courts. Justice Clark's opinion referred to the New Jersey Supreme Court's remarks in the Van Duyne case (see p. 129). He stated that a fundamental error of the trial court in the Sheppard case was that it failed to use its power to control the publicity. The trial judge's fatalistic attitude and his failure to take the appropriate steps that were available to him to control the publicity problem were a fatal error.

The Supreme Court then ventured the opinion that the available procedures "would have been sufficient to guarantee Sheppard a fair trial." The Court did not, therefore, consider whether or not it would be appropriate to use sanctions against the press.

The Court specifically enumerated the steps that could have been taken by the trial court to avoid interference by the press with the judicial process. The presence of the press could have been limited when it appeared to be acting in a prejudicial manner. The trial court should have adopted strict rules governing the newsmen's use of the courtroom. The number of reporters could have been limited and their physical location could have been set up in a less disruptive way. The press's conduct in the courtroom itself could have been controlled more strictly by the judge.

But mainly, Justice Clark said, the court should have made efforts to control "the release of leads, information, and gossip to the press by police officers, witnesses and the counsel for both sides." Emphasizing that the fault derived from the court's lack of control and was not due to the press's overindulgence, the Court stated that "effective control of these sources—concededly within the court's power—might well have prevented the divulgence of inaccurate information, rumors, and accusations that made up much of the inflammatory publicity. . . . More specifically, the court might well have proscribed extra-judicial statements by any lawyer, party, witness, or court official which divulged prejudicial matters."

Moreover, the Court went on, the trial judge might have "requested the appropriate city and county officials to promulgate a regulation with respect to dissemination of information about the case by their employees. . . . In addition, reporters . . . could have been warned as to the impropriety of publishing material not introduced in the proceedings. . . . In this manner, Sheppard's right to a trial free from outside interference would have been given added protection without corresponding curtailment of the news media. Had the judge, the other officers of the court, and the police placed the interest of justice first, the news media would have soon learned to be content with the task of reporting the case as it unfolded in the courtroom—not pieced together from extra-judicial statements."

Furthermore, the Supreme Court reiterated, the available procedural techniques should have been resorted to. For example, "sequestration of the jury was something the judge should have raised sua sponte with counsel. . . ." Observing that the reversal of a case is merely a palliative and not a cure, the Clark opinion called upon trial courts to "take such steps by rule and regulation that will protect their processes from prejudicial outside interferences. Neither prosecutors, counsel for defense, the accused, witnesses, court staff, nor enforcement officers coming under the jurisdiction of the court should be permitted to frustrate its function." And, as if calling for the adoption of the suggested New Jersey rule, and implying that the bar should clean its own house before it criticizes the press, the majority opinion concluded: "Collaboration between counsel and the press as to information affecting the fairness of a criminal trial is not only subject to regulation, but is highly censurable and worthy of disciplinary measures."

Conclusion

Nelles and King (see p. 278 above) have collected and analyzed all contempt by publication cases up to 1928, pointing out that the decisions reflected a continuation of philosophical differences over the concept of judicial power, as well as over the appropriate extensiveness of press freedom in this country.

In fifty-eight cases holding publications contemptuous, thirty of them were incident to political situations, and forty-two impugned the fairness of the court or judge, indicating that personal feelings of the judges were much in evidence.

Over the years, gradual but steady eradication of the rationales for summary contempt have developed:

The Supreme Court upheld the right of Congress to limit the judicial contempt power, thus showing that it could not be inherent.

Twentieth-century scholarship[31] showed that summary powers were not immemorially used, as Wilmot had peremptorily stated.

A famous treatise on criminal law[32] showed that necessity as a rationale for summary contempt procedures is fatuous.

Finally, the early experiences of states like New York and Pennsylvania showed that courts could survive efficiently without sweeping contempt powers. The use of the contempt power, then, far from being a universal quality in the administration of justice, was really nothing more than an expedient device for justice's administrators.

Nelles and King argued that any law that allows punishment of disrespectful publications is unscientific and does not consider the good as well as the bad effects of partisan publications. "The elimination of outside influence by publications seems impracticable where it would be most desirable, and undesirable in many cases where it might be practicable." For example, while it might be desirable to eliminate coverage in sensational jury cases involving sex or gruesome crime, the chances

---

[31] The original and classic study of the history of the contempt power was done by Sir John Fox in *Contempt of Court* (1927). This book brought together a famous series of articles by the author, which appeared in the early 1900's in the *Law Quarterly Review*.

[32] Livingston's *The Complete Works on Criminal Procedure* (1873) is a classic study of criminal law and jurisprudence which analyzed in a perceptive and polemic way what the author felt to be the false rationales for the summary contempt power.

of eliminating it are most unlikely. In cases involving criticism of judges, while restriction might be practicable, it really is not desirable.

In an analysis of the contempt by publication cases between the time of the 1831 statute and 1928, the Nelles and King study showed that only fifteen of the fifty-eight reported publications held punishable related to a case on or near trial by jury. Five of the fifteen related to pending jury trial cases; another five related to grand jury proceedings. Thirty-eight had no relation to jury proceedings. In their words, "It seems not unlikely that the punishments had more tendency than the publications to bring the administration of justice into disrepute."

A review of the facts of all state and Federal cases from 1831 to 1928 where particular publications out of court were held punishable as contempts shows that the publications rarely were such as to prejudice a jury; almost all involved descriptions of bias or prejudice or aspersions about the integrity of the courts. Thus, though the rationales for the use of contempt by publication doctrine to protect fair trials rely on the need to protect out-of-court influences upon verdicts, most of the cases involved criticism of courts and judges.

In 1953, Lois G. Forer won the American Bar Association's Ross Prize Essay on the subject "A Free Press and a Fair Trial." In her article, along with her own proposals, she analyzed the contempt by publication cases from 1928 through 1953.

She pointed out that of the twenty-five reported contempt cases involving radio, press, or speech in the period between 1928 and 1953, *no* cases arose out of the publication of inadmissible evidence. Of these reported cases, fourteen involved press criticism of courts, often specifically naming judges. In these cases, the use of the contempt power was rationalized as necessary to protect the administration of justice from being brought into disrepute and to preserve the public confidence in the courts. Few cases involved press interference with trials in any serious sense.[33]

---

[33] A breakdown of the cases between 1928 and 1953 shows the sources of the use of the contempt by publication power to have been the following: a letter to the foreman of a jury, a Chamber of Commerce Committee resolution which was published urging the removal of a traffic court judge (the contemnor was acquitted), press and radio charges critical of a labor injunction and demanding that the judge be removed (also an acquittal), press criticism of a judge's order to the jury that they return a verdict for the plaintiff in a civil case (the conviction was reversed), the inducing of a litigant to withdraw an action (also reversed on ap-

There have been then a hundred American contempt by publication cases in about a hundred and fifty years. An analysis of them, in general, and of the leading cases specifically, shows the inapt and unsuccessful use of the contempt power to curb press misconduct in the area of criminal justice.

The contempt power has been abandoned in America as a vehicle for controlling press publication about trials—at least where there is no jury. The Supreme Court will, however, reverse convictions on due process grounds when publicity is so extreme and pervasive that it appears to permeate the decision-making process—at least in jury cases. The press will be allowed to criticize judges' decisions, law, and the trial process, immune from punishment for contempt. But, while allowing editorialization, appellate courts will show more concern to protect defendants from the effects of prejudicial publications, especially when they emanate from public officials or participants in the trial. While the Supreme Court, like much of the organized bar, has become increasingly critical of press coverage of crime and trial news, it does not appear poised to punish the press for what it sees as misconduct of this nature. Rather, it is likely to seek new procedures and revitalize existing ones to cope with the problems raised by prejudicial reporting.

---

peal), the use of discourteous language in the courtroom by an attorney, press criticism of a court's decision, an attorney's criticism of the court, disobedience of a court order not to publish testimony until the trial of a companion case was concluded (an acquittal), violation of a court order prohibiting communications to creditors, two communications to grand jurors by an attorney who was under investigation, publication of an article accusing a union of being gangster-run while the union was under receivership (resulted in acquittal), institution of contempt proceedings against the press in which the proceedings criticized pending litigation (resulted in acquittal), a pamphlet criticizing a city court, criticism of a final decision of a court (resulted in acquittal), a letter by a trustee criticizing a bankruptcy plan of a court, newspaper comments about a claim in an appellate court, criticism of a pending civil action (resulted in acquittal), and press criticism of a judge.

PRESS AND PREJUDICE AT DALLAS

Dallas was the extreme of extremes—the act, the public response, the press treatment, and the bar's reaction to that treatment. As an issue in the free press, fair trial controversy, the news coverage of President John F. Kennedy's assassination deserves special attention, for although bad cases are supposed to make bad law, sometimes useful results come from an examination of a bad case, which in this context is the extreme one.

We have suggested that some of the criticism of press coverage of crime and the administration of justice and many of the remedies that have been proposed are products of a blinkered view; they drive with singleminded intensity for a fair trial by an impartial jury, indifferent to the injuries to other values inflicted by the process.

The extreme example of that attitude, it seems to us, was the complaint about press coverage of the assassination and its presumed effect on a trial of Lee Harvey Oswald had he survived to be tried. Its exposition in the Report of the President's Commission on the Assassination of President Kennedy (Warren Commission) did more than any other act to revive the debate about free press, fair trial and give it its present vigor.

The case against the press, made in various forms by the American Bar Association, local bar groups, law school faculties, and others, as well as by the Warren Commission, came in its most concise form in a declaration by the American Civil Liberties Union: "It is generally conceded that as a result of the conduct of the Dallas police and the communications media when Oswald was taken into custody, he could not have had a fair trial anywhere in the United States."

Arguing the same theme, the Warren Commission described the chaos caused by reporters, cameramen, and radio and television equipment in the Dallas police station, explained how it interfered with efficient police operations, noted the consequent harassment of Oswald and the corrosion of security processes to the point that Jack Ruby was able to enter the police station basement, unnoticed in the crowd of newsmen, and take Oswald's life.

The facts are not in dispute[1] and, in any event, are not relevant to the subject about to be discussed. What *is* germane for examination here is the information about the crime released by the law enforcement officials at Dallas and published by the press. About that, the Warren Commission wrote:

> The Commission agrees that Lee Harvey Oswald's opportunity for a trial by 12 jurors free of preconception as to his guilt or innocence would have been seriously jeopardized by the premature disclosure and weighing of the evidence against him.
>
> The problem of disclosure of information and its effect on trials is, of course, further complicated by the independent activities of the press in developing information on its own from sources other than law enforcement agencies. Had the police not released the specific items of evidence against Oswald, it is still possible that the other information presented on television and in the newspapers, chiefly of a biographical nature, would itself have had a prejudicial effect on the public. . . .
>
> The Commission recognizes that the people of the United States, and indeed the world, had a deep-felt interest in learning of the events surrounding the death of President Kennedy, including the development of the investigation in Dallas. An informed public provided the ultimate guarantee that adequate steps would be taken to apprehend those responsible for the assassination and that all necessary precautions would be taken to protect the national security. It was therefore proper and desirable that the public know which agencies were participating in the investigation and the rate at which their work was progressing. The public was also entitled to know that Lee Harvey Oswald had been apprehended and that the State had gathered sufficient evidence to arraign him for the murders of the President and

---

[1] Where responsibility rested for the sorry state of affairs, whether it was an inevitable result of contemporary press operations or whether it could have been avoided, are, however, questions very much in dispute. Our own conclusion is that the chaos was not inherent, that a firm and unpanicked police administration could have established order and proper procedure (Gladwin Hill, a veteran *New York Times* reporter who was an eyewitness of the scene, came to the same conclusion in a persuasive letter to the editor of the *Times,* published October 2, 1964). The formula for coping with a flood of press attention to a sensationally newsworthy event is not complicated. It has been set forth in "Orderly Procedures for Mass Coverage of News Events," a small brochure produced by the Joint Media Committee on News Coverage Problems, a group created by newspaper and broadcasting news executives in response to the suggestions of the Warren Commission.

Patrolman Tippit, that he was being held pending action of the grand jury, that the investigation was continuing, and that the law enforcement agencies had discovered no evidence which tended to show that any other person was involved in either slaying.

However, neither the press nor the public had a right to be contemporaneously informed by the police or prosecuting authorities of the details of the evidence being accumulated against Oswald. Undoubtedly the public was interested in these disclosures, but its curiosity should not have been satisfied at the expense of the accused's right to a trial by an impartial jury. The courtroom, not the newspaper or television screen, is the appropriate forum in our system for the trial of a man accused of a crime.

If the evidence in the possession of the authorities had not been disclosed, it is true that the public would not have been in a position to assess the adequacy of the investigation or to apply pressures for further official undertakings. But a major consequence of the hasty and at times inaccurate divulgence of evidence after the assassination was simply to give rise to groundless rumors and public confusion. Moreover, without learning the details of the case, the public could have been informed by the responsible authority of the general scope of the investigation and the extent to which State and Federal agencies were assisting in the police work.[2]

The statement presents two issues for examination. The lesser if more specific one is whether publication did in fact give rise to "groundless rumors and public confusion." The more basic question is whether, at such a cataclysmic moment, it was, in the words of one set of press critics, an unjustified "obsession that everybody has a right immediately to know and see everything,"[3] or, as the Warren Commission put it, that "neither the press nor the public had a right to be contemporaneously informed . . . of the details of the evidence being accumulated against Oswald."

As background to consideration of these questions, it is useful to recall the impact of the assassination on the nation. That can be done, and with great precision, thanks to an impressive national survey of public opinion undertaken immediately after the tragedy by a group of qualified scholars. The results were presented in a book, *The Kennedy Assassina-*

[2] *Official Warren Commission Report on the Assassination of President John F. Kennedy* (Washington: U.S. Government Printing Office, 1964), pp. 239–240.

[3] Letter to the *New York Times*, November 27, 1963, by a group of Harvard Law School professors.

tion and the American Public: Social Communication in Crisis.[4] Some of its findings:

> More than 90 per cent of the American people knew of the shooting of President Kennedy within an hour after the event; more than half heard the news in the first 30 minutes, before the President was pronounced dead.
>
> Conflicting stories and wild rumors began to circulate at once about the number of shots and where they came from and, with Oswald's arrest, about his Soviet connections. Speculation was instant: was he innocent, did he do it alone, was he mad, or was he the agent of a Communist conspiracy? Alternately, was he the tool of a right wing plot?
>
> The impact on the public was tremendous. More than half of those who heard the news could not continue their normal occupation for the rest of the day; they professed never in their lives to have had the same sort of feelings. One of their responses was to glue themselves to the television set: the average adult spent 8 hours on Friday, the day of the assassination, 10 the next day, and 8 each on Sunday and Monday watching television. On those days at least one-fourth of the adult population spent as much as 13 hours looking at television.
>
> "There were times during those days when a *majority of all Americans* were apparently looking at the same events and hearing the same words from their television sets—participating together, at least to that extent, in a great national event. Nothing like this on such a scale had ever occurred before."
>
> And never was there a clearer demonstration of how large a segment of the population has a predilection for the conspiratorial theory of history. One-fourth of the 1,384 persons interviewed suspected the work of a Communist, Castroite, or other leftist; half as many had the immediate reaction that the shot was fired by a segregationist or a representative of the right wing. Twelve per cent thought the assassin was paid to kill the President, another 11 per cent thought he had been persuaded to do it by some unspecified group.

[4] Bradley S. Greenberg and Edwin B. Parker, eds. (Stanford: Stanford University Press, 1965).

Of those interviewed, 47 per cent immediately worried about the fact of the assassination on "the political situation" in this country. Forty-four per cent worried about "our relations with other countries" and 41 per cent "how the United States would carry on without its leader."

Gladiyn Hill, the West Coast correspondent of the *New York Times*, has asked how in such a situation, with an anguished and worried citizenry, "any shred of information could have been superfluous."[5]

"Significantly," Hill wrote, "no one has been able to allege what would have been the press's worst possible dereliction under the circumstances: that the public was *insufficiently* informed. Failing this, the carpers had to twang on a more baroque contention: that the public was told too much."

Referring to the items of news about Oswald's arrest that the Warren Commission suggested were the totality of what was proper for the Dallas police to have released, Hill declared: "Seven facts. Regarding the most extraordinary and momentous event in the nation's recent history, the American people were expected by the Warren Commission to have been satisfied with fewer facts than they would read about in a high school basketball game."

Indeed, the Commission blandly conceded that under its precepts the public would not have been informed in an area that would seem of crucial importance. If the Dallas police had confined themselves to the Commission's spartan formula, the Warren Report observed, "It is true that the public would not have been in a position to assess the adequacy of the investigation or to apply pressures for further official undertakings." Outweighing that loss, the Commission implied, was the fact that the too hasty and partially inaccurate news gave rise to "groundless rumors and public confusion."

What rumors did *the press* instigate or intensify? There were dozens that circulated by word of mouth; there were none that, on being given mention by the press, were not handled with caution and qualified for what they were. It was the press that exposed and quenched rumor, not the other way around.

What inaccuracies, what confusion beyond that which was the reality of the moment?

[5] *Frontier Magazine,* March, 1966.

As far as can be determined, there were five major items:

1. Reports were published that the rifle was found on the second floor of the Texas School Book Depository or in the fifth-floor staircase. By the next day, all reports agreed it was found on the sixth floor.

2. The rifle was variously reported as being an Enfield, a Mauser, a U.S. Army gun, or of Japanese make. By the next day it was reported correctly as a Mannlicher-Carcano rifle.

3. Although there was a solid consensus that three shots had been fired, there were some reports suggesting four or even five. There were some reports of four or even five bullets having been found.

4. There was an initial report that Oswald was seen at his rooming house at 12:45 P.M., only fourteen or fifteen minutes after the shots. It was finally determined that he returned about one-half hour after the slaying.

5. Dallas hospital doctors first indicated that one bullet had entered the President's throat. The Warren Commission was convinced that all came from behind, to the President's right.

We shall return later to the questions about the reported wound in the throat and the number of bullets found.

These few and for the most part minor inaccuracies, however, did not create public confusion during the crucial first several days, or even weeks, following the assassination, the period to which the Warren Commission presumably referred in its complaint against the press. Punctilious in its supply of detail and argument elsewhere, the Commission did not itemize the rumors that the press assertedly gave rise to or specify the confusion that the press's inaccuracies were supposed to have caused.

As to the facts, the conclusion of the Press-Bar Committee of the American Society of Newspaper Editors of April, 1965, remains exact: "Within 48 hours, the print and electronic media reported the Dallas story so accurately and completely that the Warren Commission, in ten months and with unlimited resources, did not alter the basic outlines of what the media had reported."

As to public confusion, the valid judgment of the press's performance seems, in the light of hindsight, not that of the Commission but that of the opinion study previously quoted. In an introduction to the book, Wilbur Schramm, Director of the Institute for Communications Research at Stanford University, declared:

It was extremely important to a shocked public to have a large and continuing flow of information on the matter that concerned them. The swift, full coverage undoubtedly grounded many rumors before they could circulate. By speaking so fully and freely of Oswald and the events in which he was involved, the media helped to reduce fears of a conspiracy and prepare people to believe the theory that a lone, disturbed man had done it. . . . One of the most important deductions from the events of late November, 1963, is that Americans trust their free press and free broadcasting system. . . . It must be said that these did not fail the American people in any important way. . . .

In the uncertainty caused by the assassination crisis, television was an important source of information that alleviated some of the anxiety. . . . It structured and clarified the extent of personal threat. . . . It gave timely reassurance by showing the existence and continuity of cherished institutions and values. It reinforced social prescriptions for correct behavior by showing the exemplary conduct of the nation's leaders. . . . And it helped narcotize behavior that might have been dangerous by exhausting the need for action.

The Warren Commission saw peril to Oswald's rights in the hypothetical case of his having survived; it may be permitted, therefore, to examine the equally hypothetical situation in the event that the Dallas officials had acted in accordance with the precepts the Commission suggested as proper for them. They would have announced only that a certain Lee Harvey Oswald had been arrested and there was sufficient evidence to arraign him for the President's murder and that of Patrolman Tippit; the investigation was continuing and there was no evidence that any other person was involved in either slaying. The only additional information that could have been released under the Commission's formula would have been Oswald's age and address, because anything more of a biographical nature—his history, his marriage, his activities on the day of the assassination or on preceding days—would have been potentially prejudicial.

To give the fullest opportunity for the realization of the Warren Commission's vision of the salutary effects on Oswald's rights, we postulate a second hypothesis: that the press thereupon maintained complete silence on all matters concerning Oswald except those announced by the officials.

The assumption is, of course, fantastic, but not nearly so implausible as what seems to be the implicit premise of the Warren Commission: that *had* press and officialdom behaved as prescribed, a public vacuum of news about Oswald, prejudicial or otherwise, would have persisted until his trial.

We grope here, of course, with a dream world, but it is not of our making and we must do the best we can to find our way in it.

A news vacuum is as abhorrent to natural man as any other vacuum is to nature. The one the Warren Commission, the American Civil Liberties Union, and the other press contemnors postulate would have been immediately filled, and by the most evil contents, those poured into it by word of mouth. And no one may minimize the dynamics of that medium—pervasive in its force, its epidemic capability, its recklessness, and, in the absence of an antidote, its credibility, even of its mutually inconsistent assertions.

The ingredients for the reports that would have carried by word of mouth were as explosive as anyone could wish:

1. On the morning of the assassination, there was a full-page advertisement in the Dallas News "welcoming" Kennedy and asking, "*Why* have you scrapped the Monroe Doctrine in favor of the Spirit of Moscow?" and "*Why* have you ordered or permitted your brother Bobby, the Attorney General, to go soft on Communists?" and more of the same;

2. Vice President Lyndon Johnson, a man until that time grossly maligned by much of the public for what were wrongly thought to be his views on civil rights, regional prejudices, and general outlook, was instantly the subject of disgusting suspicions, widely bruited;

3. It was known in Dallas and in New Orleans (where Oswald had discussed the matters at length in a radio broadcast three months earlier) that Oswald had made an abortive migration to Russia, worked there three years, had expressed pro-Communist, anti-United States sentiments, and had married a Russian woman, with whom he had returned to the United States;

4. It was known in New Orleans—Oswald had also publicized that episode in the broadcast—that he had engaged in pro-Castro activity there.

On what fertile soil the implications of those facts, inconsistent though they were, would have fallen is made clear by the opinion surveys mentioned above. It is inconceivable that rumors, exponentially multiplying in panic and irresponsibility, would not have spread through the fifty states—somewhat more slowly, to be sure, without the press to carry them, but by that same fact with less to impede their repetition or reduce their credibility.

No one can believe that the outcome would have been otherwise. Is it credible that people so riven that half of them stopped their normal activities for the rest of the day, and half remained glued to television for four days, would have buttoned their lips and closed their ears for the long months until the trial to all talk of who did it and who was Oswald? Would the citizens of Dallas, from whom the jury would have been drawn, have dutifully resisted talking and listening?

A different hypothesis, that the press would have had the good sense to find out everything it could if the Dallas officials had behaved as the Warren Commission proposed they should have, does no better to support the theory that official silence would have enhanced Oswald's chances for an impartial jury. All the ingredients that would have gone into word-of-mouth rumor would have been discovered by the press. Although they would have been treated with much more care and intense examination, and although the suspicions of official connivance and right-wing instigation would probably have been liquidated, the essential facts damaging to Oswald would have emerged: the Russian trip, the anti-United States declarations, the pro-Castro propaganda, etc.

It was surely better for Oswald's hypothetical trial that the press dealt with those facts as it did—accurately—rather than to leave them to rumor. And, to return for a moment to reality after an excursion into fantasy, what disclosure of all those facts of Oswald's life and activity did to raise a presumption of guilt was minimal—as we have contended in this book in other cases—compared to the effect of the mere fact that he was arrested.

Indeed, Oswald's exposure to the press—granted, under the most deplorable circumstances—may have done him (still in relation to the hypothetical trial) more good than harm. He had a chance, at least, to say over television, "I'm only a patsy," and to utter an exculpatory shout to newsmen: "They're holding me because I was in the Soviet Union. The police won't let me have representation." And finally, as Rostow has noted (see p. 48), press surveillance seems to have kept him from the traditional tender overnight treatment of the Dallas police with its usual results of a "voluntary" confession.

We have guessed at the consequences for Oswald had the Dallas law enforcement officials confined their public statements to the items

under the Warren Commission rubric. What guess may one make about
the consequences for the nation?

Our guess is that they would have been dreadful. The single greatest fear following the shooting—a fear so real and terrifying that the
new President's entourage went to great lengths to keep his movement
secret—was that the act was part of a conspiracy. In the light of the
right-wing environment of Dallas (Vice President and Mrs. Johnson had
been assaulted there in 1960 and Adlai Stevenson had been spat upon
a month before the assassination), and the left-wing history of Oswald,
the wildest rumors could have been believed. Unfortunately, some still
are, but happily only by a small minority in America.

In the first day or two following the murder, "Incomplete information about the assassination, speculation about the possible conspiracy
of unknown magnitude, and thoughts that the supposedly real killer
might be at large all contributed to an ominous atmosphere at Dallas,"
a television reporter on the scene reported.[6]

Along with Professor Schramm, we are convinced that the complete
flow of information that emerged, even with its occasional and in our
view inconsequential initial inaccuracies, was the single most effective
means to quench the rumors of conspiracy and reassure the public.

We cannot agree with what must be the implicit assumption of
the Warren Commission, that an undetailed, unsupported assertion
of the Dallas officials that "the law enforcement agencies had discovered
no evidence which tended to show that any other person was involved
in either slaying" would have been an adequate reassurance. On the
contrary, we suggest that that unadorned announcement, followed by
silence until the trial, would have been the most effective agent that can
be imagined for spreading rumors and public confusion.

Unless, of course, the press—and the Warren Commission—were all
wrong about Oswald's having acted alone and about the absence of a
conspiracy.

"Confusion" on that score was first created by a political scientist and
a historian, Jack Minnis and Staughton Lynd, in an article entitled
"Seeds of Doubt" in the *New Republic* of December 21, 1963. If it said
anything, it said that Oswald could not have done the act alone. A
mysterious conspiracy, which the authorities were trying to hush up,

[6] Tom Pettit, in Bradley S. Greenberg and Edwin B. Parker, eds., *The Kennedy
Assassination and the American Public* (Stanford: Stanford University Press, 1965).

was implied. Their evidence, having to do mainly with the wound in Kennedy's throat, was soon proved false.

Or so it seemed. Since then, however, other articles and books[7] have appeared, all implying if not directly asserting the existence of a conspiracy. Whether that conclusion is correct or false, we cannot now judge. We can only note that if it is false, then the press performed a most profound service to the nation in helping restore its calm and preventing what one can imagine, without drawing too long a bow, could have been some terrible consequences to various political groups and organizations, to Mrs. Lee Harvey Oswald, and to a few remarkably decent and humane people who befriended her. If the conspiracy contention is true, however, then the press did a miserable job, but one that would not have been made better if it had behaved exactly as the Warren Commission seems to have wished it to behave. If there was in fact a conspiracy, the press will be subject to criticism for failing in its function, but the Warren Commission will not be one of those in a position to make it.

It is doubtless possible to contrive a set of rules and regulations (assuming no First Amendment inhibitions) that would prevent the press from publishing anything that might prejudice a jury summoned to try the case of some future defendant charged with having assassinated the President of the United States. But for anyone who attempts to formulate them, the task will be difficult indeed. A thousand contingencies must be foreseen and measures created to handle them; an enormous list of forbidden news items must be set down; a complicated set of restrictive procedures must be ordained for the operation of the press. And all of these measures and categories and procedures must be applied continually, at all times and for all defendants, for surely no one would argue that only an accused Presidential assassin should enjoy the safeguards that are deemed necessary to assure an unprejudiced jury.

It will be fair to ask the man drafting the rules to bear in mind their effect on the workings of the democracy and the structure of an open society—not only at the time of a Presidential assassination, should that tragedy ever come again, but on every other day.

[7] Inter alia, Mark Lane, *Rush to Publish* (New York: Holt, Rinehart, and Winston, 1966); Edward J. Epstein, *The Warren Commission and the Establishment of Truth* (New York: Viking, 1966); Harold Weisberg, *Whitewash: The Report on the Warren Report* (Hyattstown, Md.: published by the author, 1966).

INDEX

A

Accardo, "Tony": *see* Accardo case
Accardo case: 23–24
Acton, Lord: 51
Adams, J. Bodkin: *see* Adams case
Adams case: 148–150, 151n.; contempt power and, 275–276
Afro-American (Baltimore): 89
Almon case: 276–278
American Bar Association: 245, 313; Canons of Professional Ethics, 127–128, 211–212; Kennedy assassination, 315; Ross Prize essays, 122 (1965), 313 (1953); on television reporting, 211–212, 215; *see also* Reardon Committee; Reardon Report
American Bar Association Journal: 210n., 212n., 228n., 239n.
American Civil Liberties Union: 200, 220; Kennedy assassination, 315, 322; on televising trials, 215
American Commonwealth, The (Bryce): 45
American Jury, The (Kalven-Zeisel): 57, 68, 91n., 108
American Museum of Natural History (N.Y.): 183, 184
American Psychologist: 246n.
Aristophanes: 51
Arizona Republic: 270
Army-McCarthy hearings: 229; *see also* McCarthy, Senator Joseph R.
Association of Broadcasters (Ore.): statement on crime news coverage, 126, 255
Atlantic Monthly: 47n.
Attorneys general: on frequency of prejudicial publicity, 257–263

B

Baker, Robert ("Bobby"): 169
Baltimore Radio case: *see State v. Baltimore Radio Show*
Beall, J. Glenn: 167
Beck, David: *see* Beck case
Beck case (*Beck v. Washington*): 283, 284, 300–302
Bedford, Sybille: 148n., 203
Bentham, Jeremy: 52
Billie Sol Estes v. State of Texas: see Estes case
Birch Society: 187n.
Bittinger, D. W.: 164, 165
Black, Justice Hugo: 71, 237; Bridges case, 286; Estes case, 215, 222; *Times-Mirror* case, 285
Blackstone: 277
Blade (Toledo): Gosser case, 24–29; guide lines for crime news coverage, 124–125
Blake, Gene: 44
Blythin, Judge: 18
Book Week: 48n., 52n.
Borchard, Edwin N.: 22n.
Bowles, Carl Cletis: 161, 162
Boykin, Frank W.: 168
Brennan, Justice William J., Jr.: 169; Estes case, 215–216, 222, 223
Bridges, Harry: *see* Bridges case
Bridges case (*Bridges v. California*): 71–72, 116, 122, 282, 284–287
Brim, Orville G., Jr.: 246n.
Broder, Dale: 105n.
Brown, Edmund G: 162
Brown, John: 4
Bryce, Lord: 45, 145, 200
Buchanan, James: 278
Burywaise, Elvin: 181, 182

327

C

K

I

J

L